RÉGION ET DÉVELOPPEMENT

n° 47-2018

Varia

L'Harmattan

REVUE RÉGION ET DÉVELOPPEMENT

Revue fondée en 1995 par Gilbert Benhayoun et Maurice Catin

Revue semestrielle référencée dans ECONLIT et dans IDEAS (REPEC)

Site web : www.regionetdeveloppement.org

ISSN 2117-0843

5-7, rue de l'Ecole-Polytechnique, 75005 Paris

http://www.editions-harmattan.fr

ISBN : 978-2-343-15701-6

EAN : 9782343157016

Région et Développement

n° 47 - 2018

Varia

Région et Développement

n° 47-2018

www.regionetdeveloppement.org

Scientific network centrality of European regions: the role of territorial resources

Lorenzo CASSI*, Emilie-Pauline GALLIÉ, Agénor LAHATTE***, Valérie MERINDOL******

Abstract - This article provides an original framework for analyzing networks of scientific collaborations in Europe at regional level. Which are the determinants of the observed clustering phenomenon? Which is the role of the territories? The aim of this article is to provide empirical evidence in order to answer to these questions. For this, we base our analysis on scientific collaborations between European regions in eight different disciplines (e.g. Medicine, Chemistry...) over the period 2001-2011. A normalized centrality measurement is proposed. We test the impact of territorial resources and field scientific characteristics on regions centrality in each of the analyzed discipline. Firstly, the analysis highlights a strong heterogeneity between disciplines, showing the need of carrying out specific investigation for each of them. Second, the results show the different roles played by local resources, according to the disciplines. Finally, the article discusses the implications of these results in terms of science and innovation policies.

JEL Classification
O3, R5, CL5

Key-words
Scientific network
European regions
Centrality
Territorial resources
Science and innovation policies

We would like to thank the reviewers for their comments and suggestions which helped us to improve this article.

* Paris School of Economics - Université Paris 1 Panthéon-Sorbonne ; OST du HCERES ; Lorenzo.Cassi@univ-paris1.fr
** IGAENR ; emilie-pauline.gallie@education.gouv.fr
*** OST du HCERES ; agenor.lahatte@hceres.fr
**** Paris School of Business, newPIC chair ; valerie@merindol.net

INTRODUCTION

Actors able to reach more central network position will more likely benefit from network (Burt 1992; Borgatti 2005), in terms of knowledge access and diffusion, of performance and influence on the others actors (Gilsing et al., 2008; Maggioni et al., 2007; Ponds et al., 2010). That is why stimulating the network participation of scientific institutions localized in a specific region is important from a regional policy perspective.

To investigate the characteristics and the centrality of scientific networks, regions are often considered as a relevant unit of analysis (Autant-Bernard et al., 2007), even if they encompass several universities and public research organizations that develop specific collaborations depending on their specialization, size and strategy.

The determinants of scientific networks centrality have been investigating in the literature in several ways (Wanzenbock et al., 2015; Sebestyén and Varga, 2013). The geographic perspective analysis is developed around two main approaches: the internal capacity and the territorial one.

First, centrality depends on the resources of the actor itself. In the case of regions, it means the R&D and scientific resources of the institutions localized in the region represent a driver for network centrality (Autant Bernard et al, 2007; Barber et al., 2011). Internal capacity is required not only to engage in collaborations, but also to benefit from knowledge transmitted via network inter-linkages. Some scholars pointed out that the region's strength in knowledge production is one of the most crucial factors for developing central position in knowledge networks (Broekel and Brenner, 2011; Grossman and Helpman, 1991).

Second, spatial dimension is associated to the impact of geographical proximity on the development of actors' collaboration (Boschma and Frenken, 2010). Scientific institutions are embedded in economic and technological environment. This territorial embeddedness gives the opportunity to access to nearby resources localized in the regions and the surrounding territories (Wanzenock et al., 2015; Berge et al., 2015). Spatial embeddedness could affect a region's network position due to spillover mechanisms resulting from economic dependencies, agglomeration dynamics or core-periphery structures in nearby regions (see Feldmann and Kogler, 2010; Breschi and Lissoni, 2009).

In this sense, scientific network centrality of regions depends not only on internal resources of the universities and research organizations, but also on the various regional resources nearly accessible (Wanzenbock et al., 2014). The focus of this study is to investigate how the combination of these resources affects the region's scientific centrality in Europe.

In line with Hoekman et al. (2010), we explore how the scientific centrality of a region depends on economic and scientific regional attributes and how this could vary depending on the scientific field under analysis. As disciplines are based on different production and knowledge diffusion patterns (e.g. Bonaccorsi, 2008), we assume that driving factors determining the centrality of a region can vary according to discipline. Our analysis attempts contribute to this literature in two main ways. First, it contributes to the debate around the regional policy supporting local scientific activities. We underline some major challenges for regional policymakers wanting to bring regional scientific communities closer to the center of the European network. Boosting collaboration can be effective if the actual driving factors are activated Second, we simultaneously take into account both the general characteristics of the territory and the specific scientific characteristics of each discipline (i.e. intra-discipline variables), as well as potential inter-discipline effects. So we contribute to identify the specificities of scientific disciplines in the regional policy perspective.

For our study, we use data from Web of Sciences (henceforth WoS) from 2000 to 2011 covering eight broad scientific disciplines. For each discipline, we calculated the valued degree centrality for each European region. In order to make meaningful comparisons between disciplines, we propose an original normalization method. Based on the rich-club phenomenon approach, a threshold value for each distribution is identified, and the degree of centrality for each region is normalized accordingly. To control for spatial effect, we follow the empirical strategy adopted by Wanzenbock et al. (2014) and a panel version of Spatial Durbin Model (henceforth SDM) is applied to our degree of centrality data.

The paper is organized as follows: the second section briefly presents the literature that should be taken into account together to analyze the determinants of regional network centrality. Here, we present the literature covering the determinants of regional resources and we make some assumptions about their impact on scientific network centrality. The third section presents the data and methods, namely the network construction and the econometric model adopted. The fourth section presents the empirical exercise and main results for each of the eight scientific disciplines analyzed. The last section offers a conclusion, discussing the main results and implications for policymakers.

1. THE DIFFERENT SCALES OF TERRITORIAL RESOURCES AS DRIVING FACTORS OF SCIENTIFIC NETWORK CENTRALITY

Economic and geographic literature shows that territorial resources can play an important role to understand how economic actors develop (Asheim et al., 2005). Based on this literature, we identify some questions concerning the impact of local resources on the centrality of regions within the European scientific network that deserve more research than what actually done. We organize the analyses around three main dimensions: the internal resources of the region (2.1) and the spillovers within a region (2.2) and between a region and the surrounding ones (2.3).

1.1. The scientific/internal resources as driving factors of scientific centrality

Academic literature focusses on regional innovation system diversity and trajectories in terms of their R&D and innovation capabilities (Asheim, 2006; Pinto, 2009). This diversity is frequently presented as a dichotomy between core/leader vs. periphery/follower in regional innovation systems (Doloreux et al., 2008; OECD, 2011). Regions with low capabilities and performance are often not well integrated into the European research area. For (regional or European) policymakers, the challenge is therefore to support peripheral regions in moving out of their isolation (Doloreux et al., 2008; Hewitt-Dundas et al., 2011). Based on this literature, we wonder which factors could influence centrality.

The scientific centrality of an actor depends first on the resources of the actor itself. In the case of regions, it means that the R&D and scientific resources of the institutions localized in the region can be a driver for network centrality (Autant Bernard et al., 2007; Barber et al., 2011). Internal capacity is required not only to engage in collaborations, but also to benefit from knowledge transmitted via network inter-linkages. Some scholars pointed out that the region's strength in knowledge production is one of the most crucial factors for developing central position in knowledge networks (Broekel and Brenner, 2011; Grossman and Helpman, 1991). According to this literature, scientific resources can be analyzed in terms of financial resources dedicated to research institutions, which represent the critical mass, i.e. scientific production, and in terms of scientific excellence, i.e. impact or visibility (Zitt et al., 2000; Tjissen et al., 2007). In order to reduce disparities, regional policy actions are designed to increase the scientific capacity of research institutions on the one hand and push the pursuit of scientific excellence on the other

(Benneworth et al., 2007). For R&D policy, one of the main challenges is about the equilibrium between scientific production and scientific excellence. In other words, is the scientific production which makes a region more central or/and the quality of its production? Answering to this question could help to orientate the R&D policy.

This question must be analyzed at the disciplines level. Indeed, the impact of scientific regional resources on centrality may vary between disciplines because knowledge production dynamics differ between scientific regimes. Bonaccorsi (2008) shows that some key differences between disciplines exist because the resources required for their development are different. The author identifies what he calls technical complementary that includes physical infrastructures. Disciplines like physics and astrophysics require significant infrastructures while such an investment plays a relative minor role in biology or chemistry (Bonaccorsi, 2008; Genuth et al., 2010). We assume that while regional policymakers have an increasing role in scientific policy (Perry, 2007; Crespy et al., 2007), bolstering scientific resources does not have the same impact among the disciplines.

1.2. The local spillovers effects on scientific centrality

Beyond internal resources, the literature shows the impact of various types of spillovers (such as knowledge spillovers or industry spillovers, cf. for instance Capello, 2009 for a review) on the development of the local actors.

Thus, from the Regional Innovation System (RIS) perspective, regional scientific development depends on the proximity and interactions between public and private research (Kratke et al., 2009). Scientific capabilities are more concentrated in regions characterized by high levels of private R&D and economic growth (Asheim et al., 2006). We therefore assume that regional economic and innovative capacities contribute indirectly to strength the development of regional scientific institutions and, a fortiori, of the centrality of the regional scientific institutions.

However, the impact of this support may vary between disciplines. Bonaccorsi (2008) states that one of the key differences between disciplines is based on institutional complementarities: public and private interactions vary between disciplines and these interactions do not have the same impact on all disciplines. For instance, for applied scientific activities, the private sector may play a more important role than for fundamental research activities: in medicine as in engineering science, collaborations between public and private research are essential for producing new scientific results, while for mathematics or fundamental physics this is definitely less the case (Todt et al., 2007; Merito et al., 2007).

Moreover, the analysis at the discipline level, allows us to test the effects of some possible "inter-discipline spillovers" in an adaptation of inter-industry spillovers. Indeed, as shown at the industry level, what is it done in one sector can positively influence the development of other sectors. We make the assumption that the more the region is central in different scientific disciplines, the higher the probability to be central in one specific discipline is.

1.3. Surrounding territorial resources as spillovers and their impact on network centrality

A large literature shows the influence of surrounding regions on a region's own outcome such as economic growth, gas emission or knowledge production (Jaffe, 1989; Feldman, 1994; Autant-Bernard, 2001). In the literature, local knowledge spillovers influence the development of surrounding regions. Because of growth spillovers (for instance Arora and Vamvakidis, 2005), a region growth depends also on outcome and behavior of neighboring regions. In both cases, the main idea is that the proximity between regions creates opportunities for interactions that influence the development of the regions. However, if knowledge spillovers are rather considered as having positive effects, in some cases, surrounding territorial R&D has a negative impact on regional knowledge production (Autant-Bernard, 2012), negative effects which may result from core-periphery relations between neighboring regions. In other cases, the presence of large infrastructure such as an airport (Percoco, 2010) could contribute to generate spillover over the surrounding regions. Thus a large panel of activities can have a spillover effect on other regions. From the policymaker perspective, the variety of positive and negative spillovers associated with the surrounding regions introduces some challenges for implementing horizontal multi-governance (Koschatzky et al., 2007): when is it possible for regions to cooperate? When are they competing?

In this context, as for knowledge production or economic growth, we suppose that spatial spillovers could have an impact on the capacity of scientific communities to become more central in the European network. Such spatially lagged characteristics are referred to as accessibility or connectivity measures (Ponds et al., 2010). High accessibility between two regions implies a high level of opportunities for interaction, and therefore a high level of potential (negative or positive) spillovers between two regions. In this context, we consider that spillovers from surrounding regions can also impact the way regions collaborate. Following Wanzenbock et al. (2014), we assume that "spatial connectivity affects a region's network position due to spillover mechanisms resulting from the spatial concentration of industries, knowledge-intensive sectors and organizations and the resulting economic dependencies and core-periphery structures between nearby regions" (p.343) (see, e.g. Feldman and Kogler, 2010).

Results regarding territorial spillovers may vary significantly between disciplines. If it is true that technical and institutional complementarities affect the development of disciplines (Bonaccorsi, 2008; Mora Valentine et al., 2002), we assume that they are very likely to work differently depending on the geographical scale. More specifically, technical complementarities seem to depend on huge investments more related at a "macro-region" level, if not related at a country policy level. The administrative borders of regions could therefore be too narrow. We expect positive or negative externalities from neighbouring regions.

The identification of scale has clear implications in terms of policy, namely with regard to the appropriate policymaker intervention level. When local resources are rolled up with regional ones, regional policymakers can play a key role in supporting economic development (Tödling et al., 2005). Conversely when surrounding regions influence local development, regional policymakers have to develop various forms of collaboration with others levels of public administration in order to support economic development (Medeiros, 2013). According to this perspective, therefore, policymakers have to address horizontal and vertical multi-governance challenges (Koschatzky et al., 2007). Our empirical analysis would propose different level of intervention according to the discipline considered.

2. REGIONAL NETWORKS: DATA AND METHODS

2.1. Data

In order to investigate the European scientific system, we focus on the existing collaboration between regions (NUTS2) in 8 broad scientific disciplines (see Table 1) defined by OST (2010) as an aggregation of Thomson Reuters Scientific Categories[1]. Data of co-publications among regions (EU27) used and citations associated

---

[1] The articles published in multidisciplinary journals are reallocated to these disciplines using the Thomson Reuters re-assignation procedure to subject categories.

come from the Web of Science (WoS) database, which contains information from most journals covering all scientific fields. We retrieve all scientific articles, letters, notes and reviews published between 2000 and 2011 and related to research collaborations between EU regions. A publication is considered as research collaboration between regions if it contains at least two different institutional addresses corresponding to two different NUTS2 regions. The publications co-authored by intra-regional institutions are therefore excluded and our study is limited to bilateral and multilateral inter-regional co-authorship. Our sample is based on four sets of smoothed data corresponding to 3-year periods: 2000-2002, 2003-2005, 2006-2008, and 2009-2011. Our empirical study covers 265 regions across 27 European countries. As publications are mainly written by public researchers, the network studied can be considered as the public scientific network.

Table 1: The Scientific Disciplines

Fundamental biology	Physics
Medicine	Science of the universe
Applied biology / ecology	Engineering sciences
Chemistry	Mathematics

2.2. Methods

We use the data on scientific publications co-authored by inter-regional institutions to build a network, by discipline and by period, where the actors /nodes are the regions and the links between them are co-publications. The value of the link between two regions is given by the number of collaborations in common in a given discipline over the period under analysis. We are therefore considering a weighted network.

The centrality of each region is captured by its degree of centrality. However, since we are considering a weighted network, referring to the degree of centrality can pose problems, as shown by Opsahl et al. (2010). In a weighted network, the degree of centrality is given by the sum of the weight of actor's links: in our case it would correspond to the number of inter-regions collaborations carried on by the focal region. However, this approach means that we completely lose the information about the number of partners: the same value of centrality (e.g. ten) can correspond to very different scenarios (e.g. one partner with which you have collaborated ten times or ten collaborations with ten different partners). Opsahl et al. (2010) propose a definition of the degree in a weighted network that is able to grasp both aspects of collaboration: quantity (i.e. degree) and strength. The weighted degree of centrality for actor i is therefore defined as the following:

$$C_D^{w\alpha}(i) = k_i \times \left(\frac{s_i}{k_i}\right)^{\alpha} = k_i^{(1-\alpha)} \times s_i^{\alpha} \quad (1)$$

where ki is the number of partners and si the sum of the strength of links between players, and α is the weighting parameter for each of the two aspects. We decide to set α as equal to 0.5 because we have no specific reasons to assign more importance to one aspect over another.

For meaningful comparison between degrees of centrality across eight different disciplines and across time, we propose a methodology to normalize the degree of centrality based on the rich-club phenomenon. Following the approach developed by Zhou and Mondargon (2004) and generalized by Serrano (2008), it is possible to check whether there is a breakpoint over the degree of centrality distribution of a discipline and so establish if regions are structured around a core (i.e. rich club) and a periphery[2].

Table 2: Weighted Links

Discipline		# Pairs of regions	Mean	Median	Max
	2000-2002				
Fundamental biology		12106	3.041	1.000	236.333
Medicine		13728	5.031	1.000	390.333
Applied biology/eco		7670	1.463	0.667	61.667
Chemistry		9897	2.167	0.667	183.000
Physics		10006	6.191	1.333	358.333
Science of the univ		8858	2.150	0.667	118.667
Engineering science		8739	1.726	0.667	127.667
Mathematics		3820	0.839	0.333	22.000
	2003-2005				
Fundamental biology		13270	3.342	1.000	243.000
Medicine		16197	6.072	1.333	534.667
Applied biology/eco		9233	1.579	0.667	77.000
Chemistry		10757	2.307	1.000	211.667
Physics		11063	7.202	1.333	429.667
Science of the univ		10775	3.272	1.000	198.333
Engineering science		10336	2.041	0.667	165.667
Mathematics		4504	0.941	0.333	38.333
	2006-2008				
Fundamental biology		15286	4.040	1.000	297.333
Medicine		18161	7.851	1.333	699.000
Applied biology/eco		11863	1.881	0.667	94.333
Chemistry		12053	2.527	1.000	265.333
Physics		12638	7.836	1.667	517.667
Science of the univ		13243	4.906	1.000	303.333
Engineering science		11558	2.157	0.667	218.000
Mathematics		5301	1.054	0.667	50.000
	2009-2011				
Fundamental biology		17745	5.341	1.333	393.333
Medicine		20729	10.145	2.000	1009.667
Applied biology/eco		14881	2.418	1.000	136.667
Chemistry		13007	2.789	1.000	322.333
Physics		13507	13.216	2.000	585.333
Science of the univ		16211	6.782	1.667	419.000
Engineering science		12428	2.418	1.000	259.667
Mathematics		6060	1.152	0.667	70.667

Once the degree of centrality has been calculated for each region, CDwα(i), we look at the characteristics of its distribution in order to identify the existence of a core-periphery structure (Serrano, 2008). To say that a network is characterized by

[2] This is only a necessary condition. The most central regions only constitute a core if the links between them are particularly intensive, i.e. the number of links between core members is greater than "the corresponding value in a randomized version of the graph that preserves the degree distribution" (Serrano, 2008, p. 4). Once this second condition is satisfied, it is possible to claim that the network analysed displays a core-periphery structure.

such a structure, a necessary condition is the presence of a break-point in the complementary cumulative distribution of actors' degrees of centrality.[3] Once the break-point is identified, the degree of centrality of each region in a specific discipline in a given period is divided by the corresponding value. This methodology allows us to take into account on the one hand the difference between disciplines in terms of number of collaborations, and on the other hand, the difference over time of number of collaborations that could impact on the value of centrality.

Table 3: Core Characteristics

Discipline		Min degree	Core size	Core share
	2000-2002			
Fundamental biology		191.053	87.000	0.328
Medicine		279.564	89.000	0.336
Applied biology/eco		79.297	93.000	0.351
Chemistry		141.539	89.000	0.336
Physics		306.844	61.000	0.230
Science of the univ		116.565	85.000	0.321
Engineering science		113.287	79.000	0.298
Mathematics		28.337	90.000	0.340
	2003-2005			
Fundamental biology		207.958	92.000	0.347
Medicine		351.994	92.000	0.347
Applied biology/eco		98.919	89.000	0.336
Chemistry		152.116	92.000	0.347
Physics		387.457	55.000	0.208
Science of the univ		194.048	77.000	0.291
Engineering science		138.444	83.000	0.313
Mathematics		32.660	96.000	0.362
	2006-2008			
Fundamental biology		260.898	93.000	0.351
Medicine		433.188	92.000	0.347
Applied biology/eco		134.005	100.000	0.377
Chemistry		178.863	90.000	0.340
Physics		400.932	60.000	0.226
Science of the univ		271.980	74.000	0.279
Engineering science		163.310	80.000	0.302
Mathematics		46.733	83.000	0.313
	2009-2011			
Fundamental biology		339.274	97.000	0.366
Medicine		529.426	99.000	0.374
Applied biology/eco		177.837	107.000	0.404
Chemistry		206.753	86.000	0.325
Physics		578.575	66.000	0.249
Science of the univ		366.999	83.000	0.313
Engineering science		180.849	86.000	0.325
Mathematics		48.819	97.000	0.366

[3] More technically, it is necessary to (i) compute the log-CCDF (complementary cumulative distribution function) of log-degree; (ii) "use a piece-wise linear regression of log-degree and log-CCDF using a moving threshold to get best fit for power law coefficients" (Zelnio, 2012, p. 604).

2.3. Network and core identification

We build 32 networks: eight disciplines/networks for each of the four periods. Table 2 shows the main distribution links values, i.e. s_i of equation 1.

We applied the methodology described in this section to the 32 networks in order to detect if there is a breakpoint, and, if so, its value. All of them show this structural breakpoint. Table 3 shows the minimum value and the number of regions that are on the right tail of the distribution (i.e. core).

The critical threshold of the core represented by the minimum degree increases over time for each domain. Both these factors reflect the network dynamics in the different fields studied. The differences between disciplines are striking. For instance, the minimum degree for Physics is ten times that for Mathematics, with the other six disciplines report values between the two extremes. Another difference concerns the relative size of the core. The main differences are among disciplines, where for instance Applied Biology is between 50 or more per cent greater than Physics. Less important are differences within the same discipline over time. This can be interpreted as sign of a certain inertia of the status of core member. In any case, the descriptive statistics show that these differences should be taken into account and raise questions over analysis that covers all disciplines together.

2.4. The determinants of centrality

The aim of our empirical exercise is to identify driving factors of regional position in the inter-regional scientific co-publications network. In order to compare results over different disciplines, we consider the degree centrality of the region normalized relative to the minimum degree necessary to belong to the core to be the dependent variables. This normalization allows us to compare the results in terms of magnitude of the coefficients. Otherwise they would be meaningless.

Moreover, we intend to control for spatial effect, in particular to check if the regions close to region i affect its potential to be central. To do so, we use an analytical framework that accounts for spatial knowledge spillover effects in our co-publications network analysis of EU regions (Autant-Bernard, 2012). A panel version of SDM (Elhorst, 2003 and 2012; Wanzenbock et al., 2014) is applied to our degree of centrality data. This model turns out to be more appropriate in empirical analysis for calculating the magnitude of direct impacts and indirect or spatial spillover effects (Autant-Bernard and LeSage, 2011; Elhorst, 2012). It makes it possible to distinguish between direct, indirect and total effects.

The panel SDM is written as follows:

$$y_t = \rho W y_t + X_t \beta_1 + W X_t \beta_2 + u_t$$

$$u_t = \mu + \tau_t + \epsilon_t$$

where y_t is an Nx1 vector containing degree of centrality in a discipline normalized relative to the minimum degree for belonging to the core, for each region (i=1,..., N) (Table 3) at time t where t=1, 2, 3, 4. Each of these four periods corresponds to 3-year of observations, namely 2000-2002, 2003-2005, 2006-2008, and 2009-2011. X_t is an NxK matrix of exogenous explanatory variables including a constant term. W is an NxN non-negative matrix of known constants describing the connections between regions. W, generically labelled spatial weight matrix (see, e.g., Anselin 1988) is constant over time, with the element of W in row i and column j denoted by w{ij}. The components of W are given by: w{ij}=0 for all i=j by assumption since no spatial unit can be considered its own neighbour, and w{ij}=1 if region i and region j are contiguous (i.e. they have a border in common) and w{ij}=0 otherwise. W is row-standardised, meaning that the row elements sum up to 1. Wy_t corresponds to Nx1 vector of the spatially-lagged dependent variable and WX_t is an NxK spatial lag matrix of K independent variables. The centrality of each region is then assumed to rely on weighted average centrality of its neighbouring regions and a weighted average of its neighbours' exogenous explanatory variables. The rho parameter associated with spatial lag of y_t is the spatial autoregressive coefficient and reflects the strength of the spatial interaction; β_1, β_2 denote Nx1 vectors of response parameters of predictors X and their spatial lag respectively. u_t denotes a Nx1 vector of error terms, with μ region specific fixed effects, τ_t period specific fixed effects and ε_t an Nx1 vector of normally distributed, homoscedastic and uncorrelated errors. The Maximum Likelihood procedure is applied to the spatial Durbin model (Elhorst, 2003) for estimating regression parameters based on fixed effects.

The explanatory variables, i.e. X_t, selected can be classified in two different groups: regional economic resources and scientific activities. With regard to the first, we considered some economic data for the period 1995-2011 retrieved from the Eurostat website in June 2013. In particular, for each region, we downloaded: the GDP per capita relative to the EU27 average, normalized to 100; the R&D expenditure level (% of GDP), broken down by Public and Private sector[4]. We opted to capture the relative degree of development of a region by a normalized measure of GDP per capita because this is the main criterion for identifying the target regions for the European Cohesion policy (i.e. a region with less than 75% of average GNP per capita). Finally, we selected an input variable such as human resources in Science and Technology (thousands of people) that is supposed to capture the research effort in each region and therefore its size.

The second set of variables measures scientific activities. Over all periods under observation, data on publications of regions in each discipline are taken into account. Two measures are defined: (i) the share of the discipline out of the total scientific production of the regions and (ii) the relative impact of each region's output in each discipline This is measured by the average number of citations received by the region in a given discipline benchmarked against the average number of citations received by the EU in the same domain. These two measures should capture respectively the quantity and quality of the results of the scientific efforts of each region in a specific field. They should make it possible to define the objective of a regional scientific activities policy. Is it reaching a sufficient critical mass? Or is the quest for excellence the silver bullet? Are they two sides of the same coin? Finally, we have defined a variable which counts how many other disciplines the region is already in the core in order to capture some inter-disciplinary spillovers, if there are any. This variable is calculated on the base of the network analysis explained previously.

3. RESULTS

Tables 4 and 6 presents the estimated coefficients for the eight disciplines, while, following Wanzenböck et al. (2014), Tables 5 and 7 present the average impact estimates for each discipline on the magnitude and significance of direct, indirect and total impacts on a region network position that would arise from a change in one unit of our regional characteristics, averaged over space and time. More specifically, the direct impacts measure the effects of region-internal characteristics on a region's network centrality, while the indirect impacts estimate the sum of spatial spillover effects, i.e. influences of changes in region-external characteristics. The overall influence of distinct characteristics on regional network centrality at the regional level is given by the total impact. LeSage (2009) shows that there are two

[4] To overcome a minor problem of missing data for some regions in Eurostat data, we use the median ratio procedure as suggested by Hollanders et al. (2012).

possible (equivalent) interpretations of the total effects. One interpretation (the one that we adopt in our discussion) reflects how changing an explanatory variable of all regions by some constant amount would affect the centrality of an average region. LeSage and Pace (2009) label this as the average total impact on an observation. The total effect includes both the average direct impact plus the average indirect impact. The second interpretation measures the total cumulative impact of a change in each explanatory variable in region i on the centrality of all neighboring regions, which Lesage and Pace (2009) label the average total impact from an observation.

Before looking at each of the eight regressions, it is worth noting that geographical space has a role in explaining core membership in six out of the eight disciplines analyzed. The estimates for the spatial autoregressive parameter (i.e. rho) are highly significant and positive for Fundamental Biology, Medicine, Applied Biology, Chemistry, the Science of the Universe and Engineering Sciences but not for Physics and Mathematics.

Table 4: Estimation results of fixed effects panel SDM (first set of disciplines)

	Fundamental biology		Medicine		Applied biology/ecology		Chemistry	
	coef.	t	coef.	t	coef.	t	coef.	t
GNP per capita	0.0008	0.8340	0.0023*	2.4710	0.0034***	3.5710	0.0007	0.7540
Number Fields Core Membership	0.0243***	4.8640	0.0158***	4.2500	0.0507***	4.6820	0.0324***	4.9990
Human resources in S&T	-0.0002	-1.0670	0.0001	0.4880	-0.0001	-0.3480	-0.0003**	-2.6490
Public R&D expenditures	0.1750**	3.1890	0.0992*	2.2450	0.1010	1.4000	0.1210*	2.2320
Private R&D expenditures	0.0118	0.6050	0.0530**	2.7640	0.0339	1.0060	0.0228	0.9290
Relative Impact	0.0927***	3.9990	0.0421***	3.8260	0.0767***	3.9780	0.0263	1.7880
Publication Share by field	0.5880**	3.0700	0.3040***	4.2630	0.9040***	4.3590	0.4770***	3.7130
W x GNP per capita	0.0019	1.6150	0.0014	1.4720	0.0030*	2.1450	0.0008	0.6620
W x Number Fields Core Membership	0.0150	1.4220	0.0014	0.1360	-0.0046	-0.3290	0.0262**	2.6420
W x Human resources in S&T	0.0002	1.1920	0.00004	0.3690	0.0003*	2.1750	0.0001	1.0840
W x Public R&D expenditures	0.0775	0.9750	-0.0268	-0.4620	-0.0313	-0.3170	-0.0188	-0.2280
W x Private R&D expenditures	0.0376	0.9480	0.0429	1.1190	0.0516	0.7830	0.0571	1.4920
W x Relative Impact	0.0493	1.2230	0.0014	0.0630	-0.0330	-0.8070	-0.0015	-0.0490
W x Publication Share by field	0.1080	0.3740	-0.0491	-0.3610	-0.1020	-0.3020	-0.7040***	-3.777
ρ	0.1030*	2.2370	0.3480***	6.3250	0.2790***	7.5200	0.1950***	4.9480
Observations	1060		1060		1060		1060	
Log Likelihood	1451.6000		1668.2000		1010.2000		1436.9000	

* $p < 0.05$, ** $p < 0.01$, *** $p < 0.001$

The first column of Table 5 presents impact measures for Fundamental Biology. With regard to direct impact, we observe that a region's capacity for scientific knowledge production is decisive for its centrality. It is unsurprising that the quantity (number of publications) and quality (relative impact) of scientific production in the discipline have a positive impact on centrality in fundamental biology. Moreover, the public R&D expenditure and being core in other disciplines also play an important role. With regard to indirect effects, we observe no spatial spillover impacts on a region's network centrality. This result differs from findings in previous literature on the spatial dimension of knowledge production which consider the existence of spatial spillovers from surrounding regions. In fundamental biology, surrounding resources would not directly impact centrality. The total impact estimation confirms direct impact results. Moreover, being in a rich region or surrounding by rich regions, also positively influence the centrality of a region. Total impact estimates suggest that activities in the field and the level of public R&D expenditure particularly influence network positioning in this discipline. These results suggest that in Fundamental Biology, in order to be central, regions need a large amount of regional scientific resources.

The second column of Table 5 presents impact measures for Medicine. Every variable except Human Resources in Science and Technology has a significant positive impact. Direct impact estimates suggest that regional production in the field is significantly an important capacity factor for being central in Medicine.

Being surrounding by rich regions (i.e. regions with higher GDP per capita) contributes to being a central region. This result confirms the significance of economically based spillover effects for centrality in scientific networks (Wanzenböck et al., 2014). Such spatial dependencies may for example arise due to the location of universities, which often tend to be located in regions surrounding urban centres, with further consequences on cross-regional commuting flows between regions.

Table 5: Marginal effects estimates of changes in SDM regressors (first set of disciplines)

	Fundamental biology	Medicine	Applied biology/ecology	Chemistry
	Mean	Mean	Mean	Mean
Direct effects				
GDP per capita	0.0009	0.0025**	0.0037***	0.0008
Number Fields Core Membership	0.0244***	0.0162***	0.0507***	0.0335***
Human resources in S&T	-0.0002	0.0001	-0.00004	-0.0003**
Public R&D expenditures	0.1750**	0.0985*	0.0989	0.1200*
Private R&D expenditures	0.0126	0.0587**	0.0384	0.0260
Relative Impact	0.0933***	0.0432***	0.0755***	0.0261
Publication Share by field	0.5820**	0.3050***	0.9030***	0.4430***
Indirect effects				
GDP per capita	0.0021	0.0032*	0.0052**	0.0010
Number Fields Core Membership	0.0194	0.0100	0.0129	0.0391**
Human resources in S&T	0.0002	0.0001	0.0004*	0.0001
Public R&D expenditures	0.1060	0.0117	-0.0014	0.0065
Private R&D expenditures	0.0419	0.0902	0.0811	0.0734
Relative Impact	0.0656	0.0236	-0.0141	0.0052
Publication Share by field	0.1700	0.0781	0.1850	-0.7440***
Total effects				
GDP per capita	0.0030***	0.0057***	0.0089***	0.0017
Number Fields Core Membership	0.0438***	0.0262	0.0636**	0.0727***
Human resources in S&T	-0.00002	0.0001	0.0004	-0.0002
Public R&D expenditures	0.2820**	0.1100	0.0975	0.1260
Private R&D expenditures	0.0545	0.1490*	0.1190	0.0994
Relative Impact	0.1590***	0.0668	0.0614	0.0313
Publication Share by field	0.7520*	0.3830	1.0890*	-0.3010

* $p < 0.05$, ** $p < 0.01$, *** $p < 0.001$

Given the total impact estimates for our regional characteristics in Medicine, the pattern observed for direct effects has been partly reversed. Total impact estimates for Medicine show only significant positive effects for a region's GDP and private R&D expenditure. Positive capacities based on effects due to the level of public R&D expenditure, being core in other fields and activities and visibility in Medicine are removed when region-internal and external impacts are considered together in our regional arrangement. These results suggest the importance of being in a rich region or surrounded by rich regions where firms do R&D.

In Applied Biology (third column Table 5), the economic level of the region, the effect of being core in other fields and activities and visibility positively influence the centrality of the region. Direct impact estimates suggest that regional production in the field is one of the most important factors. Positive spatial spillover impacts on a region's network centrality can be observed for the estimates for GDP and Human Resources in Science and Technology. Thus network centrality seems to be related to the economic strength of neighboring regions. Total effects confirm the importance of the economic level of the region and surrounding regions. Moreover, the number of disciplines in which the region is core is an important factor. However, the most important impact is the production of publications in Applied Biology. Quantity of scientific output matters. Regional quality is not any more significant, which suggests that it is important to be surrounded by dynamic regions but not ones which are too good.

Table 6: Estimation results of fixed effects panel SDM (second set of disciplines)

	Physics		Science of the Universe		Engineering science		Mathematics	
	coef.	t	coef.	t	coef.	t	coef.	t
GDP per capita	0.0018*	2.2480	0.0013	0.8540	0.0017	1.7740	-0.0004	-0.2610
Number Fields Core Membership	0.0455***	4.4370	0.0810***	4.8210	0.0363***	4.6780	0.0573***	4.4870
Human resources in S&T	0.0001	0.6160	-0.0003	-1.3330	-0.0002	-1.1440	-0.0001	-0.6130
Public R&D expenditures	0.0617	0.9390	0.0027	0.0290	0.1710**	2.8140	0.2540*	2.3230
Private R& D expenditures	-0.0018	-0.0630	-0.0366	-0.7910	0.0121	0.5010	-0.0182	-0.3690
Relative Impact	0.129***	5.2520	0.1780***	5.0340	0.0399**	3.1100	0.0269**	2.7540
Publication Share by field	0.8150***	4.1380	0.6520	1.6280	0.6040***	4.3700	1.8330***	3.6260
W x GDP per capita	0.0008	0.6320	0.0050*	2.3380	0.0021	1.5520	0.0022	1.1420
W x Number Fields Core Membership	0.0145	0.9360	-0.0046	-0.1690	0.0184	1.6370	-0.0137	-0.5470
W x Human resources in S&T	-0.00002	-0.1530	0.0002	0.7840	0.0003*	2.0670	0.0003	1.6550
W x Public R&D expenditures	-0.1700	-1.8400	-0.1920	-1.3740	-0.1340	-1.4100	-0.1210	-0.7710
W x Private R&D expenditures	0.0255	0.622	0.0929	1.092	0.0414	0.857	0.147*	2.171
W x Relative Impact	-0.0762*	-2.4060	-0.0896	-1.6820	0.0513	1.8430	0.0082	0.3840
W x Publication Share by field	-0.4760	-1.7030	0.7680*	2.0810	0.0254	0.1070	0.7170	0.6590
ρ	0.0535	1.5320	0.1270**	3.0560	0.1930***	4.5700	0.0480	1.2550
Observations	1060		1060		1060		1060	
Log Likelihood	1043.6000		657.2000		1256.5000		667.1000	

* $p < 0.05$, ** $p < 0.01$, *** $p < 0.001$

For network centrality in Chemistry (last column of Table 5), the regional level of publications has a positive impact. More surprisingly, the relative impact of the region is not significant. This means that the quality of publications does not contribute to increasing a region's degree of centrality. It is the only field with such a result. The number of fields in which the region is already core and the level of public R&D expenditure positively affect centrality. Finally, although it is low, the level of Human Resources in Science and Technology has a negative impact, which is puzzling. In the Chemistry network, a positive spatial spillover impact can be observed for estimates of the number of core fields in surrounding regions. By contrast, the level of publications in Chemistry has a strong negative impact. This suggests that surrounding regions need to be leaders in other fields but not too productive in chemistry. Negative effects may, for instance, result from core-periphery relations between neighboring regions (Wanzenböck et al., 2014). The total impact reduces this negative spillover effect since only the number of core fields is significant. In

Chemistry, the production of publications and their visibility would not be so important from a pan-European perspective. By contrast, being core in different fields and surrounded by regions in different fields makes a significant contribution to increasing a region's centrality.

For network centrality in Physics (first column Table 7), at the regional level, the field's quantity of production and quality largely contribute to the centrality of the region. Being core in other fields and the level of GDP influence centrality as well. The only significant spillover effect has a negative impact and it is the relative impact of the surrounding regions. At the total effect, only being core in other disciplines and the GDP per capita are still significant. Direct and indirect effects for both quantity and quality in physics cancel each other out. This suggests a core-periphery structure of the location of the activities in physics. To be central, a region needs to be surrounded by dynamic regions in economic activities and sciences (other than in physics).

Table 7: Marginal effects estimates of changes in SDM regressors (second set of disciplines)

	Physics Mean	Science of the Universe Mean	Engineering science Mean	Mathematics Mean
Direct effects				
GNP per capita	0.0018*	0.0015	0.0018*	-0.0003
Number Fields Core Membership	0.0451***	0.0802***	0.0369***	0.0564***
Human resources in S&T	0.0001	-0.0003	-0.0002	-0.0001
Public R&D expenditures	0.0580	-0.0039	0.1660**	0.2480*
Private R&D expenditures	-0.0013	-0.0334	0.0142	-0.0159
Relative Impact	0.1270***	0.1750***	0.0421**	0.0266**
Publication Share by field	0.8000***	0.6590	0.6020***	1.8150***
Indirect effects				
GNP per capita	0.0009	0.0055*	0.0028	0.0021
Number Fields Core Membership	0.0181	0.0070	0.0306*	-0.0109
Human resources in S&T	-0.00001	0.00015	0.0003	0.0003
Public R&D expenditures	-0.1740	-0.2110	-0.1210	-0.1110
Private R&D expenditures	0.0272	0.0995	0.0533	0.1520*
Relative Impact	-0.0721*	-0.0753	0.0703*	0.0104
Publication Share by field	-0.4650	0.9430*	0.1690	0.7990
Total effects				
GNP per capita	0.0027*	0.0070***	0.0046***	0.0018
Number Fields Core Membership	0.0632**	0.0872*	0.0675***	0.0456
Human resources in S&T	0.00008	-0.00015	0.00012	0.00021
Public R&D expenditures	-0.1160	-0.2150	0.0448	0.1370
Private R&D expenditures	0.0260	0.0661	0.0675	0.1370
Relative Impact	0.0550	0.0994	0.1120**	0.0370
Publication Share by field	0.3360	1.6020**	0.7700**	2.6140*

* $p < 0.05$, ** $p < 0.01$, *** $p < 0.001$

In the Science of the Universe (second column Table 7), the experience of being core in other disciplines and above all the relative impact of the region positively influence the centrality of the region. A positive spatial spillover impact can be observed for estimates of the GDP and scientific production in the field. Being surrounded by rich regions which produce many publications in Science of the Universe contributes to centrality. The total impact confirms the importance of the economic and scientific level of surrounding regions. Moreover, the number of disciplines in which the region is core is important. However, the positive effect of relative impact is removed. This means that to be central in the Science of the Universe a region needs to be surrounded by regions with a high level of scientific production but low relative impact (that means not too good).

For the Engineering Sciences network (third column Table 7), almost all the estimates are significant. This means that financial (GDP and Public R&D expenditures) and scientific resources (being core, production and quality of the research in engineering sciences) are the region-internal drivers. In particular, scientific production and public R&D expenditure have a strong impact. These impacts are reinforced by scientific production and the experience in being core in the surrounding regions. By contrast, public R&D expenditure has negative spillover effects even if it is not significant. This one is strong enough to cancel out the direct impact of public R&D expenditure in the total impacts.

For the Mathematics network, (last column Table 7), the resources dedicated to public R&D influence the centrality of regions. The main impact is largely due to the level of scientific production in the discipline. It is a surprise to note a positive spillover impact of surrounding private R&D expenditures. The total impact, only and largely accounts the level of scientific production. The relative impact is no more significant as both direct and indirect impacts seem to balance each other out.

4. DISCUSSION

This research brings several results according to the impacts of scientific and territorial resources on European regions network centrality. It highlights the differences between disciplines and stresses the importance to take into account territorial resources at various geographical scale.

The observed heterogeneity across disciplines shows how important it is to carry out disaggregated analysis. For instance, Wanzenbock et al. (2014), which adopted the same econometric methods but analyzed the scientific network at an aggregated level, found different results in terms of the effects of surrounding regions. Analyzing scientific networks without regard to disciplinary specificities could erase and hide important differences.

Thus, our results show that according to the disciplines, the role of internal resources differs and does not automatically improve the scientific network centrality. For instance, in fundamental biology, it is worthwhile to invest in both production and excellence to increase centrality. In mathematics, it is better to focus on excellence; the effort for scientific production would be useless at the global level. Finally, in physics, none investment on scientific internal resources gives some positive effects on centrality.

In more general terms, the observed heterogeneity raises the issue of the different roles that regional resources can play and consequently the different implications for policymaking. First of all, let us return to the interpretation of the results in the SDM method used. On the one hand, it is possible to use the direct effects and the indirect effects. This analysis can determine what influence each independent variable, i.e. the normalized degree of centrality. However, on the other hand, it is necessary to check if the results are still significant overall and, then to look at the sign and magnitude of the overall effect. Indeed only the analysis of the total effects makes it possible to identify which (direct or indirect) effect dominates.

The results can be organized around the various possible combinations between positive, zero or negative direct and indirect effects. In our opinion, each combination can be interpreted in terms of the role a territory could play. Three cases have been observed:

- The parameters of the direct and the indirect effects for a factor have the same sign. A strengthening territorial effect is in play. For example, if the parameter is positive, increasing the scientific production of the region and its neighbors increases the centrality of the focal region.

- The parameters of the direct and indirect effects for a factor are a different sign: there is a competitive effect between territories. For instance, the increase of its own scientific production would increase the centrality of the region but an increase by surrounding regions would have a negative effect on it centrality.

- The parameter of the direct effect is significant but, that of the indirect effect is not (or vice-versa): we assume that there is independence between regions. For instance, increasing regional scientific production would increase centrality but growth of scientific production among nearby regions would no impact on centrality.

These three possible combinations should be compared with the total effects results in order to verify if overall, territorial effects are still in operation or not.

In fundamental biology, territory seems generally independent, the indirect effect parameters are not significant and the total effects parameters, which are significant, are more or less the same as those of the direct effects. However, in engineering science, territory has a reinforcing role – the parameters of the direct and indirect effects, as well as those of total effects are positive. The surrounding regions have a reinforcing role and support local effects. This is particularly true for the quality of the science. This result shows that in this discipline, administrative territory boundaries should not be applied consistently in order to develop collaboration on scientific activities.

For the other disciplines, we have no overall result but different cases according to the variable taken into account. In mathematics, territories are more competitive than complementary. Indeed, the surrounding regions have a negative impact and, when we look at the total effect, only scientific production has a significant effect. In many cases (such as quality, private R&D, public R&D), the direct and indirect effects cancel each other.

In medicine, territories are in competition (even if we do not observe significant spillover effects), except in terms of economic development. Indeed, only economic factors (private R&D and GDP) are significant at the total effect level. This could mean that regions can become more central if they are surrounded by rich regions with private R&D activities but no science activities. The economic territory would be larger than the administrative region and play a reinforcing role. With regard to scientific activities, the regions would compete with each other.

In Science of the Universe, territory plays a particularly important role because the factors of the surrounding regions contribute the most (GDP and scientific production) to the centrality of the region, it is already core in other disciplines.

For the remaining four other disciplines, there are several similarities. We therefore propose to discuss them by the factors driving centrality rather than by the disciplines. One of the most interesting results is the impact of scientific activities (quantity or number of publications and quality or relative impact) in the field performed by surrounding regions. The territories are in competition for excellence in research. Indeed, for Physics, Science of the Universe, Applied Biology (and also in Mathematics and Medicine), the quality of the surrounding regions have a negative impact on centrality. That means that for these disciplines, there is a core-periphery structure with regard to the location of disciplines: if one region is central, the surrounding ones would do less good science. This has a clear implication in terms of research organization at a country level: it is unlikely that two regions that are good in sciences would be close to each other. Surprisingly the results are not the same for chemistry: the quality of science does not have any impact (direct or indirect).

In terms of scientific production, we observe a competition between territories in two disciplines. Indeed, scientific production has the same negative effect for physics and chemistry. If a region is surrounded by large producers in their fields, it is less central.

Being central in other disciplines (and/or complementarity between disciplines) increases centrality for almost all disciplines. Except in Mathematics and Applied Biology, there is a reinforcing effect from surrounding regions.

The diversity of the cases observed shows how important it is to carefully choose the relevant territorial scale for the development of research activities collaborations. Indeed, depending on the disciplines and factors taken into account, the territory does not play the same role. In general, our results can be summarized as follows; to explain the scientific centrality of a region, economic variables show a more strengthening complementarity between regions while scientific factors tend to be neutral or show competition between regions.

The various impacts of territories on centrality have some effects on public policy in the horizontal and vertical forms of governance approaches. Governance type should be selected according to the role played by the territory. We can therefore identify four potential cases by level of public intervention.

Table 8: Case of policy intervention

Case	Effect			Role of territories	Regional policy	Level of intervention
	total	direct	Indirect			
1	+	+	+	Reinforcing	Active	**Horizontal Multi-governance** – Incentive for coordination
2	+	+	Insignificant	Not relevant	Active	**Regional governance** – no interest in coordination
3	+	Insignificant	+	Larger scale	Not useful	**Vertical Multi-governance** – macro region level
4	+	+	-	Competition	Active, only if direct effect overcame indirect effect (less effective than case 1)	**Regional governance or nothing**

According to our results, two previously identified typical cases lead to "traditional" public policies. For fundamental biology, an independently-led regional policy will have the most chance of effectively increasing the region's centrality in the discipline.

For engineering sciences, policymakers wishing to optimize the effects of their policies need to coordinate their actions with surrounding regions. In such cases, regional policymakers have to foster horizontal multi-governance.

For other disciplines, policymakers need to carefully adapt their strategy; they have to shift from a cooperative to competitive paradigm depending on the driving factors. Table 9 summarizes when, according to the significant factors, regional policymakers should act alone and when they should cooperate. It should be noted that in our study, in the case of competition between territories direct and indirect effects cancel each other out for total effects.

For instance, to be more central in Mathematics, a region only needs to invest in the production of scientific publications. In Medicine and Applied Biology, policy-makers should develop horizontal multi-governance policies for economic factors and act at a regional level for private R&D in the case of Medicine and scientific production for Applied Biology.

Table 9: Policy intervention by scientific disciplines

Scale of the territory	Regions only	Collaboration between regions	Competition between regions	Changing scale of the territory
Policy intervention	**Regional**	**Horizontal governance**	**Regional**	**Vertical multi-governance**
Fundamental Bio	All			
Engineering sc.		All		
Physics	GDP Core			
Science of the Universe	Core			Scientific production GDP
Mathematics	Scientific production			
Chemistry		Core		
Medicine	Private R&D	GDP		
Applied Biology	Scientific production Core	GDP		

The complex picture that our analysis allows us to draw shows that policymakers should adapt their interventions according to disciplinary specificities. This is true for two main reasons: (1) not all variables play the same role for each discipline, and (2) the territorial scale of intervention can differ significantly according to the discipline and variable taken into account.

Our analysis does, however, suffer some limitations. The first concerns the data on scientific activities. Scientific co-publications only capture a part of actual scientific collaborations. Moreover, coverage of different disciplines is heterogeneous. In particular, Humanities and Social science coverage is very low in WoS and it has not been possible to analyze these disciplines too. Second, the explanatory variables are relatively few and standard. Taking into account other variables would imply reducing the number of regions analyzed, and therefore, most likely, covering the most peripheral regions less. Moreover, our research identifies that there are positive or negative spillovers on centrality according the disciplines. Further research is needed to explain these different results. Finally, the relationship between network centrality and excellence deserves further investigation.

REFERENCES

Andersson, M., Karlsson, C., Grasjo, U., 2007, "Human Capital and Productivity in a Spatial Economic System", *Annales d'économie et de statistique*, 87/88, 125-143.

Aranguren, A.J., Larrea, M., Wilson, J., 2010, Learning from the local governance of nework for innovation in the Basque Country, *European Planning Studies*, 18,1, 47-65.

Arora V., Vamvakidis A., 2005, Economic Spillovers. Exploring the Impact Trading Partners have on Each Other's Growth, *Finance and Development*, 42, 3

Asheim, B.T., (eds), 2006, Constructing regional advantage: principles, perspectives", policies, *European Commission Report*, Brussels.

Asheim, B.T., Coenen, L., 2005, Knowledge Bases and Regional Innovation Systems: Comparing Nordic Clusters, *Research Policy*, 34, 8, 1173-1190.

Autant Bernard, C., Billand, P., Frachisse, D., Massard, N., 2007, Social distance versus spatial distance in R&D cooperation : empirical evidence from European Collaboration choices in micro and nanotechnologies, *Papers In Regional Science*, 86, 495-519

Autant Bernard, C., 2001, Science and knowledge flows: Evidence from the French case, *Research Policy*, 30, 7, 1069-1078.

Autant-Bernard, C., 2012, Spatial Econometrics of Innovation: Recent Contributions and Research Perspectives, *Spatial Economic Analysis*, 7, 403-419.

Autant-Bernard, C., LeSage, J.P., 2011, Quantifying knowledge spillovers using spatial econometric models, *Journal of Regional Science*, 51, 3, 471-496.

Autant-Bernard, C., Massard, N., Charlot, S., 2008, Les déterminants géographiques de l'innovation : Diffusion spatiale des connaissances et choix de localisation, in : Madiès, T., Prager, J.-C. (Eds.), *Innovation et compétitivité des régions*, La Documentation Française, Paris, 227-265.

Barber, M.J., Fischer, M.M., Scherngell, T., 2011, The Community Structure of R&D Cooperation in Europe. Evidence from a social network perspective. *Geographical Analysis*, 43, 4, 415-432.

Benneworth, P., Hospers, G.J., 2007, The new economic geography of old industrial regions: universities as global/local pipelines, *Environment and Planning: Government and Policy*, 25,6, 779-802.

Bergé, L., Wanzenbock, I., Scherngell, T, 2015, Centrality of regions in R&D networks: Conceptual clarifications and a new measure, *Cahier du Gretha*, n° 2015-31, Université de Bordeaux.

Bonaccorsi, A., 2008, Search regimes and the industrial dynamics of science, *Minerva*, 46, 285-315.

Borgatti, S. P., 2005, Centrality and network flow. *Social Networks* 27, 1, 55-71.

Boschma, R., Frenken, K., 2010, The spatial evolution of innovation networks : a proximity"; in Boschma R., Martin R. *The Handbook of Evolutionary Economic Geography*, Edward Elgar.

Breschi, S., Lissoni, F., 2009, Mobility of skilled workers and co-invention networks: an anatomy of localized knowledge flows, *Journal of Economic Geography* 9, 4, 439-468.

Burt, R.S., 1992. *Structural holes: The social structure of competition*. Harvard University Press, Cambridge, MA.

Capello, R., 2009, Spatial Spillovers and Regional Growth: A Cognitive Approach, *European Planning Studies*, 9, 2.

Cooke, P., 2001, "Regional innovation systems, clusters, and the knowledge economy", *Industrial and Corporate Change*, 10, 4, 945-974.

Crespy, C., Heraud, J.A., Perry, B., 2007, Multilevel governance, regions and science in France between competition and equality, *Regional Studies*, 4, 8, 1069-1084.

Doloreux, D., Bitard, P., 2005, Les systèmes régionaux d'innovation : discussion critique, *Géographie, Economie et Société*, 7, 21-36.

Doloreux, D., Dionne, S., 2008, Is regional innovation system development possible in peripheral regions? Some evidence from the case of La Pocatiere Canada, *Entrepreneurship and Regional Development*, 20, 259-283.

Elhorst, J.P., 2003, Specification and estimation of spatial panel data models, *International Regional Science Review*, 26, 3, 244–268.

Elhorst, J.P., 2012, Dynamic spatial panels: models, methods, and inferences, *Journal of Geographical Systems*, 14, 5–28.

Feldman, M.P., Kogler, D.F., 2010, Stylized facts in the geography of innovation, in Hall B.H. and Rosenberg N., *The Handbook of the economics of innovation*, Elsevier.

Feldman, M. P., 1994, *The Geography of Innovation*, Kluwer Academic Publishers, Boston.

Frenken, K., Hardeman, S., Hoekman, J., 2009, Spatial scientometrics: towards a cumulative research program, *Journal of infometrics*, 3, 222-232.

Gallie, E.P., Legros, D., 2007, How do spatial spillovers diffuse in science-industry interactions? The case of French biotech sector, *Economics of Innovation and New Technology*, 16, 8, 635-652.

Gelsing, L., 2010, Innovation and the development of industrial networks, in Lundvall B.A. (ed) *National systems of innovation: toward a theory of innovation and interactive learning*. Anthem Press, London.

Genuth, J., Chompalov, I., Shrum, W., 2010, How experiments begin: the formation of scientific collaborations, *Minerva*, 38, 311-348.

Gilsing, V., Nopoteboom, B., Vanhaverbeke, W., Duysters, G., van den Oord, A., 2008, Network embeddedness and the exploration of novel technologies: Technological distance, betweenness centrality and density, *Research Policy*, 17, 10, 1717-1731.

Hamdouch, A., Depret, M.-H., 2009, Surveying the Literature on Territorial Innovation Systems: A Suggested Interpretation Framework, *SSRN Working Papers Series*.

Hazir, C.S., Autant-Bernard, C., 2014, Determinants of cross-regional R&D collaboration: some empirical evidence from Europe in biotechnology, *Annals of Regional Science*, 53, 369-393.

Hewitt-Dundas, N., Roper, S., 2011, Creating advantage in peripheral regions: The role of publicly funded R&D centres, *Research Policy*, 40, 6, 832-841.

Hoeckman, J., Frenken, K., Tijssen, R.J., 2010, Research collaboration at a distance: changing spatial patterns of scientific collaboration within Europe, *Research Policy*, 39, 662-673.

Hollanders, H., Derbyshire, J., Lewney, R., Tijssen, R., Tarantola, S., Rivera Leon, L., 2012, Methodology report, Regional Innovation Scoreboard 2012.

Jaffe, A. B., 1989, "Real effects of academic research", *American Economic Review*, 79, 5, 957-970.

Karlsson, C., Grasjo, U., Andersson, M., 2006, Regional knowledge Accessibility and regional economic growth, *Conference of the European regional Science Association*, Volos, Greece.

Koschatzky, K., Kroll, H., 2007, Which side of the coin ? The regional governance of science and innovation, *Regional Studies*, 41, 8, 1115-1127.

Kratke, S., Brandt, A., 2009. Knowledge Networks as a Regional Development Resource: A network Analysis of the interlinks between scientific institutions and regional firms in the Metropolitan region of Hannover, Germany, *European Planning Studies*, 17,1, 43-63.

LeSage, J.P., 2009, An introduction to spatial econometrics, *Revue d'économie industrielle*, 123, 19-44.

LeSage, J.P., Pace, R.K., 2009, *Introduction to Spatial Econometrics*, C R C Press, Boca Raton, New York.

Maggioni, M. A., Nosvelli, M., Uberti, T. E., 2007. Space versus networks in the geography of innovation: A European analysis. *Papers in Regional Science*, 86 , 3, 471-493.

Mattsson, P., Laget, P., Nillson, A., Sundberg, C.J., 2008, Intra-EU vs. extra-EU scientific co-publication patterns in EU, *Scientometrics*, 75, 3, 555-574.

Mederos, E., 2013, Euro-Meso-Macro : The new regions in Iberian and European Space, *Regional Studies*, 47, 8, 1249-1266.

Merito, M., Bonaccorsi, A., 2007, Co-evolution of physical and social technologies in clinical practice: the case of HIV treatments, *Research Policy*, 36, 7, 1070-1087.

Mora-Valentin, E.M., Montoro-Sanchez, A., Guerras-Martin, L.A., 2002. Determining factors in the success of R&D cooperative agreements between firms and research organizations, 28 *The EBA conference, Regional integration, agglomeration and international business*, Athens, Greece.

Morrison, A, Rabellotti, R, Zirulia, L., 2013, When do global pipelines enhance the diffusion of knowledge in clusters?, *Economy Geography*, 89, 77-96.

OECD, 2011, Regions and innovation policy, *OECD Review of Regional Policies*, OECD Publishing.

OECD, 2013, Regions and Innovation: Collaborating across Borders, *OECD Reviews of Regional Innovation*, OECD Publishing.

Opsahl, T., Agneessens, F., Skvoretz, J., 2010, Node centrality in weighted networks: Generalizing degree and shortest paths, *Social Networks*, 32, 245-251.

Percoco, M., 2010 , Airport Activity and Local Development: Evidence from Italy, *Urban studies,* 47, 11.

Perry, B., 2007, The multi-level governance of science policy in England, *Regional Studies*, 418, 1051-1067.

Pinto, H., 2009, The diversity of innovation in the European Union: Mapping latent dimensions and regional profiles, *European planning studies,* 17, 2, 303-326.

Ponds, R., Oort, F.V., Frenken, K., 2010, Innovation, spillovers and university-industry collaboration: an extended knowledge production function approach. *Journal of Economic Geography* 10, 2, 231-255.

Ponds, R., van Oort, F. Frenken, K., 2010, Innovation, spillovers and university industry collaboration: an extended knowledge production function approach, *Journal of Economic Geography*, 10, 231-255.

Serrano, M., 2008, Rich-club vs rich-multipolarization phenomena in weighted networks, *Physical Review*, E 78.

Tijssen, R.W., Van Leeuwen, T.N., 2007, Research cooperation within Europe: bibliometric views of geographical trends and integration processes. in Torres-Salinas, D. Moed H. (eds), *Proceeding trends and integration, proceedings of the ISSI 2007*, CINDOC CSIC, Madrid, 744-758.

Tödling, F., Trippl, M., 2005, One size fits all? Towards a differentiated regional innovation policy approach, *Research Policy*, 34, 1203-1219.

Todt, O., Gutierrez-Garcia, A., Fernandez de Lucio, I., Castro-Martinez, E. 2007, The regional dimension of innovation and the globalization of science: the case of biotechnology in a peripheral region of the European Union, *R&D management*, 37, 65-74.

Wanzenbock, I., Scherngell, T., Lata, R. 2015, Embeddedness of European regions in European Union-Funded Research and Development Networks: a spatial econometric perspective, *Regional Studies*, 49, 10, 1685-1705.

Wanzenböck, I, Scherngell, T, Brenner, T., 2014, Embeddedness of regions in European knowledge networks. A comparative analysis of inter-regional R&D collaborations, co-patents and co-publications, *The Annals of Regional Science*, 53, 337-368.

Zelnio, R., 2012, Identifying the global core-periphery structure of science, *Scientometrics*, 91, 601-615.

Zhou, S., Mondragon, R.J., 2004, The Rich-Club Phenomenon in the Internet Topology, *IEEE Communications Letters,* 8, 180-182.

Zitt, M., Bassecoulard, E., Okubo, Y., 2000, Shadows of the past in international cooperation: collaboration profiles of the top five producers of science", *Scientometrics*, 47, 3, 627-657.

La centralité des régions européennes dans les réseaux scientifiques : le rôle des ressources territoriales

Résumé - Cet article fournit un cadre original pour examiner les réseaux de collaborations scientifiques au niveau des régions européennes. Quels sont les facteurs qui conduisent au phénomène de clusterisation observé ? Quel est le rôle des territoires ? L'objectif de cet article est d'apporter des résultats empiriques permettant de fournir des éléments de réponse à ces questions. Pour cela, nous nous appuyons sur l'analyse des collaborations scientifiques entre les régions européennes dans huit disciplines différentes (Médecine, Chimie...) sur la période 2001-2011. Une mesure de la centralité normalisée est proposée. Nous testons l'impact des ressources territoriales et des spécificités scientifiques sur la centralité des régions dans chacune des disciplines. L'analyse met en avant une forte hétérogénéité entre les disciplines, montrant l'importance de réaliser des analyses spécifiques pour chacune d'elles. Les résultats montrent également les différents rôles que jouent les ressources locales, selon les disciplines. Enfin, l'article discute de l'implication de ces résultats en termes de politiques de la science et de l'innovation.

Mots-clés

Réseaux scientifiques
Régions européennes
Centralité
Ressources territoriales
Politiques de la science et de l'innovation

Région et Développement

n° 47-2018

www.regionetdeveloppement.org

La relation croissance-chômage en Tunisie : validation de la spécification non linéaire de la loi d'Okun

Abdessalem GOUIDER*, Ridha NOUIRA, Faouzi SBOUI*****

Résumé - Ce travail propose de tester pour l'économie tunisienne la validité de la relation d'Okun appliquée à des données annuelles de PIB réel et de chômage couvrant la période 1980-2015. Il est vérifié l'existence d'une relation non linéaire entre la croissance et le chômage : le chômage cyclique est plus sensible aux variations du PIB (*output gap*) en phases de récession qu'en phases d'expansion. L'analyse de la relation de causalité non linéaire entre le chômage et la croissance montre une causalité significative dans un seul sens allant de l'*output gap* au chômage.

Classification JEL

C13, C49, C52, E24

Mots-clés

Chômage
Loi d'Okun
Modèle NARDL
Tunisie

Les auteurs remercient le rapporteur anonyme et la rédaction de la revue pour leurs commentaires qui ont aidé à l'amélioration de cet article.

* College of Economics and Administrative Sciences, Al-Imam Mohammad Ibn Saud Islamic University (IMSIU), Saudi Arabia and Gabes University (Tunisia); abdgouider2011@gmail.com.

** Unité de Recherche EAS, Université de Mahdia, FSEG de Mahdia, Université de Monastir ; nouira.ridha75@gmail.com.

*** Unité de Recherche MOfid, Université de Sousse, FSEG de Mahdia, Université de Monastir ; sbouif@yahoo.fr.

INTRODUCTION

Dans un contexte de chômage massif, la relance de la croissance économique est souvent avancée comme une solution adéquate. Cependant, l'augmentation du taux de croissance n'implique pas nécessairement la diminution du taux de chômage et ce pour diverses raisons. Tout d'abord, la population active peut croitre à un taux plus élevé que celui de l'emploi. Ensuite, la croissance économique peut avoir un faible contenu en emploi selon la croissance de la productivité (Huang et Lin, 2008).

En 1962, Arthur Okun s'est intéressé à la relation entre la croissance économique mesurée par le taux de croissance du PIB réel et le chômage aux Etats-Unis. Cette relation dite « loi d'Okun » permet de déterminer le seuil de croissance à partir duquel le taux de chômage commence à diminuer. Okun conclut qu'une croissance de 1% du PIB réel aux Etats-Unis permet de réduire le taux de chômage de 0,4%. En outre, lorsque le taux de croissance atteint 3%, le taux de chômage tend à se stabiliser. Au-delà de 3%, les emplois créés conduisent le taux de chômage à diminuer.

Les premiers travaux testant la relation d'Okun ont adopté une modélisation linéaire de la relation croissance-chômage [Gordon (1984) ; Clark (1989); Prachowny (1993) ; Moosa (1997) ; Attfield et Silverstone (1997,1998) ; Crespo Cuaresma (2003)]. Des études plus récentes ont remis en cause l'hypothèse de linéarité de la relation d'Okun au profit de spécifications non linéaires qui supposent l'asymétrie de la relation croissance-chômage en phases d'expansion et de récession [Lee (2000), Huang et Chang (2005), Cuaresma (2003), Fouquau (2008), etc.]. Les contractions de l'économie ont des effets plus forts et rapides sur le chômage alors que les phases d'expansion ont des effets plus progressifs. Ainsi, en supposant l'absence de contraintes réglementaires sur le licenciement, dès l'entrée en récession les employeurs vont réagir rapidement en se séparant d'une partie de leur personnel. A l'inverse, quand l'économie prend le chemin de la reprise, les entreprises demeurent prudentes à recruter des employés car elles doutent de la durabilité de la reprise.

L'étude de la relation croissance-chômage est intéressante dans le contexte tunisien. La Tunisie a toujours enregistré des taux de chômage à deux chiffres malgré le fort investissement en éducation et les réformes économiques adoptées depuis la fin des années 1980. En outre, le chômage en Tunisie revêt un caractère structurel dans la mesure où la part des chômeurs de longue durée (plus d'un an) a connu une hausse considérable. Ainsi, la croissance économique réalisée pendant les dernières décennies n'a pas généré suffisamment de postes de travail pour absorber les nouveaux demandeurs d'emplois, notamment les femmes et les jeunes diplômés.

L'aggravation du taux de chômage, un des facteurs principaux ayant conduit aux évènements survenus en Tunisie à partir de mi-décembre 2010, a relancé le débat sur la relation entre le taux de croissance et le taux de chômage. L'objectif principal de ce travail est justement de mesurer la sensibilité du chômage aux variations du taux de croissance du PIB en Tunisie, ce qui revient à estimer le coefficient d'Okun et vérifier sa validité.

Cet article est structuré comme suit. La première section donne un survol de la littérature sur la relation d'Okun. La deuxième section présente les caractéristiques de la relation entre la croissance économique et le chômage en Tunisie. La troisième section décrit la méthodologie adoptée. Les tests empiriques, les résultats et les interprétations correspondantes sont présentés dans la quatrième section.

1. REVUE DE LA LITTÉRATURE SUR LA RELATION D'OKUN

Arthur Okun a été le premier à expliquer la relation négative entre la croissance et le chômage. Il a proposé deux types d'approches pour modéliser la relation entre le chômage et le PIB réel : la version en « différences premières » qui relie la variation du PIB réel aux variations du taux de chômage observé et la version « gap » qui relie les variations cycliques du PIB aux variations cycliques du chômage[1]. Depuis, plusieurs travaux ont tenté de vérifier la validité de cette relation dans d'autres pays autres que les Etats-Unis, mais aussi de tenir compte des éléments négligés par Okun tels que la présence de changement structurel et d'asymétrie dans cette relation (non linéarité de la loi d'Okun). Bien qu'ils se distinguent au niveau du choix de la fréquence des données, de la version à tester, des filtres à utiliser pour le calcul des variables potentielles, etc., la majorité de ces travaux se sont attachés à prouver la non linéarité de la relation d'Okun.

Dans ce sens, Frank et Stengos (1989) ont indiqué l'incapacité des tests classiques de Box-Pierce et de Ljung-Box à détecter la dépendance temporelle rattachée aux séries générées par des processus non-linéaires. Egalement, Froot et Rogoff (1995) et Lothian et Taylor (1996) ont mis en évidence l'inadéquation des tests traditionnels (tests de racine unitaire, tests de cointégration) dans le cas de la non-linéarité. Ainsi, en supposant la non linéarité des séries économiques, les conclusions que l'on pourrait tirer concernant leur stationnarité sont erronées si l'on raisonne dans un cadre linéaire.

Le recours aux spécifications non linéaires de la relation croissance-chômage est justifié par l'incapacité de la modélisation linéaire à tenir compte du changement de régime, des ruptures de tendance et d'asymétrie du cycle. Par exemple, la linéarité ne permet pas de capter la dynamique du chômage au cours d'une crise économique de grande ampleur (période de grande récession). Pour tenir compte de cette non-linéarité qui implique l'asymétrie du coefficient d'Okun, une vaste littérature empirique a été développée [Lee (2000), Harris et Silverstone (2001) ; Sögner et Stiassny (2002) Huang et Chang (2005) ; Huang et Chang (2005) ; Holmes et Silverstone (2006); Huang et Lin (2006) ; Fouquau (2008) ; Beaton (2010), etc.].

En utilisant les données trimestrielles relatives à l'économie canadienne pour la période 1960-2002, Huang et Chang (2005) testent la validité de la loi d'Okun en adoptant une approche en changement structurel avec seuil. Tenant compte de la non linéarité de la relation d'Okun, les deux auteurs ont trouvé que les coefficients d'Okun sont significativement plus élevés en valeur absolue dans les périodes de récession que dans les phases d'expansion. Ce résultat a été conforté par Knotek (2007) qui a montré que le coefficient d'Okun s'affaiblit au cours des phases d'expansion par rapport aux périodes de récession.

De même, Cuaresma (2003) considère que la relation négative entre la production et le chômage peut prendre une forme non linéaire dans la mesure où les changements du niveau de la production peuvent produire des changements asymétriques du niveau de chômage. Utilisant une spécification non linéaire de la relation entre le chômage cyclique et la production cyclique pour l'économie américaine, Cuaresma a trouvé que l'effet de la croissance du PIB sur le chômage est asymétrique et que le chômage cyclique est plus sensible à l'écart de production lorsque l'économie se situe dans des phases de récession.

En utilisant un modèle en panel non dynamique de 20 pays de l'OCDE sur la période 1970-2004, Fouquau (2008) obtient des résultats conduisant au rejet de l'hypothèse de linéarité de la relation croissance-chômage et confirme l'existence d'une asymétrie dans la relation d'Okun.

D'autres extensions du travail pionnier d'Okun (1962) se sont intéressés à vérifier la présence de changement structurel et d'asymétrie dans la relation croissance-chômage au niveau des sous-groupes de la population active répartie selon le genre, l'âge, la région, etc. Dans ce cadre, Boda et Považanová (2015) ont utilisé un modèle

[1]Le PIB cyclique est mesuré par la différence entre le PIB observé et le PIB potentiel alors que le chômage cyclique est la différence entre le taux de chômage observé et le taux de chômage naturel.

VAR structurel pour vérifier dans quelle mesure la variable genre peut être à l'origine d'une asymétrie de la relation croissance-chômage pour quatre pays à savoir le Portugal, l'Italie, l'Espagne et la Grèce. En utilisant des données trimestrielles sur la période 1998-2014, ces auteurs ont conclu que la variable genre peut effectivement être à la base d'une asymétrie de la loi d'Okun, le chômage des hommes réagissant différemment que le chômage des femmes aux fluctuations cycliques de la production.

Zanin (2014) a examiné la relation d'Okun différemment pour les hommes et les femmes selon les classes d'âge pour les pays de l'OCDE. En se référant à des données qui couvrent la période 1998-2012, il trouve que les groupes d'âge les plus jeunes (et particulièrement la population masculine jeune) sont les plus sensibles aux fluctuations économiques par rapport aux cohortes les plus âgées.

Villaverde et Maza (2009) ont analysé la relation croissance-chômage pour les régions espagnoles sur la période 1980-2004 en se référant à la version « gap » de la loi d'Okun. Ils ont conclu que la relation inverse entre le chômage et la croissance est valable pour la majorité des régions mais les coefficients d'Okun sont très différents ce qui renvoie à la non linéarité de la relation d'Okun. Selon Villaverde et Maza, cette disparité par région du coefficient d'Okun est expliquée en partie par des disparités régionales de la croissance de la productivité.

2. RELATION CROISSANCE-CHÔMAGE EN TUNISIE

En Tunisie, la relation croissance-emploi a connu au moins deux évolutions historiques. Avant 1986, ce sont principalement les entreprises publiques, malgré leurs difficultés financières et leur manque de compétitivité, qui créent l'essentiel de l'emploi. Le marché du travail est alors soumis à des politiques très rigides ayant entrainé un sureffectif de main-d'œuvre particulièrement dans les entreprises publiques et les administrations. A partir de 1986, un programme de mise à niveau a été mis en place afin de restructurer les entreprises publiques en difficulté et réhabiliter le rôle du secteur privé. Le code du travail a alors connu d'importantes réformes qui ont visé plus de flexibilisation des relations de travail et une meilleure protection sociale des travailleurs. Un désengagement progressif de l'Etat au profit du secteur privé a permis de réduire l'offre d'emplois dans le secteur public mais aussi de faire apparaître de nouvelles formes de travail qui ont accentué la précarité de l'emploi (travail à temps partiel, contrats à durée déterminée, etc..).

Par ailleurs, l'économie tunisienne a connu de profondes mutations depuis l'indépendance. Dominée longtemps par les activités agricoles, la production nationale s'est diversifiée, notamment via le renforcement de la part des industries manufacturières, dont la productivité relative reste faible, et des services (voir Annexe 1). Malgré la diversification progressive de l'économie tunisienne marquée par un secteur de services en expansion continue, employant plus de la moitié de la main-d'œuvre occupée et contribuant à raison de 62% du PIB en 2014, un déséquilibre chronique entre l'offre et la demande de travail s'est toujours manifesté, se traduisant par un taux de chômage à deux chiffres. Le taux de chômage est de 15,4% en 2015 (BCT, 2015). Il touche davantage les diplômés de l'enseignement supérieur. Ces derniers demeurent la catégorie la plus vulnérable avec un taux de chômage de 31,4% en 2015 (PNUD, 2016). Les femmes rencontrent plus de difficultés que les hommes pour s'insérer dans le marché du travail. Le taux de chômage des femmes est de 22,6% contre 12,5% pour les hommes (BCT, 2015).

Le chômage en Tunisie est le résultat d'un déséquilibre qui est à la fois quantitatif, provenant de l'incapacité de l'appareil productif à créer suffisamment d'emplois en regard de l'évolution de la population active disponible[2], et qualitatif reflétant l'inadéquation entre la formation acquise et les besoins en qualifications des entreprises. Ce chômage revêt un caractère largement structurel. Selon l'OCDE (2015), la proportion des chômeurs de longue durée constitue 44,6% du total des chômeurs en 2014, soit un taux beaucoup plus élevé que celui par exemple observé en moyenne dans les pays de l'OCDE (22,4%). En outre, le délai d'insertion professionnelle des jeunes ayant terminé leurs études est estimé à 6 ans.

L'économie tunisienne souffre depuis 2010 d'un sérieux problème au niveau de sa capacité à créer des emplois dans la mesure où la croissance du PIB s'est ralentie. Les créations annuelles d'emplois sont passées de 72 000 postes d'emplois en moyenne par an entre 2000 et 2010 à environ 35 000 emplois par an entre 2010 et 2015.

Figure 1 : Relation entre le taux de croissance du PIB et le taux de chômage en Tunisie (1975-2015)

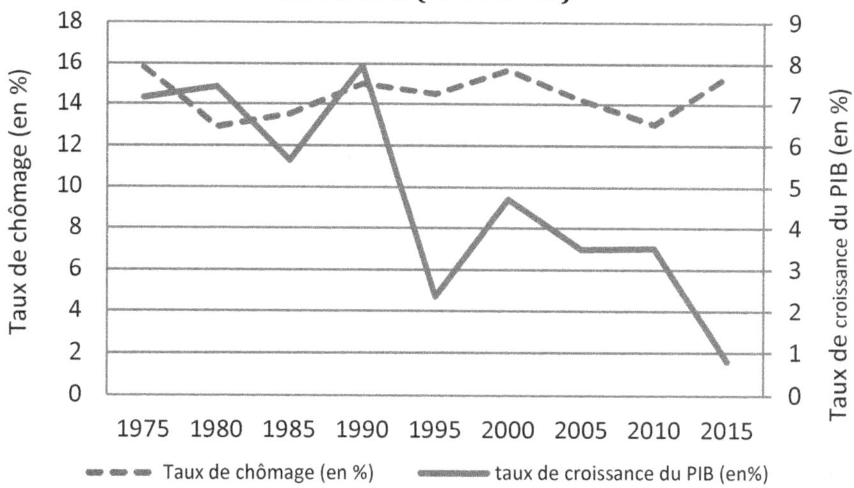

Source : représentation des auteurs à partir des données de l'Institut National de la Statistique et de la Banque mondiale.

La figure 1 confronte l'évolution historique du taux de croissance du PIB à celle du taux de chômage en Tunisie. L'évolution des taux de croissance et du chômage en Tunisie n'atteste pas la présence d'une relation régulière et stable entre ces deux variables. L'économie tunisienne a connu des phases d'expansion qui n'ont pas été suivies par une réduction du chômage. De même, les phases de récession ne se sont pas nécessairement accompagnées par une augmentation du chômage. Par exemple entre 1985 et 1990 l'économie tunisienne a connu une nette croissance du PIB, pourtant le chômage n'a cessé de s'aggraver passant de 13,5% en 1985 à 15% en 1990 (le même constat peut être fait pour la période d'expansion 1995-2000). Ainsi, une conjoncture économique favorable (périodes d'expansion) n'est pas systématiquement synonyme d'un niveau de chômage plus faible. De même, une conjoncture économique défavorable (périodes de récession) peut ne pas aggraver le chômage. C'est le cas pour la période entre 2000 et 2005 lorsque le taux de chômage a diminué malgré le ralentissement du taux de croissance. Cette analyse montre bien que la

[2] Selon l'Observatoire National de l'Emploi et des Qualifications, l'économie n'a créé en moyenne que 61 000 emplois durant les six dernières années alors que près de 81 000 nouveaux demandeurs d'emploi viennent s'ajouter par an.

relation entre la croissance et le chômage en Tunisie n'est pas stable et que la relation d'Okun se déforme au cours des périodes de récession et de reprise. Le taux de chômage peut alors présenter un comportement asymétrique. Ce constat justifie notre ambition de tester la validité de la loi d'Okun et de vérifier la non-linéarité de cette relation en Tunisie.

3. MÉTHODOLOGIE

Ayant constaté l'instabilité de la relation croissance-chômage en Tunisie et les spécifications non linéaires dans la littérature pour expliquer cette relation, nous nous référons au modèle non linéaire autorégressif avec retards échelonné (NARDL) proposé par Shin, Yu et Greenwood-Nimmo (2014). Ce modèle a le mérite de tester les asymétries de court et de long terme. En outre, il a l'avantage de permettre de mélanger des variables I(0) et I(1) et de tester directement l'existence d'une relation de cointégration de long terme.

Il convient de rappeler que la relation inverse entre le chômage et la croissance du PIB a été modélisée par Okun à l'aide de deux types d'équations. La première, dite version en « différences premières », peut se présenter comme suit :

$$\Delta u = C + \beta \Delta pib + \varepsilon \tag{1}$$

avec Δ la différence première de la variable ; u est le taux de chômage ; pib est le logarithme du PIB réel. β mesure de combien varie le taux de chômage en points de pourcentage lorsque le PIB réel varie de 1%.

La seconde, dite « version gap », relie les écarts du taux de chômage et du PIB observé respectivement au taux de chômage naturel et au PIB potentiel. Cette version se présente sous la forme suivante :

$$u - u^* = c + \beta^*(pib - pib^*) + \varepsilon \tag{2}$$

avec u^* et pib^* sont respectivement le taux de chômage naturel et le PIB potentiel. La différence $(pib - pib^*)$ est appelée écart de production (*output gap*).

Le coefficient d'Okun β^* mesure de combien varie le taux de chômage cyclique lorsque l'*output gap* varie de 1%. Comme l'a indiqué Knotek (2007), la difficulté associée à la « version gap » réside essentiellement au niveau de la détermination du taux de chômage naturel et du PIB potentiel qui ne sont pas directement observables. Une large gamme de méthodes ont été retenues pour mesurer ces variables telles que le filtre de Hodrick-Prescott (1997) (Marinkov-Geldenhuys, 2007 ; Moosa, 2008), le filtre de Baxter-King (Freeman, 2001 ; Chang, 2005), le filtre de Beveridge-Nelson et le filtre de Kalman (Moosa, 1997 ; Silvapulle et al., 2004).

La robustesse des résultats sera examinée en testant les deux versions de la relation d'Okun et en utilisant différents filtres pour le calcul de la production potentielle. De même, pour tester la sensibilité du coefficient d'Okun à l'hypothèse de linéarité de la relation chômage-croissance ainsi qu'au choix de la version à vérifier et au filtre adopté, les résultats issus d'une modélisation linéaire seront comparés à ceux issus d'une modélisation non linéaire.

Nous estimerons les deux versions de la loi d'Okun dans le contexte de l'économie tunisienne en utilisant des données annuelles couvrant la période 1980 -2015[3].

Dans la « version gap », le PIB potentiel et le taux de chômage naturel sont généralement mesurés à l'aide d'un filtre. Dans ce travail, nous nous limitons à trois types de filtre pour calculer ces séries : le filtre de Hodrick et Prescott (HP), le filtre de Butterworth (BW) et le filtre de Christiano-Fitzgerald (CF).

---

[3] Ces données sont obtenues auprès de l'Institut National de la Statistique.

4. VALIDATION EMPIRIQUE DE LA LOI D'OKUN

4.1. Tests de stationnarité

Avant l'estimation des équations (1) et (2), il convient de tester la stationnarité des séries. L'application d'un test de stationnarité qui ne tient pas compte de la non linéarité aux séries générées par des processus non-linéaires peut donner des résultats erronés. Pour cette raison, deux types de test de stationnarité sont appliqués : le test de racine unitaire stationnaire (DF-GLS) proposé par Elliott, Rothenberg et Stockle (1996) et le test de FADF–SB proposé par Furuoka (2017) qui envisage trois types de non-linéarité[4]. Les tableaux 1 et 2 récapitulent les résultats des tests de stationnarité. *gaphp, gapbw et gapcf* sont les écarts de la production par rapport à son niveau potentiel calculés en utilisant respectivement les filtres de HP, BW et CF ; *varcroi* est la variation du log de PIB réel. *chomhp, chombw et chomcf* sont les écarts du taux de chômage par rapport à son niveau naturel calculés respectivement à l'aide des filtres de HP, BW et CF ; *varcroi* est la variation du taux de chômage.

Tableau 1. test de stationnarité pour la variable taux de croissance

		gaphp	*gapbw*	*gapcf*	*varcr*	Valeurs critiques		
	Statistiques					1%	5%	10%
Test linéaire								
	DF-GLS	-3.57**	-3.17	-4.14**	-3.89**	-4.17	-3.48	-3.19
Test non linéaire								
	FADF	-3.71[1]	-3.86[1]	-4.1[1]*	-3.8[1]	-5.13	-4.44	-4.1
	ADF-BS	-3.62*	-3.4*	-3.7*	-6.06**	-4.56	-3.86	-3.51
	FADF-BS	-4.3[1]	-4.6[1]*	-4.5[1]*	-4.4[1]*	-5.39	-4.7	-4.36

*,**,*** *le coefficient est significatif respectivement à 10%, 5% et 1%.* [ ] *la valeur de k, fréquence de Fourier.*

Tableau 2. test de stationnarité pour la variable taux de chômage

		chomhp	*chombw*	*chomcf*	*varch*	Valeurs critiques		
	Statistiques					1%	5%	10%
Test linéaire								
	DF-GLS	-3.97**	-3.7**	-3.04	-4.06**	-4.17	-3.48	-3.19
Test non linéaire								
	FADF	-3.8[2]*	-4.1[2]*	-3.46[2]	-4.1[1]*	-4.85	-4.14	-3.75
	ADF-BS	-3.65*	-3.69*	-3.13	-4.32**	-4.48	-3.74	-3.42
	FADF-BS	-4.1[2]	-3.9[1]	-4.6[2]*	-4.6[2]*	-5.45	-4.7	-4.32

*,**,*** *le coefficient est significatif respectivement à 10%, 5% et 1%.* [ ] *la valeur de k, fréquence de Fourier.*

Les tableaux 1 et 2 montrent que les résultats des tests de stationnarité (linéaire et non linéaire) sont hétérogènes. Ceci nous contraint de trancher sur l'ordre d'intégration de ces séries bien qu'elles soient toutes stationnaires en différences premières (voir annexe 3, tableau A-2 et A-3). En effet, les résultats sont sensibles au type du filtre utilisé pour calculer la variable potentielle (HP, BW,CF) ainsi qu'au type du test adopté (linéaire ou non). Par exemple, si on applique le test linéaire sur la variable *output gap* calculée à partir de filtre HP, on a une stationnarité de la variable *output gap* à 5% ce qui revient à dire que la variable *gaphp* est I(0). Par contre,

[4] Ces trois types de non linéarité engendrent trois tests statistiques (voir annexe 2 pour plus d'explication).

en se basant sur les statistiques FDAF et FADF-BS du test de stationnarité non linéaire, cette variable est I(1). De la même manière, pour le test de stationnarité (DF-GLS) et en utilisant le même filtre (BW), il apparaît une stationnarité en niveau de la variable *output gap* et une non stationnarité pour la variable taux de chômage. D'où le risque de régresser deux variables intégrées d'ordre différent [I(0) et I(1)].

La méthode ARDL apparaît comme la meilleure technique pour estimer la relation d'Okun puisqu'elle a l'avantage de tester des relations de long terme entre des variables dont les ordres d'intégration sont différents (Acikgoz et Mert, 2010). Afin de mettre en œuvre la sensibilité du coefficient d'Okun à l'hypothèse de linéarité ou non de la relation chômage-croissance et pour tenir compte de l'asymétrie de cette relation, nous l'estimerons également par la technique NARDL.

4.2. Estimation du coefficient d'Okun : une analyse linéaire et non linéaire

Le modèle autorégressif à retard échelonné (ARDL), développé par Pesaran, Shin et Smith (2001), est une technique économétrique utilisée pour tester les relations de long terme entre des variables qui ne sont pas intégrées de même ordre [I(0) ou I(1)]. Cette technique a l'avantage d'obtenir de meilleures estimations sur des échantillons de petite taille.

Dans le but d'établir la relation de long terme entre le chômage et la croissance en Tunisie, nous reformulons les équations (1) et (2) sous le modèle ARDL comme suit :

$$\Delta chom_t = \mu + \sum_{i=1}^{p} \delta_{1i} \Delta chom_{t-i} + \sum_{i=1}^{p} \delta_{2i} \Delta gap_{t-i} + \gamma_1 chom_{t-1} + \gamma_2 gap_{t-1} + \varepsilon_t \quad (3)$$

Selon cette équation, on a une relation de cointégration si les coefficients γ_1 et γ_2 sont statistiquement différents de zéro. L'hypothèse nulle de ce test est $H_0: \gamma_1 = \gamma_2 = 0$ (pas de relation de long terme). L'hypothèse de cointégration est testée en utilisant le test de Fisher dont la valeur calculée est comparée aux valeurs critiques tabulées par Pesaran et al. (2001). L'hypothèse d'absence d'une relation de cointégration est rejetée lorsque la valeur calculée de la statistique F de Fisher est supérieure à la valeur critique. Le coefficient de long terme correspondant au coefficient d'Okun est alors $\beta = \gamma_2/-\gamma_1$.

Le modèle NARDL est une version non linéaire du modèle ARDL. Dans ce modèle on reprend la représentation autorégressive de Pesaran et al. (2001) et en y incorporant des effets asymétriques à court et à long terme afin de tenir compte de l'asymétrie de la relation chômage-croissance. En suivant la méthodologie de Shin, Yu et Greenwood-Nimmo (2014), on décompose la variable *output gap* en ses sommes partielles positives (gap_t^+) et négatives (gap_t^-) :

$$gap_t^+ = \sum_{j=1}^{t} \Delta\, gap_t^+ = \sum_{j=1}^{t} \max(\Delta gap_j, 0)$$

$$gap_t^- = \sum_{j=1}^{t} \Delta\, gap_t^- = \sum_{j=1}^{t} \min(\Delta gap_j, 0)$$

où Δgap_t^+ traduit les augmentations dans le taux de croissance alors que Δgap_t^- traduit les diminutions.

Afin de tenir compte de l'asymétrie, l'équation (3) est modifiée comme suit :

$$\Delta chom_t = \mu + +\gamma_1 chom_{t-1} + \gamma_2^+ gap_{t-1}^+ + \gamma_2^- gap_{t-1}^- + \sum_{i=1}^{p-1} \delta_{1i} \Delta chom_{t-i}$$

$$+ \sum_{j=0}^{p} \delta_{2j}^+ \Delta gap_{t-j}^+ + \sum_{j=0}^{p} \delta_{2j}^- \Delta gap_{t-j}^- + \varepsilon_t \quad (4)$$

La technique de NARDL nous permet de tester directement s'il existe une relation de cointégration de long terme en utilisant la méthodologie des "bounds tests". Cette technique propose deux statistiques. La première (t_{BDM}) permet de tester la significativité du coefficient γ_1 ($\gamma_1 = 0$), alors que la seconde (F_{PSS}) permet de tester la significativité des coefficients $\gamma_1, \gamma_2^+ et\ \gamma_2^-$ ($\gamma_1 = \gamma_2^+ = \gamma_2^- = 0$).

Le coefficient d'Okun qui mesure la sensibilité du chômage à la croissance n'est autre que le coefficient de long terme. Dans le modèle NARDL, ce coefficient est calculé de la manière suivante : $\beta^+ = \gamma_2^+ / -\gamma_1$ et $\beta^- = \gamma_2^- / -\gamma_1$.

On peut s'attendre à ce que le coefficient associé aux écarts de PIB négatifs (β^-) soit d'une plus grande ampleur en valeur absolue que celui associé aux écarts du PIB positifs (β^+).

Le tableau 3 récapitule les résultats de l'estimation des modèles ARDL linéaire et non linéaire. Ces modèles permettent à la fois de tester l'existence d'une relation de cointégration entre les variables du modèle ainsi que l'estimation de la relation de long terme. Pour le modèle linéaire, les résultats sont les mêmes quel que soit le type de filtre utilisé pour calculer la variable potentielle à savoir l'existence d'une relation de cointégration entre le taux de chômage et la croissance.

Tableau 3: Résultat des modèles ARDL et NARDL

	Analyse linéaire				Analyse non linéaire			
	Test de cointégration de Pesaran et al. (2001) (ARDL)				Test de cointégration de Shin et al. (2014) (NARDL)			
	Cointégration	Coefficient		Cointégration	Coefficient			
	F	$\hat{\beta}$	t-Stud	t_{BDM}	$\hat{\beta}^+$	p-value	$\hat{\beta}^-$	p-value
$(chomhp, Gaphp)$	8.77**	-0.84	-0.96	-3.6339**	-0.85	0.03	-1.02	0.06
$(chombw, Gapbw)$	6.81**	-0.73	-0.87	-3.2962**	-0.83	0.008	-0.99	0.02
$(chomcf, Gapcf)$	7.90**	-1.01	-1.57	-6.2737**	-0.8	0.01	-0.94	0.09
$(varch, varcr)$	17.7**	-0.04	-0.03	-4.7726**	-0.81	0.11	-0.98	0.1
Valeur critique à 5%	4.04 si I(0) 4.78 si I(1)			-3.22				

L'estimation de cette relation de long terme montre que le coefficient d'Okun est négatif mais il n'est pas significatif. Ce résultat signifie que l'économie peut par exemple croître sans réduire le chômage. Ce constat corrobore l'analyse descriptive présentée précédemment dans laquelle il apparaît qu'en Tunisie les périodes d'expansion ne sont pas nécessairement suivies par une baisse du chômage.

Mais cette hypothèse de linéarité de la relation chômage-croissance en Tunisie paraît peu pertinente pour modéliser la relation d'Okun.

En admettant la non linéarité de la relation d'Okun, et en supposant l'existence de deux régimes dans cette relation (hypothèse d'asymétrie du coefficient d'Okun), le modèle NARDL prouve qu'il existe une relation de cointégration entre le chômage et la croissance. En effet, le coefficient de long terme estimé (coefficient d'Okun) est négatif et il est significatif. La loi d'Okun est ainsi vérifiée quel que soit le filtre utilisé. Ces résultats montrent également que la valeur du coefficient d'Okun diffère selon que l'économie fonctionne en régime d'expansion (écart positif) ou en régime de récession (écart négatif). Plus précisément, ce coefficient s'affaiblit, en valeur absolue, au cours des phases d'expansion par rapport aux phases de récession. D'après les estimations du modèle asymétrique, en moyenne et quel que soit le filtre utilisé, les coefficients associés aux écarts de production négatifs et positifs varient, respectivement, entre -1,02 et -0,94 et entre 0,85 et -0,8. Le chômage cyclique est plus sensible aux écarts de PIB réel négatifs que positifs. Par exemple, en utilisant le filtre HP et en période de récession, si le taux de croissance du PIB réel diminue de 1% le chômage augmente de 1,02%. En revanche, en période d'expansion, une croissance du PIB de 1% ne réduit le chômage que de 0,85%.

Les résultats obtenus à partir des modèles ARDL et NARDL permettent de tirer trois conclusions. D'abord, le choix du filtre employé pour calculer la variable potentielle n'influence que marginalement la valeur des résultats obtenus. Ensuite, les résultats sont très sensibles à l'hypothèse de linéarité qui, selon, peut valider ou non la loi d'Okun. Cette loi n'est pas validée si on retient l'hypothèse de linéarité de la relation chômage-croissance. Enfin, les résultats obtenus sont cohérents avec les travaux de Cuaresma (2003) et de Knotek (2007) qui ont montré que le chômage cyclique est plus sensible à l'écart de production lorsque l'économie se situe dans des phases de récession.

4.3. Une analyse non linéaire de la causalité entre le chômage et la croissance

Après avoir vérifié que l'hypothèse de non linéarité de la relation chômage-croissance est la plus adaptée, nous testons l'existence d'une relation de causalité entre le chômage et la croissance économique en appliquant un test de causalité non linéaire qui tient compte de l'asymétrie de la relation d'Okun. Le test de Hristu-Varsakelis et Kyrtsou (2010) est utilisé pour pallier l'inconvénient des tests de causalité linéaire. Dans ce test, les auteurs adoptent le modèle bivarié de Mackey-Glass (MG). Celui-ci est spécifié de la façon suivante :

$$X_t = \alpha_{11}\frac{X_{t-\tau_1}}{1+X^{c_1}_{1-\tau_1}} - \gamma_{11}X_{t-1} + \alpha_{12}\frac{Y_{t-\tau_2}}{1+Y^{c_2}_{1-\tau_2}} - \gamma_{12}Y_{t-1} + \varepsilon_t \quad (5)$$

$$Y_t = \alpha_{21}\frac{X_{t-\tau_1}}{1+X^{c_1}_{1-\tau_1}} - \gamma_{21}X_{t-1} + \alpha_{22}\frac{Y_{t-\tau_2}}{1+Y^{c_2}_{1-\tau_2}} - \gamma_{22}Y_{t-1} + u_t \quad (6)$$

avec τ_i le nombre de retard déterminé par le critère de Schwarz et c_i une constante. Ce test se présente sous deux versions, symétrique et asymétrique, et distingue entre les valeurs positives et négatives des variables. Le principe de ce test est le même que celui du test de causalité linéaire de Granger sauf que le modèle à estimer est celui de MG. Si on cherche à tester si la variable Y cause la variable X, on doit tester la significativité du coefficient α_{12}. S'il y a une relation de causalité non linéaire entre Y et X, il faut que α_{12} soit significativement différent de zéro. La statistique de ce test est la suivante :

$$S_F = \frac{(S_c - S_u)/n_c}{S_u/(T-n_u-1)} \sim F(n_c; T - n_u - 1) \quad (7)$$

S_c est la somme des carrés des résidus du modèle contraint ($\alpha_{12} = 0$) ; u est la somme des carrés des résidus du modèle sans contrainte ; $n_c = 1$ est le nombre des coefficients à contraindre égalisant zéro ; $n_u = 4$ le nombre des paramètres dans le modèle non contraint.

Dans ce qui suit, on s'est contenté de la version symétrique du test de Hristu-Varsakelis et Kyrtsou (2010). Pour la version asymétrique, il suffit de remplacer dans les équations (5) et (6), la variable Y_t par Y_t^+ (ou Y_t^-) avec Y_t^+ les valeurs positives de Y_t (ou Y_t^- les valeurs négatives de Y_t).

Les résultats du test de causalité non linéaire sont présentés dans le tableau 4. Ils prouvent l'existence d'une relation de causalité non linéaire dans un seul sens allant de *l'output gap* au chômage. En effet, la statistique du test de Hristu-Varsakelis et Kyrtsou, pour les différents filtres employés, est significative uniquement pour la relation de causalité qui va du taux de croissance vers le taux de chômage et non pas dans le sens inverse. D'où la confirmation de l'hypothèse selon laquelle le chômage est très sensible à la modification de *l'output gap*. En période d'expansion, l'écart entre la production réelle et son niveau potentiel augmente, et le chômage cyclique diminue. Cependant cette diminution est moins importante que l'augmentation du chômage survenue en période de récession lorsque le PIB croît moins vite que la production potentielle.

Tableau 4. Test de causalité non linéaire : modèle MG

	Relation symétrique		Relation asymétrique	
	F	P-value	F	P-value
Gaphp → Chomhp	3.59*	0.07		
Chomhp → Gaphp	0.91	0.84		
$Gaphp^+$ → Chomhp			4.56**	0.02
$Gaphp^-$ → Chomhp			7.29***	0.003
Gapbw → Chombw	3.29*	0.1		
Chombw → Gapbw	0.04	1		
$Gapbw^+$ → Chombw			3.67*	0.06
$Gapbw^-$ → Chombw			3.32*	0.07
Gapcf → Chomcf	5.95**	0.02		
Chomcf → Gapcf	1.01	0.5		
$Gapcf^+$ → Chomcf			10.5***	0
$Gapcf^-$ → Chomcf			1.68	0.2
varcr → varch	19.7***	0		
varch → varcr	0.6	0.71		
$varcr^+$ → varch			3.31*	0.08
$varcr^-$ → varch			4.14***	0

5. CONCLUSIONS

Compte tenu de l'instabilité de la relation croissance-chômage en Tunisie, une loi d'Okun peut être mise en évidence en utilisant des spécifications non linéaires. L'estimation du modèle linéaire aboutit à la non-significativité du coefficient de la loi d'Okun alors que son estimation à partir du modèle NARDL, qui tient compte de l'asymétrie de la relation chômage-croissance en phases d'expansion et de récession, donne des résultats significatifs. L'étude confirme ainsi que le chômage cyclique tunisien est plus sensible aux écarts de PIB réel négatifs que positifs. En outre, l'application des tests de causalité non linéaire montre que c'est l'*output gap* qui influence significativement le chômage et non l'inverse.

De là, on peut suggérer qu'un des enjeux des politiques économiques en Tunisie devrait porter non seulement sur une amélioration du contenu en emplois de la croissance économique mais aussi sur la promotion de suffisamment d'emplois qualifiés pour faire face à l'afflux croissant des diplômés. L'absorption de cette catégorie de demandeurs d'emploi permettrait parallèlement d'augmenter la productivité du travail qui a été toujours nettement en dessous de son potentiel.

Du côté de l'offre, face à la faible capacité du secteur public à créer suffisamment d'emplois pour atténuer l'acuité du chômage, notamment des diplômes de l'université, les politiques économiques à mettre en œuvre gagneraient à privilégier le soutien du secteur privé et à promouvoir l'entrepreneuriat. Dans ce sens, il serait efficace de subventionner la création d'entreprises et d'assainir l'environnement des affaires afin de booster l'investissement privé. De même, les institutions du marché du travail devraient évoluer pour alléger la rigidité qui sape la volonté et la capacité des entreprises à embaucher des jeunes. Du côté de la demande d'emploi, le recadrage du système éducatif s'avère indispensable en vue de mieux adapter la formation aux besoins du système productif.

D'une manière générale, les politiques actives d'emploi devront cibler plus particulièrement les jeunes diplômés, les femmes et certaines régions défavorisées dans lesquelles le taux de chômage a atteint des niveaux alarmants. En ce sens, en s'inspirant de l'approche adoptée par Dixon et al. (2017), un prolongement à cette étude serait d'estimer la relation d'Okun en utilisant les taux de chômage désagrégés selon l'âge, le genre et la région.

REFERENCES

Acikgoz, S., Mert, M. (2010). "The Endogeneity of the Natural Rate of Growth: An Application to Turkey," *Panoeconomicus*, SavezekonomistaVojvodine, Novi Sad, Serbia, 57(4), 447-469.

Attfield, C., Silverstone, B. (1997). Okun's Coefficient: A Comment. *Review of Economics and Statistics*, 79, 326-329.

Attfield, C., Silverstone, B. (1998). Okun's law, Cointegration and Gap Variables. *Journal of Macroeconomics*, 20, 625-637.

Banque Africaine de Développement (2014), Tunisie : Document de stratégie pays intérimaire 2014 -2015.

Basu, D., Foley, D.K. (2013), Dynamics of output and employment in the US economy. *Cambridge Journal of Economics*, 37(5), 1077-1106.

Beaton, K. (2010). Time variation in Okun's law: A Canada and US comparison. Bank of Canada, Working Paper, 7, 3-15.

Boda, Považanová (2015), Gender asymmetry in Okun's law in the four PIGS countries, *Procedia Economics and Finance*, 30, 111-123

Christiano, L.J., Fitzgerald, T.J (1999), "The Band Pass Filter" NBER Working Paper No. W7257.

Clark, P. (1989). Trend Reversion in Real Output and Unemployment. *Journal of Monetary Economics*, 40, 14-32.

Cuaresma J. C. (2003), Okun's Law Revisited, *Oxford Bulletin of Economics and Statistics*, 65, 4 (2003) 0305-9049, 439-451.

Dixon R., Lim G.C., Van Ours J.C. (2017). Revisiting Okun's relationship, *Applied Economics*, 49, 28, 2749-2765.

Fouquau J. (2008), Threshold effects in Okun's Law: a panel data analysis, *Economics Bulletin*,Vol. 5, 33, 1-14

Frank, M., Stengos, T. (1989), "Measuring the Strangeness of Gold and Silver Rates of Return", *Review Of Economic Studies*, 56, 553-567.

Freeman, D. (2001). Panel tests of Okun's law for ten industrial countries. Economic Inquiry, 39, 511-523.

Froot, K. A., Rogoff, K., (1995). Perspectives on PPP and long-run real exchange rates. In: Grossman, G., Rogoff, K. (Eds.), *Handbook of International Economics*, Vol. III. North-Holland, Amsterdam, 1647-1688.

Furuoka, F. (2017), "A New Approach to Testing Unemployment Hysteresis", *Empirical Economics*, 53,3, 1253-1280.

Gordon, R. (1984). Unemployment and Potential Output in the 1980s. Brookings Paper on Economic Activity, 2, 537-586.

Harris, R., Silverstone, B. (2001). Testing for asymmetry in okun's law: A cross country comparison. *Economics Bulletin*, 5, 1-13.

Hodrick, R., Prescott, E. (1997). Postwar us Business Cycles: An Empirical Investigation. *Journal of Money, Credit and Banking*, 29, 1-16.

Holmes, M., Silverstone, B. (2006). Okun's law, asymmetries and jobless recoveries in the United States : a Markov Switching approach. *Economics Letters*, 92, 293-299.

Hristu-Varsakelis, D., Kyrtsou, C. (2010). "Testing for Granger Causality in the presence of Chaotic Dynamics", *Brussels Economic Review*, 53 (2), 323-327.

Huang H. C., Chang Y.K. (2005), Investigating Okun's law by the structural break with threshold approach: evidence from Canada, *The Manchester School*, 73, 5, 599-611.

Huang, H., Chang, Y. (2005). Investigating Okun's law by the structural break with threshold approach: evidence from Canada. *The Manchester School*, 5, 599-611.

Huang, H., Lin, S. (2006). A flexible nonlinear inference to Okun's relationship. *Applied Economics Letters*, 13, 325-331.

Huang, H., Lin, S. (2008), Smooth-Time-Variyng Okun's Coeffcient, *Economic Modelling*,

Institut National de la Statistique (2012), Enquête nationale sur la population et l'emploi

Institut National de la Statistique (2014), Recensement Général de la Population et de l'Habitat 2014, Principaux indicateurs.

Institut Tunisien des Etudes Stratégiques (2016), La Tunisie en 2025, Rapport économique complet.

Knotek, E. (2007). How useful is Okun's law. *Economic Review*, Federal Reserve Bank of Kansas City, 4, 73-103.

Lee J. (2000), The Robustness of Okun's Law: Evidence from OECD Countries, *Journal of Macroeconomics*, Spring 2000, 22, 2, 331-356.

Lothian, J. R., Taylor, M. P. (1996) "The recent float from the perspective of the past two centuries". *Journal of Political Economy*, 104, 488-509.

Mackey, M.C., Glass, L., (1977). "Oscillation and chaos in physiological control systems", *Science*, 197, 287-289.

Marinkov, M., Geldenhuys, J.-P. (2007). Cyclical Unemployment and Cyclical Output: an estimation of Okun's Coefficient for South Africa. *South African Journal of Economics*, 75, 373-390.

Moosa, I. (1997). A cross-country comparison of Okun's coefficient. *Journal of Comparative Economics*, 24, 335-356.

Moosa, I. (2008). Economic Growth and Unemployment in Arab Countries: Is Okun's law Valid ? *Journal of Development and Economic Policies*, 10, 5-24.

OCDE (2015), *Investir dans la jeunesse en Tunisie : Renforcer l'employabilité des jeunes pendant la transition vers une économie verte*, Edition OCDE, Paris

Okun, A.M. (1962), Potential GNP: its measurement and significance. In: Proceedings of the Business and Economics Statistics Section, *American Statistical Association*, 98-104.

Palley, T. (1993). Okun's law and the asymmetric and changing behavior of the USA economy. *International Review of Applied Economics*, 7, 144-162.

Pesaran, M. H., Shin, Y., Smith, R.J., (2001). "Bounds Testing Approaches to the Analysis of Long-run Relationships. *Journal of Applied Econometrics, 16*, 289-326.

Prachowny, M. (1993). Okun's law: Theoretical Foundations and Revised Estimates. *Review of Economics and Statistics*, 75, 331-336.

Shin, Y., Yu, B., Greenwood-Nimmo, M. (2014), Modelling asymmetric cointegration and dynamic multipliers in an ARDL framework. In: Horrace, W.C., Sickles, R.C. (Eds.), Festschrift in Honor of Peter Schmidt. Springer Science & Business Media, New York (NY).

Silvapulle, P., Moosa, I., Silvapulle, M. (2004). Asymmetry in Okun's law. *Canadian Journal of Economics* 37, 2, 353-374.

Sögner, L., Stiassny, Alfred (2002), An analysis on the structural stability of Okun's law–a cross-country study, *Applied Economics*, 34, 14, 1775–1787.

Villaverde J., Maza A. (2009), The robustness of Okun's law in Spain, 1980–2004, Regional evidence, *Journal of Policy Modeling*, 31, 289-297.

Zanin L. (2014), On Okun's law in OECD countries: An analysis by age cohorts, *Economics Letters*, 125, 243-248.

ANNEXE 1

Tableau A-1 : Contribution des secteurs économiques au PIB et part dans l'emploi (en%)

	Croissance du PIB (en %)	Agriculture		Industrie		Services	
		% du PIB	% de l'emploi total	% du PIB	% de l'emploi total	% du PIB	% de l'emploi total
1980	7,4	16,3	33,4	35,9	33,4	47,7	29,1
1990	7,9	17,7	25,8	33,6	33,6	48,6	39,1
2000	4,7	11,3	**	30,2	**	58,5	**
2010	3,5	8,2	17,8	31,5	33,0	60,3	49,2
2014	2,3	8,8	14,8	29,3	33,4	61,9	51,6

Source : WDI et rapports de l'INS.

ANNEXE 2
Test de stationnarité non linéaire de Furuoka

Furuoka (2017) propose les modèles suivants :

Modèle A : $\Delta y_t = c + \beta t + \rho y_{t-1} + \sum_{i=1}^{p} \gamma_i \Delta y_{t-i} + u_t$

Modèle B : $\Delta y_t = c + \beta t + \delta_1 \sin\left(\frac{2\pi kt}{T}\right) + \delta_2 \cos\left(\frac{2\pi kt}{T}\right) + \rho y_{t-1} + \sum_{i=1}^{p} \gamma_i \Delta y_{t-i} + u_t$

Modèle C : $\Delta y_t = c + \beta t + \delta DU_t + \theta D(T_B)_t + \rho y_{t-1} + \sum_{i=1}^{p} \gamma_i \Delta y_{t-i} + u_t$

Modèle D : $\Delta y_t = c + \beta t + \delta_1 \sin\left(\frac{2\pi kt}{T}\right) + \delta_2 \cos\left(\frac{2\pi kt}{T}\right) + \delta DU_t + \theta D(T_B)_t + \rho y_{t-1} + \sum_{i=1}^{p} \gamma_i \Delta y_{t-i} + u_t$

avec $DU_t = \begin{cases} 0 \ si \ t < T_B \\ 1 \ si \ t > T_B \end{cases}$; $D(T_B)_t = \begin{cases} 0 \ si \ t = T_B \\ 1 \ si \ t \neq T_B \end{cases}$; T_B est la date du choc.

L'auteur a introduit la transformation au sens de Fourier dans les modèles B et D. k est l'approximation de fréquence de Fourier. Furuoka suppose que le paramètre k prend les valeurs 1 ou 2 au max.

Les modèles A et C sont respectivement les modèles de test d'ADF et de test de Zivot. Les statistiques de ces tests sont respectivement ADF et ADF-SB. Pour les deux autres modèles B et D, l'auteur intègre un trend non linéaire de type transformation de Fourier. Les statistiques de ces modèles sont respectivement FADF et FADF-SB.

ANNEXE 3
Résultats du test de stationnarité sur les variables en différences premières

Tableau A-2. Pour la variable variation du taux de croissance

		Δgaphp	Δgapbw	Δgapcf	Δvarcr	Valeurs critiques		
	Statistiques					1%	5%	10%
Test linéaire	DF-GLS	-6.71	-6.35	-7.28	-6.14	-4.17	-3.48	-3.19
Test non linéaire								
	FADF	-5.92[1]	-6.63[1]	-6.86[1]	-6.35[1]	-5.13	-4.44	-4.1
	ADF-BS	-6.36	-5.98	-6.27	-8.38	-4.56	-3.86	-3.51
	FADF-BS	-6.78[1]	-6.26[1]	-6.56[1]	-6.14[1]	-5.39	-4.7	-4.36

Tableau A-3. Pour la variable variation du taux de chômage

		Δchomhp	Δchombw	Δchomcf	Δvarch	Valeurs critiques		
	Statistiques					1%	5%	10%
Test linéaire	DF-GLS	-6.23	-6.17	-6.68	-6.38	-4.17	-3.48	-3.19
Test non linéaire								
	FADF	-5.97[2]	-6.47[2]	-7.23[2]	-6.59[1]	-4.85	-4.14	-3.75
	ADF-BS	-5.98	-6.35	-7.12	-6.68	-4.48	-3.74	-3.42
	FADF-BS	--6.23[2]	-6.39[1]	-6.84[2]	-6.12[2]	-5.45	-4.7	-4.32

The Unemployment- Growth Relationship in Tunisia: Validity of the non-linear specification of the Okun's law

Abstract - This work proposes to test the validity of the Okun-relation for the Tunisian economy applied to annual data of real GDP and unemployment covering the period (1980-2015). The existence of a non-linear relationship between growth and unemployment is verified: the cyclical unemployment is more sensitive to the output gap in the recession phase than in the expansion phases. The analysis of the non-linear causality relationship between unemployment and growth shows a unidirectional causality from the "output gap" to the unemployment.

Key-words
Unemployment
Okun's law
NARDL model
Tunisia

Région et Développement
n° 47-2018
www.regionetdeveloppement.org

Understanding the effect of international remittances on undernourishment in Sub-Saharan Africa: A spatial model approach

Hamed SAMBO*

Abstract - This paper investigates the impact of remittances on undernourishment in Sub-Saharan Africa using panel data from 35 countries spanning the years 2001-2011. The generalized moments estimator under the presence of spatial autoregressive parameter was used after taking into account the spatial interaction between countries. We find that remittances contribute to the reduction of undernourishment in Sub-Saharan African. However, the elasticity of calorie consumption to remittances is low. Moreover, the impact of remittances is more pronounced in intermediate income deciles countries than in the countries in lower income deciles and higher income deciles.

JEL Classification
P22, P24, O15, O55

Key-words
Remittances
Undernourishment
Spatial Model
Sub-Saharan Africa

* Centre d'Economie de l'Université Paris Nord (CEPN), Université Paris 13.
hamed.sambo@univparis13.fr

1. INTRODUCTION

For years, the relationship between income and nutrition has yielded a debate among researchers in development economics. According to the Engel curve, a rise of consumers incomes leads to a substitution of food quantity for food quality, which implies an increase in demand for calories. Therefore, the elasticity of calorie consumption to income is greater than zero (Subramanian & Deaton, 1996). However, different studies have found that this elasticity is closed to zero (Behrman & Deolalikar, 1987; Bouis & Haddad, 1992), meaning that an increase of income doesn't lead to a significant increase in calorie consumption. More recently, based on facts in India, Deaton & Drèze (2009) have found that in spite of high growth rate of per capita income and per capita consumption, per calorie consumption has been falling for a quarter of the century. One explanation given by the authors is that an increase of per capita income has probably led to a move out from agricultural sector to modern sector, resulting to a fall of calorie consumption for physical heavy which in turn reduce the total calorie consumption. Indeed, considering that people use calories for two purposes, own nutrition and heavy physical labor, Deaton & Drèze (2009) argues that, in a single labor market with common wage, the relationship from strength to income through work and calorie consumption will induce a positive relationship between income and calorie consumption. However, a rise of real wages will induce a decline of physical labor leading to a fall in calorie consumption for work even as the calorie consumption for improving nutritional status is increasing but still inadequate. However, this analysis does not take into account the preferences of individuals for other aspects of food, namely taste, appearance, odor, status value or cultural preference. When these preferences are taken in account, it is likely that additional incomes do not induce a significant improvement in calorie intake even though there is a rise in food consumption (Behrman & Deolalikar, 1987). This is because a part of the money is spent to get more calories and the other to get tasty foods which are more expensive.

More recently, Banerjee & Duflo (2011) have provided a detailed analysis of the food consumption behavior of poor households. They argue that people eat little not because they are too poor to buy foods but because it is not clear that the additional productivity translates into higher earnings if employers do not know that a well-nourished worker is more productive. Indeed, if employers pay the same wage to all workers, then there would be no reason to eat more and get stronger. People also don't know that their good nutrition leads to a better health for their children. Therefore, poor choose their foods not for their nutritional values, but for how good they taste. Under, these arguments, it is not surprising that, with additional income, poor choose to consume tasty foods rather than nutritive foods. Another fact that Banerjee & Duflo (2011) pointed out is that there are other things more important in the lives of poor than food due to social pressures or social contexts, especially in developing countries. These things include weddings, dowries, and christenings. Given that too many others pressures and desires competing with food, it is then likely to see that poor do not eat any more or any better when their income goes up.

In recent years, migrant remittances have experienced strong growth in developing countries, outpacing public development aid. Since these transfers are directly sent to individuals and act in the form of supplementary income, the question that arises, given the relationship between income and calorie consumption, is whether they have an effect on calorie consumption in developing countries. According to the new economics of labor migration, the migration decision is made along households in order to minimize their risks and overcome limitations occurred as a consequence of the failures of the national markets (Stark, 1991). In turn, families abroad send remittances which have a positive impact on the economics of poor. The effect of remittances on poverty is well-documented in the economic literature. Researchers agree that remittances contribute to the reduction of poverty in receiving countries (Imai & al., 2014; Margolis & al., 2015; Bang & al., 2016). However, as described above, the reduction of poverty don't necessarily lead to an additional calorie consumption. In addition, most of these studies have focused on monetary poverty instead of a multidimensional poverty, which includes at some extent the outcomes of good nutrition. Other studies have analyzed the effect of remittances on food consumption. Adams & Cuecuecha (2013) have found in their study in Ghana that food consumption increase with the receipt of remittances. However, households receiving remittances spend less at the margin on food. Remittances have also been found to dampen the impact of the positive food price shock and food price instability on household consumption in vulnerable countries for which the majorities are in Sub-Saharan Africa (Combes & Ebeke, 2011; Combes & al., 2014). However again, these studies do not make it possible to know the real impact of remittances on the calorie consumption. Existing studies on the relationship between remittances and nutrition are more directed towards nutritional or health status of children (Hildebrandt & al., 2005; Antón, 2010) rather than global undernourishment.

This paper attempt to fill this gap in the literature by investigating the impact of remittances on undernourishment in Sub-Saharan Africa, the region which hosts most developing countries. Indeed, despite the continuous decrease of undernourishment in Sub-Saharan Africa, the region is the one with the largest proportion of undernourished in the world. According to FAO (2015), between 2014 and 2016, 23.2% of the population was estimated to be undernourished in Sub-Saharan Africa, compared to 12.1% in Asia and 5.5% in Latin America and the Caribbean (LAC). At the same time, remittances received in Sub-Saharan Africa were estimated to 34.8 billion USD in 2015 (World Bank).

The analysis is conducted on the panel of 35 Sub-Saharan African countries. To estimate the impact of remittances on undernourishment, we use the generalized moments estimator for autoregressive spatial panel developed by Kapoor & al. (2007). The reason behind this choice was the possibility to account for random shocks (price spikes, droughts, floods...) which are usually spatially autocorrelated. Indeed, when spatial units are spatially autocorrelated, usual panel regression models produce an inconsistent estimate of the parameters (Le Gallo, 2007).

Our findings suggest that the reception of remittances results in a decrease of the proportion of undernourished in Sub-Saharan Africa. This result is explained by the fact that most of the households that receive remittances in Sub-Saharan Africa dedicate them to consumption. However, the elasticity of nutrition to remittances is very small but overpasses that to GDP per capita. Remittances were also found to be a hedge against flood shocks in Sub-Saharan Africa. We also find that GDP per capita, domestic credit, and private investment contribute to a reduction of the proportion of undernourished in the region. In addition, having a great share of agricultural land also leads to a significant reduction of the proportion of under- nourished in Sub-Saran Africa. Grouping countries by decile of per capita GDP, we found that the impact of remittances on undernourishment is low in both the top and the bottom GDP per capita deciles. However, the impact is much higher in decile 4 for which the per capita GDP is between 420 USD and 518 USD. This result can be explained by the fact that people in bottom deciles countries compared to those in decile 4 can not afford migration costs leading to less migration and fewer remittances in bottom deciles. In addition, the countries in the bottom deciles are those suffering the most from undernourishment. In top deciles countries, the money received from migrants is more devoted to education, healthcare and investment rather than consumption. This explains the less effect of remittances in the top decile countries.

The paper is structured as follows, Section 2 describes the trend of four income flows and that of the prevalence of undernourishment from 1990 to 2015, and Section 3 provides an understanding of the use of remittances in Sub-Saharan Africa. A description of the data and the methodology is presented in Section 4. In Section 5, we outline the main results and conclude in Section 6.

2. INCOME FLOWS AND UNDERNOURISHMENT IN FIVE SELECTING COUNTRIES FROM 1990-2015

In this section, we analyze the trends of four income flows and that of undernourishment[1] in five sub-Saharan African countries from 1990 to 2015. We focus on two types of income flows: external flows which include official development assistance, foreign direct investment and remittances; and one internal income flow, a country per capita GDP. Figure 1 shows that, compared to Burkina Faso and Kenya, where undernourishment has not declined significantly from its 1990 level, in Djibouti, Niger, and Ethiopia, there has been a sharp drop from 1994. All five countries, however, have experienced considerable growth in per capita GDP since 2000. Per capita GDP growth, therefore, does not explain the decline in undernourishment observed from 1994. However, it can not be denied that it contributed to the decline in the level of undernourishment from 2000 onwards in some countries. For example, Ethiopia, the country with the highest per capita GDP growth over the period, is also the country that has seen its level of undernourishment shrink considerably, catching up and even falling below the level of undernourishment in Burkina Faso and Kenya. However, despite Kenya's strong per capita GDP growth, nutrition has not improved significantly in the country. Moreover, Niger, which saw its level of undernourishment decline significantly from 1994 onwards, experienced only a small increase in its per capita GDP. Theories that support that the income elasticity of calorie consumption is close to zero are verified for Kenya (Behrman & Deolalikar, 1987; Bouis & Haddad, 1992) while those in favor of zero elasticity can be confirmed for Ethiopia (Subramanian & Deaton, 1996). If the per capita GDP has a controversial effect on undernourishment in the 5 countries, what about migrant's transfers?

Figure 1 shows a strong correlation between migrant remittances and per capita GDP, with the growth phases of GDP per capita coinciding with those of mgrants' remittances. In addition, countries with high growth rates are also those with high remittances. Since the trend in long-distance transfers is the same as that of GDP per capita for all countries, the same conclusions can be drawn as before. This is justifiable because remittances operate in the form of supplementary income to the household, although the uses may be different. The literature also shows that migrant remittances have a positive impact on economic growth (Pradhan & al., 2008; Nsiah & Fayissa, 2013; Driffield & Jones, 2013; Zghidi & al., 2016).

While migrant remittances and per capita GDP have contributed to the decline in undernourishment in some countries from 2000 onwards, it does not explain the decline in undernourishment observed in 1994 in Djibouti, Niger, and Ethiopia. Thus, what explains this decline in 1994? One possible explanation would be that, following the increase in undernourishment in 1990 (Figure 1), aids has increased to save countries from a probable famine (very high undernourishment), which explains why the decline in 1994 coincides with the decline in development aid (Figure 1). If we assume that development aid played a role in reducing undernourishment in 1994, what about foreign direct investment (FDI)?

[1] Undernourishment is measured by the FAO prevalence of undernourishment index which is defined as the probability that a randomly selected individuals from the reference population is found to consume less than 1,800 calories a day, a minimum requirement for an active and healthy life.

Figure 1: Trend of undernourishment and four income flows in selecting countries

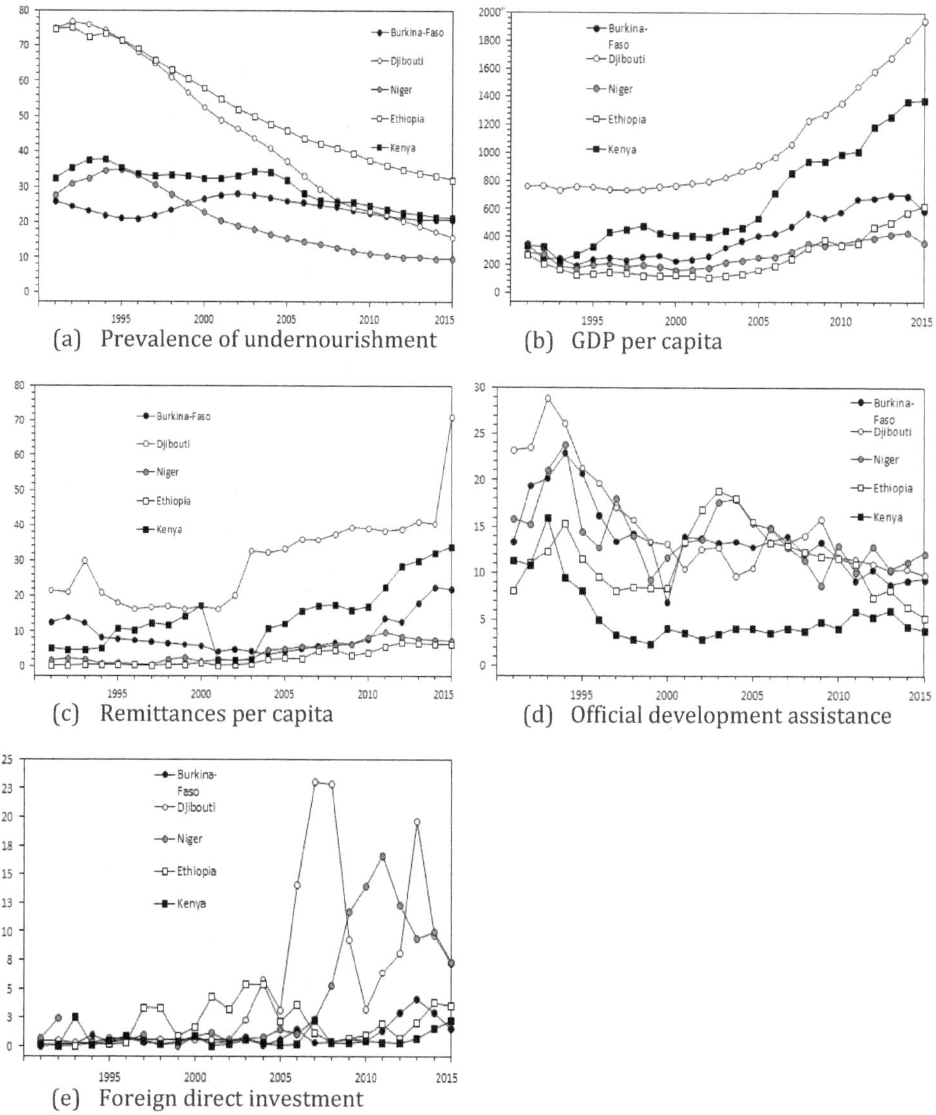

Source: Author.

The inspection of Figure 5 shows that it is difficult to establish a link between FDI and undernourishment in the five countries. The only countries where FDI has highly grown are Niger and Djibouti, starting later in 2005 after the onset of the decline in2007, did not lead to an increase in undernourishment.

Although this analysis can not be generalized to all sub-Saharan African countries, it provides an initial idea of the impact of these different income streams on undernourishment.

3. THE USES OF REMITTANCES IN SUB-SAHARAN AFRICA

As argued by Deaton (2010), learning about development requires the investigation of mechanisms. Understanding how the money sent by migrants are spent in Sub-Saharan may help to respond to the question on whether remittances contribute to the reduction of undernourishment in the region. In this section, we investigate the uses of remittances, basing on surveys that were conducted in most Sub-Saharan Africa countries.

In order to understand the development impact of remittances, in 2006, the Southern Africa Migration Project (SAMP) devised a migration-remittances survey in 5 SADC countries: Botswana, Lesotho, Mozambique, Swaziland, and Zimbabwe (Pendleton & al., 2006). The survey reveals that across the five countries, remittances are mostly used for food purchases, following school fees, clothing and transportation. Indeed, 82% of households used received money to buy foods while 52%, 52%, and 34% devoted money respectively to school fees, clothing, and transportation. However, while foods remain the main items that remittances are used for, there is a little change in the rank of other uses of money for different countries. In Botswana, Lesotho, and Zimbabwe, clothing is the second item group for which remittances are mostly devoted to (63% of households in Botswana, 76.1% in Lesotho and 57%). Regarding, Mozambique and Swaziland, school fees are the second items that remittances are spent on (49% of households in Mozambique and 55% in Swaziland). It is important to note that the households that claimed to spend their remittances on food may also use them for other purposes. Therefore, the sum of the share of household using remittances for different expenditures is not expected to be equal to 100%.

In 2008, a survey on remittances in Uganda was also conducted by the Bank of Uganda and the Uganda Bureau of Statistics. In contrast to SADC countries, it was found from this survey that remittances are mostly used in education in Uganda (27.4% of the total amount of received cash). Nevertheless, there is less difference with the share of cash used in household expenditure (food, clothing...) which counts for 22.7% of total received remittances. Building works are also one major item in which remittances-received households devote an important share of the money they received from migrants (21.2% of the total amount of received cash). Land purchase, business and saving was ranked respectively fourth, first and sixth use of remittances.

Following the survey in Uganda, in 2010, the World Bank through a Future of African Remittances Team conducted a survey in three East African countries including Uganda. The two other countries in which the survey was conducted are Ethiopia and Kenya. In contrast to the above survey, the World Bank survey of 2010 reveals that remittances are mostly spent in small business (35% of total remittances), followed by education (25% of total remittances) and daily expenses (24% of total remittances) in Uganda. However, both World Bank and Bank of Uganda's surveys show that consumption is not the first use of remittances in Uganda. The World Bank survey also showed that, in Kenya, the money received from migrants is mostly devoted to migrant physical investment (27% of total remittances), followed by new house building (18% of total remittances) and land purchase (15% of total remittances). Food purchases count only for 2% of total remittances received in Kenya. However, in Ethiopia, more than a half of total amount of remittances is devoted to daily expenses. Education and small business count respectively for 29% and 9% of the total money received from migrants in the country.

In 2010, BCEAO, a Central Bank of West African Economic and Monetary Union (WAEMU), have also performed a survey on remittances in the countries of the union: Benin, Niger, Burkina-Faso, Senegal, Togo, Mali, Guinea-Bissau and Côte d'Ivoire (BCEAO, 2013). The survey indicates that household receiving remittances spend more than a half of the received money on consumption in the region. Indeed, 54.6% of the money received is spent on consumption while 21.3% is spent on investment and 3.4% and 6.4% respectively on health-care and education.

However, heterogeneity in the use of remittances occurs within the countries of the Union. In Benin, 29.6% of remittances are devoted to consumption, 23% to property investments and 28.1% to others investments. Burkina-Faso and Côte d'Ivoire follow the same trend in the use of money received from migrants. Indeed, remittance-receiving households in Burkina-Faso spend 37.3% of remittances on consumption, 25.7% on property investments, 16.3% on other investments and 15% on education, while those of Côte d'Ivoire spend 36.2% of remittances on consumption and 29.3% on property investments.

The WAEMU's country in which the great share of remittances is spent in consumption is Senegal, with 70% of received money spent in consumption and only 7.6% in property purchase and 7.4% in education and health-care. Senegal is followed by Niger, Mali and, Guinea-Bissau in which consumption expenditures hold respectively 52.1%, 48.7% and 48% of total remittances received by each country. In Niger, only 2.8% and 0.7% of remittances are used respectively in health-care and education. In Mali, 5.2% of the money received is devoted to education while 4.2% is devoted to health-care. In Guinea-Bissau, education expenditures and health-care expenditure count respectively for 11% and 18% of total remittances. In contrast to the rest of WAEMU's countries, remittance-receiving households in Togo spend more on property investments (35.6% of the total money received). However, there is less difference with a share of money used for consumption which counts for 33% of remittances.

Although remittances are mostly spent on consumption, it is still not enough to conclude that they lead to a significant calorie consumption and thus a reduction of the proportion of undernourished in Sub-Saharan. Indeed, as underlined above rising food consumption may not necessarily provoke a significant improvement in calorie consumption which depends on the nutrients intake.

4. METHODOLOGY AND DATA

4.1. Model and estimation

The analysis of the impact of remittances on undernourishment using panel data requires a careful specification of the model to be used. In this study, the indicator employed to measure undernourishment relies on the total food supplied in the country, including food imports. Therefore, a fall in the production of foods in country *i* may affect the undernourishment of countries *j* with which *i* has food trade relationship. Undernourishment caused by a fall in food production in country *i* may then affect undernourishment in countries *j*. To simplify, we assume that *i* trades food with its neighbor countries *j*. Under this assumption, usual panel data models yield inconsistent estimate of the parameters of the model (Le Gallo, 2007; Schaffar, 2014).

In order to take into account spatial correlation between countries, we use the specification in Elhorst (2014). The model is then written as follow:

$$PoU_{it} = \lambda \sum_{j=1}^{N} w_{ij} PoU_{it} + \phi + \beta_1 Remit_{it} + \beta_2 X_{it} + c_i + \alpha_t + v_{it} \qquad (1)$$

where PoU_{it} is the prevalence of undernourishment for country *i* at time *t* (*i* =*1,.. ,N* and *t* = *1,.., T*), $Remit_{it}$ is the per capita remittances of country *i* at time *t*, and ϕ is the constant term parameter. The variable $\sum_{j=1}^{N} w_{ij} PoU_{jt}$ denotes the interaction effect of undernourishment in country i with the undernourishment in neighboring countries, w_{ij} is the i, jth element of a $N \times N$ spatial weights matrix W. X_{it} is a $1 \times (K-1)$ vector of exogenous control variables with K denoting the number of explanatory variables. v_{it} is an i.i.d error term for i and t with zero mean and variance σ^2, while c_i denotes spatial specific effects and α_t the time-period specific effects. Including spatial specific effects allows for the control of space-specific time-invariant variables whose omission could bias our results. In the same manner, time-period specific effects allow the control of all time specifics effects.

The correlation between countries may also come from interaction effects in error term. This is consistent with a situation in which random shocks are spatially cor-related. As random shocks pass through the error term, we rewrite v_{it} as follow: $v_{it} = \rho \sum_{j=1}^{N} w_{ij} v_{it} + u_{it}$. Model 1 becomes:

$$PoU_{it} = \lambda \sum_{j=1}^{N} w_{ij} PoU_{it} + \phi + \beta_1 Remit_{it} + \beta_2 X_{it} + c_i + \alpha_t + \rho \sum_{j=1}^{N} w_{ij} v_{it} + u_{it} \qquad (2)$$

To test whether this model is more appropriate to describe the data than a model without any spatial interaction effects, we use the generalized and the robust Lagrange Multiplier (LM) test proposed by Burridge (1980), Anselin (1988) and Anselin & al. (1996). The result (Table 1) indicates that only spatial error correlation have to be accepted, meaning that $\lambda = 0$ but $\rho \neq 0$ at 5 % significance level. This suggests that the countries considered in this study share common random shocks with the neighbors. This can be illustrated with the 2006-2011's horn of Africa food crisis and the 2010-2011's Sahel food crisis which affect respectively most of horn of Africa countries and most of Sahel countries located in the same area. Therefore, the model to be estimated is then:

$$PoU_{it} = \phi + \beta_1 Remit_{it} + \beta_2 X_{it} + c_i + \alpha_t + \rho \sum_{j=1}^{N} w_{ij} v_{it} + u_{it} \qquad (3)$$

Different approaches have been proposed to estimate the parameters of this model. Kapoor et al. (2007) proposed a generalization of the generalized moments estimators suggested in Kelejian & Prucha (1998) while Fingleton (2008) extend their work to develop GM estimators for spatial moving average panel data model. We use the generalized moments estimators of Kapoor & al. (2007) because it allows the disturbance terms to be both spatially and time-wise correlated as well as heteroscedastic.

The variables included in X_{it} were chosen in line with the existing literature. They include GDP per capita, Foreign Direct Investments (FDI), Official Development Assistance (ODA), public expenditures in agriculture, domestic credits, political stability, private investments, domestic food prices, food price volatility and the share of agricultural. Indeed, although the impact of income on undernourishment is controversial (Subramanian & Deaton, 1996; Behrman & Deolalikar, 1987; Deaton & Drèze, 2009; Banerjee & Duflo, 2011), there are studies showing that GDP per capita contributes to the reduction of undernourishment (Klasen, 2008). Regarding official development assistance, the literature is also controversial on their impact in developing countries. At one extreme, there are theories arguing that people are trapped in poverty in developing countries and foreign aid is the key to help them to invest in the area that will lift them out poverty-trap (Sachs, 2005). At the other extremes are theories by Easterly (2006) and Moyo (2009) arguing that foreign aids corrupt and undermine the local institution. These bad outcomes of foreign aids could lead to an increase of undernourishment since having the good institutions is one of the conditions for the reduction of undernourishment in the Sen (1981) entitlement theory. According to this theory, in an economy with private ownership and exchange in form of trade and production, the entitlement set for a given person depends on the endowment of the person and the exchange mapping. People can use their endowment to produce food or sell their labor power to get wage and buy food. The role of foreign direct investment in the reduction of undernourishment can be through the later. Indeed, foreign direct investment, especially greenfield investment, lead to a demand for workers which can be absorbed by those who want to sell their labor power to buy food. Food price, as well as food price volatility, are also the determinant of undernourishment usually cited in the literature. High food prices can lead to an increase of undernourishment (less consumption of calories) (Anríquez & al., 2013). However, Banerjee & Duflo (2011) have stated that food price has had no significant impact on calorie consumption in India from 2005. Indeed, food prices have declined in the country between 1980 and 2005, and in spite of an increase of food price in 2005, the decline in calorie consumption happened when the price of food was going down.

In order to count for the possible role of remittances in mitigating shocks, such as drought and floods, we include two dummies variables, for droughts and floods, among explanatory variables and generate the interaction terms of remittances with these dummies. The addition of interaction term is motivated by the study of Combes & Ebeke (2011) who found that remittances are a hedge against natural disasters, agricultural shocks, discretionary fiscal policy, financial and systemic banking crises, and exchange rate instability. The dummies variables on the level of income in a country were also added in the explanatory variables. They were calculated basing on the decile of per capita GDP. The thresholds, as well as the mean of per capita income, are indicated in Table 2.

Table 1: Spatial correlation tests

Ho: Error has No Spatial Autocorrelation Ha: Error has Spatial Autocorrelation		
	Statistic	P-value
LM error (Burridge)	5.9011	0.0151
LM error (Robust)	6.1813	0.0129
Ho: Spatial Lagged Dependent Variable has No Spatial Autocorrelation Ha: Spatial Lagged Dependent Variable has Spatial Autocorrelation		
	Statistic	P-value
LM error (Anselin)	0.0000	1.000
LM error (Robust)	0.2802	0.5966

Source: Author.

Estimation of equation 3 involves the specification of the $N \times N$ spatial weights matrix *W*. The choice of spatial weights matrix is a difficult task in the spatial analysis as the results may change with alternative specifications. The literature on spatial weights matrix is classified into exogenous weight matrix and parametrized weight matrix. The exogenous matrix includes binary contiguity matrix, inverse distance matrix, and k-nearest neighbors matrix. Binary contiguity matrix based on boundaries could not be used in this study since it lets islands such as Madagascar, Cabo Verde with no interaction partners. Therefore, to estimate equation 3, we use an exponential distance weights matrix which is based on a negative exponential function of distances. An exponential distance weights matrix assumes that the impact of random shocks in country *i* on neighboring countr ies *j* diminishes when the distance between *i* and *j* becomes higher. Let d_{ij} (d is a Euclidean distance based on longitude and latitude of centroid) denote centroid distances from each country *i* to all countries $\neq i$:

$$w_{ij} = \exp(-2d_{ij})$$

Table 2: Descriptive statistics on GDP per capita by decile

Decile	Mean	st dev	min	max
1	221.2387	47.24972	116.7956	275.7769
2	317.9721	26.06084	278.2105	359.1549
3	391.6511	16.81975	360.8283	417.1546
4	467.8627	31.31757	420.0534	518.3311
5	582.4032	46.40058	523.9092	671.6339
6	798.001	76.09828	676.7354	911.7183
7	1051.187	88.07473	927.173	1195.445
8	1624.384	378.1721	1197.471	2395.621
9	3403.899	569.9144	2541.343	4327.645
10	6482.726	1597.249	4390.256	10893.48

Source: Author.

4.2. Data and description

We use data from 35 Sub-Saharan African countries, spanning the years 2001-2011. Data were collected from different sources. Undernourishment is measured by the FAO (Food and Agriculture Organization of the United Nations) prevalence of undernourishment index. The index is defined as the probability that a randomly selected individual from the reference population is found to consume less than a minimum calories requirement for an active and healthy life. It relies on the Dietary Energy Consumption (DEC) which is difficult to compute due to the lack of suitable survey regularly conducted in most countries. Thus, the available DEC for human consumption in a country for one year is estimated through data on production, trade, and utilization of food commodities. The index ranges from 0 to 100, with 100 indicating a high level of undernourishment in the country. Regarding remittances, we use the World Bank's remittances data. Remittances comprise personal transfers, transfers in cash or in kind received by resident households from nonresident households, and Compensation of employees referring to the income of border, seasonal, and other short-term workers who are employed in an economy where they are not resident and of residents employed by nonresident entities. The data don't allow the understanding of which category of people (rural or urban population, rich or poor...) remittances are sent for. Thus, remittances per capita were computed by dividing the total amount of remittances received in country *i* by the population of this country. Data on political stability, domestic credits and those of official development assistance (ODA) were also collected from the World Bank database (World Development Indicators). Political stability and absence of violence are captured by an index which measures the perceptions of the likelihood of political instability and/or politically- motivated violence, including terrorism. The index is running from approximately -2.5 to 2.5, with higher values corresponding to better stability. Domestic credits, measured as a percentage of GDP, refer to the credits provided by the financial sector. They include all credits to various sectors on a gross basis, with the exception of credit to the central government, which is net. The financial sector includes monetary authorities and deposit money banks, as well as other financial corporations where data are available (including corporations that do not accept transferable deposits but do incur such liabilities as time and savings deposits).

Regarding data on macroeconomic variables such as GDP per capita and the net inflow of foreign direct investment, we used the World Economic Outlook and the IMF's balance of payment database.

Table 3: Descriptive statistics

Variable		Mean	Std. Dev.	Min	Max	Obs.
	overall	23.345	12.652	5	54.8	N = 385
Prevalence of undernourishment	between		12.203	5	50.036	n = 35
	within		3.8803	9.809	39.809	T = 11
	overall	521.11	2442.53	0.55367	20616.8	N = 385
total remittances	between		2028.49	2.510	12111.7	n = 35
	within		1399.41	-10530.6	9026.23	T = 11
	overall	38.888	71.083	0.0605	360.02	N = 385
Remittances per capita	between		69.643	1.080	298.653	n = 35
	within		18.137	-51.285	133.373	T = 11
	overall	50.668	17.8753	18.114	80.920	N = 385
Share of agricultural land	between		18.0356	18.836	80.200	n = 35
	within		1.647	41.246	57.711	T = 11
	overall	29.035	40.720	-70.377	227.783	N = 385
Domestic credit (% of GDP)	between		39.104	-12.770	175.677	n = 35
	within		12.993	-89.079	106.789	T = 11
	overall	10.590	12.090	-0.2319	115.405	N = 385
ODA	between		9.7965	0.324	48.540	n = 35
	within		7.259	-31.682	77.455	T = 11
	overall	1528.8	1951.58	116.796	10893.4	N = 385
GDP per capita	between		1828.92	235.17	7269.03	n = 35
	within		742.173	-1676.18	5153.33	T = 11
	overall	22.329	9.161	4.4038	76.12	N = 385
Private investment (% of GDP)	between		7.399	7.009	48.854	n = 35
	within		5.531	4.011	49.594	T = 11
	overall	6.493	1.776	2.12	11.69	N = 385
Domestic food price	between		1.7315	2.474	10.890	n = 35
	within		0.4865	4.941	8.2717	T = 11
	overall	-0.325	.8194	-2.375	1.185	N = 385
Political stability	between		0.763	-1.805	0.946	n = 35
	within		0.323	-1.756	0.595	T = 11
	overall	1.348	1.119	-1.406	5.858	N = 385
Public spending in agriculture	between		0.9687	0.1476	4.334	n = 35
	within		0.5824	-0.802	4.015	T = 11
	overall	13.087	9.231	-0.0599	84.5	N = 385
Food price volatility	between		5.040	5.218	26.481	n = 35
	within		7.776	-2.130	78.233	T = 11
	overall	5.0303	7.1146	-4.6180	72.841	N = 385
FDI	between		4.622	0.4877	21.915	n = 35
	within		5.459	-16.442	55.956	T = 11

Source: Author.

As for undernourishment, data on the domestic food price and the food prices volatility index were drawn from FAO's database. Domestic food price index is an indicator of the relative price of food in a country. Its computation is based on the 2011's International Comparison Program (ICP) from the World Bank and the consumer price index from the International Labour Organisation (ILO). We also use the FAO's data on agricultural land area and total land area to compute the share of agricultural land in a country. The agricultural land area is the sum area under arable land, permanent crops, and permanent pastures.

The IFPRI's (International Food Policy Research Institute) datasets on government expenditure in different sectors were used to draw data on the percentage of agriculture expenditure in total GDP of country *i*.

The binary dummy variables for droughts and floods were collected from the International Disaster Database (EMDAT), Centre for Research on the Epidemiology of Disasters (CRED).

Although most of our variables have full data, missing values were observed in domestic price index and government expenditure in agriculture. In order to extract a maximum of information from our data and avoid listwise deletion, we use the recent imputation method for time-series cross-section developed by Honaker & King (2010) to impute missing values of these variables. The purpose is not to recreate the individual missing values as close as possible to the true ones but to handle missing data in a way resulting in the valid statistical inference. The advantage of using Honacker and King's method is that, in contrast to standard methods of imputation applying to survey data, it allows for taking into account the tendency of variables which can move smoothly over time, jump sharply between some cross-sectional units like countries, jump less or be similar between some countries in close proximity, and for time-series patterns to differ across many countries. In addition, the method is based on multiple imputations which, compared to single regression (linear interpolation, unconditional mean imputation...), reflects uncertainty in the imputed values. Missing values are imputed through a bootstrapped Expected Maximum (EM) algorithm.

Table 3 reports the descriptive statistics of the data. It shows that on average, almost one in four people suffer from undernourishment in Sub-Saharan Africa during the years 2001-2011.

5. RESULTS

Table 4 reports the results of the estimation of remittances impact on undernourishment in Sub-Saharan Africa with a spatial error model. It is composed of three columns, with columns 1 and 2 indicating the results of the estimation without natural disasters, and column 2 taking into account natural disasters, namely droughts and floods.

Inspection of table 4 indicates that the impact of remittances on undernourishment is statistically significant in Sub-Saharan Africa. However, nutrition responds merely to an increase of remittances. Indeed, a 10 percent increase in remittances per individual leads to a decrease by only 1.17 percent of the proportion of undernourished in the region. As described in Section 3, in most Sub-Saharan African countries, remittances are greatly devoted to consumption, especially to food purchase. However, increasing food consumption does not systematically lead to a huge improvement of nutrition which depends on the calorie of the consumed foods. This is because food consumption depends on many factors such as taste, appearance, odor, status value or cultural preference (Behrman & Deolalikar, 1987; Banerjee & Duflo, 2011). As argued by Banerjee & Duflo (2011), due to ignorance of the real added value of good nutrition, the poorest who are the ones who suffer the most from undernourishment sometimes choose to consume tasty foods rather than nutrient-rich foods.

Like remittances, the effect of per capita GDP on undernourishment is statistically significant in Sub-Saharan Africa. However, the elasticity is very close to zero. Indeed, a 10 percent increase in GDP per capita leads to a 0.62 percent decrease of undernourishment. This finding supports the literature which underlines that the elasticity of calorie consumption to income is closed to zero (Behrman & Deolalikar, 1987; Bouis & Haddad, 1992). As described in Section 1, there have been countries that have started to reduce their level of undernourishment well before the growth of their per capita GDP. In addition, countries such as Djibouti, which have had high per capita GDP between 1980 and 2015, have remained for a long time one of the countries with a high level of undernourishment (Figure 1).

One important finding in this study is that the elasticity of calorie consumption to remittances is higher than that of GDP (Table 4). This finding can be explained by the fact that remittances are directly received by families in the home country while the reception of GDP per capita depends on how well income is distributed.

As expected, a high share of agricultural land is significantly associated with a reduction of undernourishment in Sub-Saharan Africa. Indeed, the more is agricultural land, the more is food supply and the less are undernourishment. Credits, as well as private investments, were found to contribute significantly to the reduction of undernourishment in Sub-Saharan Africa. When the share of domestic credits to GDP increase by 10 percent, the proportion of undernourished in the region decreases by 0.65 percent. This result emphasizes the role played by domestic credit (Obilor, 2013) in helping farmers to afford agriculture inputs (fertilizers, tractors...) and improve agricultural production. With respect to private investment, results in Table 4 show that a 10% increase in private investment induces a 0.58% decrease in the proportion of undernourished in Sub-Saharan Africa.

The first column of table 4 shows that official development assistance (ODA) is positively and significantly related to undernourishment in Sub-Saharan Africa. Since this finding might due to a reverse causality between official development assistance and undernourishment, we lagged ODA by one period with the intuition behind it being that current undernourishment can't cause past ODA.

Column 2 shows that ODA has no significant effect on undernourishment when it is lagged by one period. This result raises the question of the effectiveness of aids in fighting undernourishment. According to the literature, there are two theories on the effectiveness of foreign aid: the public interest theory which argues that foreign aids are necessary to fill a financing or investment gap, which in turn will lift countries out of a poverty trap (Sachs, 2005), and a public choice theory which argues that foreign aids are ineffective and possibly damaging to recipient countries (Easterly, 2006; Moyo, 2009). Aid allocation may encourage impoverishing policies since misery resulting from damaging policies leads donors more likely to grant more aid to try and alleviate the impoverished conditions (Williamson, 2010).

Like official development assistance, foreign direct investments (FDI) have no significant impact on undernourishment in Sub-Saharan Africa. Food prices, as well as food price volatility, were also found to have no significant effect on undernourishment in Sub-Saharan Africa.

Likewise, political stability, government expenditure in agriculture, droughts, and floods have no significant impact on undernourishment. The insignificance effect of floods and droughts on undernourishment in Sub-Saharan Africa is not surprising. All the countries in Figure 1 have experienced either a drought or a flood during the period 2000 to 2015. However, only the level of undernourishment in Kenya was affected by these catastrophes (Figure 1).

While droughts and floods have no significant effect on undernourishment in Sub-Saharan Africa, table 4 shows that remittances play a significant role during a period of floods as shown the significant and negative coefficient of the interaction term between remittances per capita and a dummy of floods. This result supports the finding of Combes & Ebeke (2011).

Table 4: Explaining the impact of remittances on undernourishment in Sub-Saharan Africa

	Dependent variable: Prevalence of undernourishment (N=35, T=11)					
	(1)		(2)		(3)	
	β	Elasticities	β	Elasticities	β	Elasticities
Remittances per capita	-0.0697***	-0.1161	-0.0711***	-0.1184	-0.0656***	-0.1093
	(0.0084)		(0.0084)		(0.0087)	
Share of agricultural land	-0.0866***	-0.1879	-0.0921***	-0.2000	-0.0913***	-0.1981
	(0.0324)		(0.0325)		(0.0319)	
Domestic credit (% of GDP)	-0.0503***	-0.0626	-0.0461***	-0.0573	-0.0456***	-0.0568
	(0.0147)		(0.0147)		(0.0144)	
ODA (% of GDP)	0.126**	0.0579				
	(0.0504)					
ODA (t-1)			0.0754	0.0316	0.0635	0.0266
			(0.0493)		(0.0474)	
GDP per capita	-0.0009**	-0.0580	-0.0010***	-0.0654	-0.0010***	-0.0667
	(0.0003)		(0.0004)		(0.0003)	
Private investment (% of GDP)	-0.1382*	-0.1321	-0.1236*	-0.1183	-0.1224*	-0.1171
	(0.0691)		(0.0691)		(0.0672)	
Domestic food price	0.0682	0.0192	0.1085	0.0302	0.1072	0.0298
	(0.3538)		(0.3566)		(0.3445)	
Political stability	0.11	-0.0015	0.1145	-0.0016	0.1292	-0.0018
	(0.7763)		(0.7734)		(0.7522)	
Public spending in agriculture	-0.6419	-0.0371	-0.7282	-0.0383	-0.5469	-0.0316
	(0.5434)		(0.5144)		(0.5328)	
Food price volatility	-0.0660	-0.0370	-0.0498	-0.0279	-0.0560	-0.0314
	(0.0560)		(0.0562)		(0.0552)	
FDI (% of GDP)	0.0097	0.0021	0.0322	0.0070	0.0251	0.0054
	(0.0805)		(0.0801)		(0.0785)	
Drought	1.6088	0.0091	1.6725	0.0095	1.9707	0.0112
	(1.5096)		(1.5224)		(1.5989)	
Flood	0.3484	0.0043	0.3433	0.0042	1.3985	0.0173
	(1.1121)		(1.1185)		(1.1851)	
Remittances x Drought					-0.0085	-0.0018
					(0.0191)	
Remittances x Flood					-0.0375*	-0.0121
					(0.0195)	
Constant	35.7468***		35.865***		35.630***	
Rho	0.556		0.5533		0.5599	
LM Test (Ho : Rho = 0)	9.658		9.6898		9.8897	
R^2	0.2371		0.2296		0.2276	
Ajusted R^2	0.1307		0.1222		0.1147	
Raw R^2	0.8256		0.8237		0.8230	
Ajusted Raw R^2	0.8013		0.7991		0.7971	

*Note: (): Robust standards errors, ***: Significant at 1 % level, **: Significant at 5 % level, *: Significant at 10 % level, W: Exponential distance weights matrix, LM Tests are calculated basing on Baltagi et al. (2007).*

Table 5: Explaining the impact of remittances on undernourishment by income group in Sub-Saharan Africa

Variables	Dependent variable: Prevalence of undernourishment (N=35, T=11)									
	(1)	(2)	(3)	(4)	(5)	(6)	(7)	(8)	(9)	(10)
Remittances per capita	-0.0637***	-0.0687***	-0.0695***	-0.0701***	-0.0702***	-0.0717***	-0.0701***	-0.0676***	-0.0725***	-0.0748***
	(0.0082)	(0.0082)	(0.0082)	(0.0083)	(0.0084)	(0.0088)	(0.0083)	(0.0085)	(0.0089)	(0.0087)
Share of agricultural land	-0.0579*	-0.0906***	-0.0883***	-0.0888***	-0.0897***	-0.0918***	-0.0883***	-0.0878***	-0.0876***	-0.0964***
	(0.0318)	(0.0314)	(0.0316)	(0.0317)	(0.0317)	(0.0318)	(0.0316)	(0.0315)	(0.0321)	(0.0324)
Domestic credit (% of GDP)	-0.0634***	-0.0447***	-0.0459***	-0.0452***	-0.0467***	-0.0459***	-0.0446***	-0.0458***	-0.0461***	-0.0544***
	(0.0149)	(0.0142)	(0.0143)	(0.0142)	(0.0143)	(0.0145)	(0.0142)	(0.0142)	(0.0144)	(0.0150)
ODA (t-1)	0.0859*	0.0491	0.0693	0.0666	0.0681	0.0595	0.0619	0.0636	0.0710	0.0667
	(0.0465)	(0.0474)	(0.0473)	(0.0473)	(0.0473)	(0.0473)	(0.0473)	(0.0469)	(0.0478)	(0.0485)
GDP per capita	-0.0008**	-0.0010***	-0.0010***	-0.0011***	-0.0011***	-0.0011***	-0.0011***	-0.0010***	-0.0010***	-0.0015***
	(0.0003)	(0.0003)	(0.0003)	(0.0003)	(0.0003)	(0.0003)	(0.0003)	(0.0003)	(0.0003)	(0.0004)
Private investment (% of GDP)	-0.1014	-0.1066	-0.1268*	-0.1231*	-0.1219*	-0.1124*	-0.1069	-0.1158*	-0.1233*	-0.1295*
	(0.0660)	(0.0663)	(0.0667)	(0.0669)	(0.0667)	(0.0669)	(0.0670)	(0.0662)	(0.0679)	(0.0691)
Domestic food price	0.0939	0.1338	0.0731	0.1057	0.0833	0.1567	0.1746	0.1386	0.0887	0.0602
	(0.3345)	(0.3369)	(0.3391)	(0.3410)	(0.3401)	(0.3442)	(0.3407)	(0.3368)	(0.3474)	(0.3602)
Political stability	0.5859	0-.0841	0.0624	0.1479	0.0346	-0.1239	-0.0169	-0.0506	0.0579	0.0269
	(0.7387)	(0.7311)	(0.7387)	(0.7439)	(0.7401)	(0.7425)	(0.7426)	(0.7334)	(0.7515)	(0.7762)
Public spending in agriculture	-0.6929	-0.5657	-0.5088	-0.5634	-0.5106	-0.5051	-0.5648	-0.5923	-0.5103	-0.6019
	(0.5204)	(0.5238)	(0.5275)	(0.5286)	(0.5286)	(0.5308)	(0.5279)	(0.5251)	(0.5338)	(0.5440)
Food price volatility	-0.0734	-0.0551	-0.0569	-0.0549	-0.0535	-0.0597	-0.0540	-0.0610	-0.0557	-0.0642
	(0.0539)	(0.0544)	(0.0549)	(0.0549)	(0.0549)	(0.0549)	(0.0561)	(0.0546)	(0.0557)	(0.0559)
FDI (% of GDP)	0.0497	0.0293	0.0269	0.0269	0.0229	0.0239	0.0264	0.0217	0.0231	0.0282
	(0.0773)	(0.0771)	(0.0778)	(0.0780)	(0.0778)	(0.0776)	(0.0779)	(0.0776)	(0.0787)	(0.0798)
Income group dummy	7.4186***	3.1167*	1.4974	1.6662	-1.5382	-4.7098**	-3.0513	-2.0966	0.4128	2.1485
	(1.9926)	(1.7891)	(1.7989)	(1.9888)	(1.7857)	(1.8199)	(1.8793)	(1.9387)	(2.0274)	(2.7653)
Remittances x Decile 1	0.2415									
	(0.2515)									
Remittances x Decile 2		-0.0535								
		(0.0458)								
Remittances x Decile 3			-0.0389							
			(0.0410)							
Remittances x Decile 4				-0.1383*						
				(0.0791)						
Remittances x Decile 5					-0.0015					
					(0.0226)					
Remittances x Decile 6						0.0126				
						(0.0166)				
Remittances x Decile 7							0.0002			
							(0.0266)			
Remittances x Decile 8								-0.0108		
								(0.0171)		
Remittances x Decile 9									0.0057	
									(0.0156)	
Remittances x Decile 10										0.0412*
										(0.0243)
Constant	33.402***	35.335***	36.154***	36.167***	36.366***	36.233***	35.538***	35.950***	36.059***	37.826***
	(3.9763)	(3.9613)	(3.9756)	(3.9997)	(3.9928)	(4.0186)	(3.9966)	(3.9545)	(4.1164)	(4.1807)
Rho	0.5391	0.5552	0.5509	0.5501	0.5543	0.5543	0.5565	0.5577	0.5489	0.5592
R^2	0.2841	0.2257	0.2216	0.2271	0.2248	0.2360	0.2284	0.2221	0.2244	0.2178
Raw R^2	0.8374	0.8229	0.8218	0.8233	0.8227	0.8253	0.8237	0.8218	0.8226	0.8200

*(): Robust standards errors, ***: Significant at 1 % level, **: Significant at 5 % level, *: Significant at 10 % level. W: Exponential distance weights matrix.*

Inspection of interaction between per capita remittances and income group dummies in table 5 indicates that the impact of remittances is statistically different in the income decile 4 and 10. Moreover, remittances have less effect on calorie consumption in decile 10 than decile 4.

This result can be explained by the fact that, over a certain level of income, household receiving remittances may prefer to devote a high share of the money to others uses, namely education, health, investment, rather than consumption since they have sufficient resources to afford food. For instance, in Niger and Ethiopia, the countries in which the income per individual is low, households receiving remittances spend more than 50% of received money on consumption while those of Kenya and Côte d'Ivoire, two of the countries with high per capita GDP, devote less than 40% of received money on consumption (Section 2). The effect of remittances on undernourishment is also low in countries with very low GDP per capita, decile 1-3, comparing to countries in decile 4. The possible explanation for this finding is that counting the high costs of international migration, individuals in low-GDP countries are less able to migrate and send money thereafter. As shown in table 6, the countries in deciles 1-3 are the most affected by undernourishment and, at the same time, they are the smallest receivers of remittances.

Table 6: Prevalence of undernourishment and remittances per capita by income decile

Decile	Proportion of undernourished	Remittances per capita
1	35.789	5.377
2	29.358	13.124
3	25.861	21.263
4	24.355	16.564
5	23.016	34.868
6	19.334	59.845
7	21.679	34.199
8	20.297	71.575
9	20.043	76.922
10	13.468	55.718

Source: Author.

6. CONCLUSION

The aim of this paper was to highlight the impact of remittances on undernourishment in Sub-Saharan Africa. Our findings reveal that remittances contribute to the reduction of undernourishment in the region. This result is explained by the fact that the money sent by migrants is mainly devoted to consumption in most Sub-Saharan Africa countries. However, the increase in remittances only results in a small increase in calorie consumption. This result supports the literature which argues that calorie consumption reacts very little to an increase in income. Remittances were also found to be a hedge against flood in Sub-Saharan Africa.

The study also controls for others variables that may affect the prevalence of undernourishment. Like remittances, GDP per capita, domestic credit, as well as private investment, were found to contribute to a reduction of the proportion of undernourished in Sub-Saharan Africa. In others words, the more are domestic credits and private investments, the less is undernourishment in Sub-Saharan Africa. The share of the agricultural land area in the total land area also plays a significant role in the reduction of undernourishment in the region. Having a high share of agriculture land enhances the availability of food which can be afforded with a minimum income. This minimum income is provided by the distribution of income, under low inequality of income, and the reception of money from migrants. Regarding official development assistance, our results show that they have no significant effect on undernourishment in Sub-Saharan Africa.

The impact of remittances has also been analyzed in different income deciles. The results show that remittances have a lower impact in lower income deciles and higher income deciles whereas the impact is higher in intermediate income deciles. Since migration is costly, people in low-income countries are less able to sustain it, which leads to low migration in these countries. As a result, remittances are less important in countries of low-income deciles, which are at the same time the countries suffering the most from undernourishment. Regarding the people in the countries of higher income deciles, they spend more money received from migrants on education, health, and investments than on consumption. This explains the low impact of remittances in countries of higher income deciles.

This research contributes more generally towards a broader view of the benefits of the money that migrants send to their home countries. Governments and international organizations fighting undernourishment in Sub-Saharan Africa should take into account these benefits and also encourage domestic credits as well as private investments.

REFERENCES

Adams, R. H., & Cuecuecha, A., 2013, The impact of remittances on investment and poverty in Ghana. *World Development*, 50, 24–40.

Anríquez, G., Daidone, S., & Mane, E., 2013, Rising food prices and undernourishment: A cross-country inquiry. *Food Policy*, 38, 190–202.

Anselin, L. (1988). Lagrange multiplier test diagnostics for spatial dependence and spatial heterogeneity. *Geographical Analysis*, 20 (1), 1–17.

Anselin, L., Bera, A. K., Florax, R., & Yoon, M. J., 1996, Simple diagnostic tests for spatial dependence. Regional Science and Urban Economics, 26 (1), 77–104.

Antón, J.-I. (2010). The impact of remittances on nutritional status of children in ecuador1. *International Migration Review*, 44 (2), 269–299.

Baltagi, B. H., Song, S. H., Jung, B. C., & Koh, W., 2007, Testing for serial correlation, spatial autocorrelation and random effects using panel data. *Journal of Econometrics*, 140 (1), 5–51.

Banerjee, A., & Duflo, E. (2011). *Poor Economics: A Radical Rethinking of the Way to Fight Global Poverty*. Publicaffairs New York.

Bang, J. T., Mitra, A., & Wunnava, P. V., 2016, Do remittances improve income inequality? An instrumental variable quantile analysis of the Kenyan case. *Economic Modelling*, 58, 394–402.

BCEAO (2013). Synthèse des résultats des enquêtes sur les envois de fonds des travailleurs migrants dans les pays de l'UEMOA.

Behrman, J. R., & Deolalikar, A. B., 1987, Will developing country nutrition improve with income? a case study for rural south India. *Journal of Political Economy*, 95 (3), 492–507.

Bouis, H. E., & Haddad, L. J., 1992, Are estimates of calorie income elasticities too high? A recalibration of the plausible range. *Journal of Development Economics*, 39 (2), 333–364.

Burridge, P. (1980). On the cliff-ord test for spatial correlation. Journal of the Royal Statistical Society. Series B (Methodological), 42 (1), 107–108.

Combes, J.-L., & Ebeke, C., 2011, Remittances and household consumption instability in developing countries. *World Development*, 39 (7), 1076–1089.

Combes, J.-L., Ebeke, C. H., Etoundi, S. M. N., & Yogo, T. U., 2014, Are Remittances and Foreign Aid a Hedge Against Food Price Shocks in Developing Countries?, *World Development*, 54, 81–98.

Deaton, A., 2010, Instruments, randomization, and learning about development. *Journal of Economic Literature*, 48 (2), 424–455.

Deaton, A., & Drèze, J., 2009, Food and nutrition in India: facts and interpretations. *Economic and Political Weekly*, 42–65.

Driffield, N., & Jones, C., 2013, Impact of FDI, ODA and Migrant Remittances on Economic Growth in Developing Countries: A Systems Approach. *The European Journal of Development Research*, 25 (2), 173–196.

Easterly, W., 2006, *The White Man's Burden: Why the West's Efforts to Aid the Rest Have Done So Much Ill And So Little Good.* Oxford University Press.

Elhorst, J. P. (2014). Matlab software for spatial panels. *International Regional Science Review*, 37 (3), 389-405.

Fingleton, B., 2008, A generalized method of moments estimator for a spatial model with moving average errors, with application to real estate prices. *Empirical Economics*, (1), 35–57.

Hildebrandt, N., McKenzie, D. J., Esquivel, G., & Schargrodsky, E., 2005, The effects of migration on child health in Mexico [with comments]. *Economia*, 6 (1), 257–289.

Honaker, J., & King, G., 2010, What to do about missing values in time-series crosssection data. *American Journal of Political Science*, 54 (2), 561–581.

Imai, K. S., Gaiha, R., Ali, A., & Kaicker, N., 2014, Remittances, growth and poverty: New evidence from Asian countries. *Journal of Policy Modelling*, 36 (3), 524–538.

Kapoor, M., Kelejian, H. H., & Prucha, I. R., 2007, Panel data models with spatially correlated error components. *Journal of Econometrics*, 140 (1), 97–130.

Kelejian, H. H., & Prucha, I. R., 1998, A generalized spatial two-stage least squares procedure for estimating a spatial autoregressive model with autoregressive disturbances. *The Journal of Real Estate Finance and Economics*, 17 (1), 99–121.

Klasen, S., 2008, Poverty, undernutrition, and child mortality: Some inter-regional puzzles and their implicationsfor research and policy. *Journal of Economic Inequality*, 6 (1), 89–115.

Le Gallo, J. , 2007, Économétrie spatiale : l'autocorrélation spatiale dans les modèles de régression linéaire. *Economie & prévision*, no 155 (4), 139–157.

Margolis, D. N., Miotti, L., Mouhoud, E. M., & Oudinet, J., 2015, To Have and Have Not: International Migration, Poverty, and Inequality in Algeria. *The Scandinavian Journal of Economics*, 117 (2), 650–685.

Moyo, D., 2009, *Dead Aid: Why Aid Is Not Working and How There Is a Better Way for Africa.* London: Allen Lane.

Nsiah, C., & Fayissa, B., 2013, Remittances and economic growth in Africa, Asia, and Latin American-Caribbean countries: a panel unit root and panel cointegration analysis. *Journal of Economics and Finance*, 37 (3), 424–441.

Obilor, S. I. (2013). The impact of commercial banks' credit to agriculture on agricultural development in Nigeria: An econometric analysis. *International Journal of Business, Humanities and Technology*, 3 (1), 85–94.

Pendleton, W., Crush, J., Campebell, E., Green, T., Simelane, H., Tevera, D., & De Vletter, F., 2006, *Migration, remittances and development in Southern Africa*, Southern African Migration Project.

Pradhan, G., Upadhyay, M., & Upadhyaya, K., 2008, Remittances and economic growth in developing countries. *The European Journal of Development Research*, 20 (3), 497–506.

Sachs, J., 2005, *The End of Poverty: Economic Possibilities for Our Time.* New York: Penguin Press.

Schaffar, A., 2014, Advances in spatial econometrics: an introduction. *Région et Développement*, 40, 4–9.

Sen, A., 1981, *Poverty and famines: an essay on entitlement and deprivation.* Oxford University Press.

Stark, O., 1991, *The Migration of Labor.* Cambridge: Basic Blackwell.

Subramanian, S., & Deaton, A., 1996, The demand for food and calories. *Journal of Political Economy*, 104 (1), 133–162.

Williamson, C. R., 2010, Exploring the failure of foreign aid: The role of incentives and information. *The review of Austrian economics*, 23 (1), 17–33.

Zghidi, N., Sghaier, I. M., & Abida, Z., 2016, Remittances, Institutions, and Economic Growth in North African Countries. *Journal of the Knowledge Economy*, 1–18.

Impact des transferts de fonds des migrants sur la sous-alimentation en Afrique subsaharienne : analyse à partir d'un modèle spatial

Résumé - Cet article évalue l'impact des transferts de fonds des migrants sur la sous-alimentation en Afrique subsaharienne. Menée sur un panel de 35 pays, l'étude couvre la période 2001-2011. La méthode d'estimation adoptée est celle des moments généralisés sous l'hypothèse de présence d'un coefficient spatial autorégressif. Les résultats montrent que les transferts de fonds des migrants contribuent à une réduction de la sous-alimentation en Afrique subsaharienne. Cependant, l'effet, bien que statistiquement significatif, reste minime. Les résultats montrent également que l'impact des transferts est plus prononcé dans les pays qui se situent dans les déciles de revenu intermédiaire.

Mots-Clés

Migration
Transferts de fonds
Sous-alimentation
Modèle spatial
Afrique subsaharienne

Région et Développement
n° 47-2018
www.regionetdeveloppement.org

L'IDH, la stabilité politique et l'absence de violence-terrorisme comme facteurs explicatifs de l'attractivité touristique : le cas du bassin méditerranéen

Nathalie MONTARGOT*
Abdessamad OUCHEN**

Résumé - Le présent article montre, à travers un modèle estimé pour un panel de sept pays du bassin méditerranéen, que le nombre d'arrivées de touristes peut être expliqué par l'indice de développement humain (avec ses trois dimensions : santé, éducation et niveau de vie) et l'indice de stabilité politique et d'absence de violence/terrorisme. La sûreté et la sécurité, la santé et l'hygiène, l'éducation, la formation et la disponibilité de travailleurs qualifiés et le niveau de vie apparaissent ainsi de manière générale comme de forts attributs pouvant expliquer l'attractivité touristique des destinations.

Classification JEL
C21, C23, O11, O15, R58, Z32

Mots-clés
Attractivité touristique
Bassin méditerranéen
Développement humain
Économétrie de données de panel
Stabilité politique
Violence-terrorisme

Les auteurs remercient le rapporteur anonyme et la rédaction de la revue pour leurs commentaires qui ont permis d'améliorer sensiblement cet article.

* CRM Groupe Sup de Co La Rochelle, CEREGE EA1722, Chaire ESSEC du Changement ; montargotn@esc-larochelle.fr.
** LAMAFAO, Ecole Nationale de Commerce et de Gestion de Fès, Université Sidi Mohamed Ben Abdellah Fès ; abdessamad.ouchen@usmba.ac.ma.

INTRODUCTION

L'activité économique générée par le tourisme offre une source importante de devises, de revenus et d'emplois (Claver-Cortés et al., 2007 ; Wang et Hsu, 2010). Attirer les touristes constitue donc un enjeu économique, qui apparait cependant tributaire de plusieurs facteurs qui ont été mis en évidence à travers différents modèles.

Le modèle de compétitivité touristique de Ritchie et Crouch (2003) prend ainsi en considération des facteurs comme la dotation du territoire en éléments attractifs et les ressources indispensables à l'accueil touristique, les infrastructures routières et de télécommunications, l'hospitalité de la population locale, la gestion de la qualité de l'expérience touristique, la promotion et l'aménagement du territoire. Il prend également en compte le sentiment d'insécurité que le touriste peut a priori ressentir vis-à-vis d'une destination et qui peut se répercuter négativement sur les autres facteurs.

Pour leur part, Dwyer et Kim (2003) recensent les indicateurs de compétitivité touristique suivants :

- *les ressources héritées (dotées)* qui comprennent les ressources naturelles et le patrimoine culturel ;
- *les ressources créées* qui regroupent l'infrastructure touristique, la gamme d'activités sportives, d'aventure et de loisirs, les achats et le divertissement ;
- *les facteurs de soutien* qui concernent l'infrastructure générale (relative à la santé, aux institutions financières, au système de télécommunication, à la sécurité, aux systèmes locaux de transport, au traitement des déchets et à l'approvisionnement en électricité), la qualité des services touristiques, l'accessibilité de la destination, l'hospitalité de la population locale, les liens commerciaux, sportifs, ethniques et religieux de la destination avec les marchés émetteurs de touristes ;
- *le management de la destination* qui concerne l'organisation de gestion de la destination, sa gestion marketing, l'existence d'une politique, d'une planification et d'un développement conformes à une vision formelle à long terme, le développement des ressources humaines et la gestion de l'environnement ;
- *les conditions situationnelles* comme l'environnement concurrentiel à l'échelle nationale, l'emplacement de la destination, l'environnement économique, politique et technologique au niveau mondial, la compétitivité des prix, la sécurité et la sûreté ;
- *les facteurs de la demande* qui regroupent la sensibilisation, la perception et les préférences en matière de destination ;
- *les indicateurs de performance du marché* comme les statistiques relatives au nombre de visiteurs, à leurs durées de séjour et à leurs dépenses, la contribution du tourisme à l'économie, les indicateurs de prospérité économique comme le revenu par habitant, l'investissement touristique, les prix et les politiques de soutien du tourisme par le gouvernement.

Les destinations, qu'elles appartiennent aux pays développés ou non, évoluent dans un environnement compétitif. La mesure de leur niveau de compétitivité s'avère variable selon le modèle d'évaluation retenu (Zhang et al., 2011). Le Forum économique mondial (2007, 2009, 2011, 2013, 2015 et 2017) a ainsi développé son propre modèle afin de déterminer un indice de compétitivité touristique (Travel and Tourism Competitiveness Index, TTCI). Il a permis d'établir un classement des pays tous les deux ans depuis 2007 selon les éléments suivants :

- l'environnement favorable qui concerne l'environnement des affaires, la sûreté et la sécurité, la santé et l'hygiène, les ressources humaines et le marché du travail, le déploiement des TIC ;

- la politique et les conditions favorables qui concernent le voyage et le tourisme, l'ouverture internationale, la compétitivité des prix et la durabilité de l'environnement ;
- l'infrastructure concernant le transport aérien et le service touristique ;
- les ressources naturelles, culturelles et les voyages d'affaires.

Le présent article ambitionne d'expliquer le nombre d'arrivées de touristes par un modèle différent. Nous cherchons à montrer que, au sein d'un même bassin touristique, le nombre d'arrivées de touristes dépend de deux grandes variables explicatives. D'une part, *le niveau du développement humain du pays d'accueil*, qui est la moyenne géométrique des indices normalisés pour les trois dimensions qui le composent (santé, éducation et niveau de vie) et, d'autre part, *sa stabilité politique et l'absence de violence/terrorisme*, qui traduisent la probabilité qu'un gouvernement soit déstabilisé ou renversé par des moyens inconstitutionnels, incluant la violence et le terrorisme à motivation politique (Kaufmann et al., 2010).

L'introduction d'un facteur risque, inhérent à un pays, constitue une avancée dans les approches empiriques (Sequera et Nunes, 2008). Eilat et Einav (2004), dans cet esprit, ont montré que le tourisme dépend du PIB par habitant, du commerce, du taux de change pour les pays développés. Ils ont introduit un indice de risque prenant en compte le système de classement Vigipirate et le score de la Banque mondiale évaluant la stabilité politique et l'absence de violence et de terrorisme dans le pays. Sequeira et Nunes (2008) ont quant à eux mesuré l'impact sur le tourisme des risques rencontrés par les pays (terrorisme, instabilité politique et militaire, catastrophes naturelles) sur la période 1985-2002. En se basant sur les variables provenant du *« International Country Risk »*, ils concluent qu'une augmentation d'un point du risque du pays génère 0,2 % de baisse du tourisme. Parmi l'ensemble des risques encourus, ils remarquent la plus forte influence du risque politique pour les pays fortement orientés tourisme. Rittichainuwat et Chakraborty (2009) et Fuchs et Reichel (2011) pour leur part, se sont focalisés respectivement sur le crime, le terrorisme, la maladie et les destinations à risque.

Les données relatives à la variable expliquée (nombre d'arrivées de touristes) et aux deux variables explicatives qui sont retenues dans notre modèle en panel (indice de stabilité politique et d'absence de violence/terrorisme ; indice de développement humain) sont disponibles sur les sites de la Banque mondiale et du PNUD (Programme des Nations Unies pour le Développement). L'échantillon est composé de sept pays du bassin méditerranéen, figurant parmi les 50 meilleures destinations touristiques mondiales, à savoir la France, l'Espagne, l'Italie, l'Egypte, le Maroc, la Croatie et la Tunisie, sur la période 2003 à 2013. Nous jugeons de la qualité prédictive de notre modèle à travers une comparaison entre ses prévisions, c'est-à-dire les nombres estimés d'arrivées de touristes pour les sept pays de notre échantillon et les nombres d'arrivées de touristes effectivement observés en 2014 et 2015, dates de dernières statistiques disponibles auprès de la Banque mondiale et du PNUD.

Une revue de littérature portant sur les concepts d'attractivité et de compétitivité touristiques est présentée en section 1. Elle met l'accent sur les limites des modèles utilisés, justifiant celui testé dans cette recherche. La méthodologie retenue et les résultats sont présentés en section 2. Un panel de pays d'un même bassin touristique, au climat et patrimoine naturel comparables – le bassin méditerranéen – a été sélectionné, afin de chercher à expliquer notre variable dépendante par une seule équation dans un modèle global.

1. CADRE CONCEPTUEL : ATTRACTIVITÉ, ATTRACTION ET COMPÉTITIVITÉ TOURISTIQUES

1.1. Attractivité et compétitivité touristique

L'attractivité touristique d'un territoire se mesure par le nombre d'arrivées de touristes ou par les recettes touristiques (Viceriat et al., 2007 ; Smith, 1987). L'attraction touristique tire le touriste hors de son environnement habituel (Lew, 1987). Une ressource touristique est encastrée dans l'environnement physique, culturel, social, économique ou technologique d'un lieu (Cooper et Hall, 2011). Lors d'une méta-analyse de la littérature publiée dans trois grandes revues du tourisme de 2000 à 2012 (Annals of Tourism Research, Tourism Management et Journal of Travel Research), 519 articles ont été identifiés et analysés. Scott A. Cohen et al. (2014) précisent que l'approche *push-pull* (pousser-tirer) reste la plus utilisée pour expliquer les motivations des touristes, compte tenu de sa simplicité (Dann's, 1977 ; Klenosky, 2002). Il apparait en effet que ces derniers sont poussés par leurs besoins biogènes et émotionnels à voyager et sont également tirés par les attributs de la destination (Yoon et Uysal, 2005). Les attractions touristiques constituent des ressources que les touristes désirent expérimenter et qui motivent leur déplacement (Dann's, 1977 ; Cooper et Hall, 2011). Elles comprennent les attractions culturelles (paysages urbains, musées, monuments, etc.) et naturelles (espaces sauvages) qui constituent les attractions principales et le centre attractif de la destination. D'autres facteurs temporaires (tels que les centres administratifs et commerciaux) constituent des attractions secondaires (Smith, 1980 ; Leiper, 1990).

L'attractivité est par ailleurs affectée par les conditions sanitaires de la destination ou son niveau de sécurité (Cooper et Hall, 2011). Cohen et al. (2014) montrent que les perceptions des touristes se concentrent souvent sur les risques et la sécurité, par exemple sur le crime (Barker et al., 2003, George, 2010), le terrorisme et la maladie (Rittichainuwat et Chakraborty, 2009) ou les destinations dangereuses (Fuchs et Reichel, 2011).

La littérature consacrée au tourisme considère la compétitivité touristique comme un concept relatif, multidimensionnel (de par ses dimensions économiques, politiques, sociales, écologiques et culturelles) et complexe (de par sa définition et sa mesure). Il dépend de variables quantitatives (telles que le nombre de visiteurs, la part de marché, la valeur ajoutée dégagée par l'industrie touristique, etc.) et de variables qualitatives (telles que la culture, la qualité des services touristiques, le patrimoine naturel, etc.) (Dwyer et Kim, 2003 ; Dupont, 2012). La compétitivité touristique renvoie à plusieurs aspects, tels que la position d'une destination donnée par rapport à ses concurrents, les prix des produits touristiques, la qualité de l'offre, etc. Elle peut être définie comme la capacité d'une destination à faire face à la concurrence de manière efficace et rentable sur le marché touristique, à travers son aptitude à préserver la qualité de ses ressources physiques, sociales, culturelles, et environnementales tout en restant compétitive sur le marché. Il convient de noter qu'il ne faut pas confondre la compétitivité avec l'attractivité. Cette dernière constitue en effet un préalable à la compétitivité (Dupont, 2012).

1.2. Les modèles d'attractivité et de compétitivité touristiques

Les travaux de Sequeira et Nunes (2008), Eilat et Einav (2004), Rittichainuwat et Chakraborty (2009), Fuchs et Reichel (2011) mettent en évidence l'impact négatif et significatif de la violence, du terrorisme, de l'instabilité politique et de la maladie sur le tourisme. De même que la méta-analyse de la littérature de Cohen et al.

(2014), ces travaux justifient, comme indiqué dans l'introduction générale, le choix des variables explicatives retenues dans notre modèle.

L'infrastructure d'accueil, la culture de la destination et l'accueil de la population locale constituent des attributs de l'attractivité touristique forts. Selon Ritchie et Zins (1978), Kim (1998), Gallarza et al. (2002), Enright et Newton (2004), Cracolici et Nijkamp (2008) et Jin et al. (2012), « l'infrastructure d'accueil », « la culture de la destination et l'accueil de la population locale » et « la sécurité » sont les facteurs les plus déterminants. D'après la synthèse des différents attributs de l'attractivité touristique élaborée à partir de vingt travaux par Galarneau (2015), neuf attributs reviennent dans huit travaux, à savoir : saison-climat, lieux naturels (tels que les cours d'eau et les montagnes), infrastructure d'accueil (hôtels, ports, gares, aéroports, etc.), accessibilité-transports (routes, aéroports, ports, voies ferrées, transport en commun, etc.), lieux culturels et historiques, divertissements (casinos, centres de ski, etc.), culture-accueil, événements (festivals, spectacles, etc.) et sécurité.

En vue d'éclaircir l'attraction touristique, nous pouvons partir du modèle schématique de l'environnement spatial d'une attraction touristique de Gunn (1988). Il s'agit d'un schéma composé de trois parties distinctes mais interdépendantes, à savoir le *nucleus* ou le noyau de l'attraction, l'*inviolate belt* qui est l'espace nécessaire pour mettre le nucleus dans un contexte touristique et la *zone of closure,* qui inclut les services administratifs et commerciaux nécessaires au bon fonctionnement de l'attraction, tels que l'hébergement, l'alimentation, l'information, etc.

On peut noter également le modèle de Leiper (1990), qui se base sur celui de Gunn (1988), mais considère que, plus qu'attirés, les touristes sont véritablement poussés par leur propre motivation voire leur désir de voyager vers les attractions touristiques, à travers un réseau de marqueurs (*markers*) tout au long de leur itinéraire, avant leur départ (*generating marker*), pendant leur déplacement (*transit marker*) et finalement *in situ* (*contiguous marker*). Partant de l'idée selon laquelle l'attractivité touristique d'un territoire dépend de son grand centre attractif et de son influence sur les régions avoisinantes, le modèle de Smith (1980) est similaire à celui de Leiper (1990). Il divise un territoire en trois cercles : le centre du territoire doté d'attractions, le second équipé d'un nombre d'attractions inférieur à celui du centre qui joue le rôle d'un support direct, et le troisième qui joue le rôle d'un support indirect. Les attractions des deux derniers cercles sont secondaires par rapport aux attractions principales du centre.

Par ailleurs, Caccomo et Solonandrasana (2002) distinguent deux types d'attractions : les attractions « Découverte » appelées *D-attraction* et les attractions « Evasion » appelées *E-attraction.* Si la satisfaction perdure, l'attraction sera qualifiée d'*E-attraction,* alors que si elle atteint plus ou moins rapidement un point de satiété, on parlera de *D-attraction.* Selon Botti et al. (2008), un touriste qui s'écarte de son environnement habituel pendant une longue durée va choisir une destination dans laquelle il trouvera une attraction *primaire E-attraction.* Ils indiquent également que plusieurs *D-attraction* peuvent constituer une *D-attraction* encore plus vaste, appelée une *Clustered D-attraction.*

La compétitivité touristique des destinations questionne le modèle d'évaluation utilisé et la méthode retenue (Zhang et al., 2011). De l'avis de Enright et Newton (2005), le modèle de compétitivité touristique de Ritchie et Crouch (2003) semble le plus abouti. Il comprend des critères en matière de ressources et de soutien, de management de la destination, de planification et de développement, de qualification et d'amplification des déterminants. Le premier critère est relatif aux attractions et ressources principales, telles que la dotation du territoire en éléments aptes à attirer des touristes et les ressources indispensables à l'accueil sur le territoire d'une activité touristique. Le deuxième critère est relatif aux ressources-supports telles que les infrastructures routières ou de télécommunications (éléments tangibles) et l'hospitalité de la population locale (élément intangible), destinées prioritairement à la population locale et aux touristes. En troisième lieu, le concept de *Destination Management Organization* (DMO) concerne les aspects du management de la destination (la gestion de la qualité de l'expérience touristique ou la promotion du territoire). En quatrième lieu, les aspects les plus stratégiques du management de la destination font référence à un niveau de décision supra-managérial proche de l'aménagement du territoire. En dernier lieu, le critère relatif au sentiment d'insécurité que le touriste peut ressentir a priori vis-à-vis d'une destination, peut éventuellement modifier de manière négative l'influence des autres dimensions.

En outre, le modèle de compétitivité touristique de Ritchie et Crouch (2003) montre que les destinations abondamment dotées en ressources touristiques (attractions, hôtels, restaurants...) disposent d'un avantage comparatif indéniable sur celles qui n'en possèdent qu'à un moindre degré. Cependant, le facteur travail peut directement influencer cette dotation, en créant de toute pièce des ressources (cas des événements touristiques) ou en travaillant à la mise en tourisme d'attraits patrimoniaux non encore exploités (Botti et al., 2015). A l'inverse du modèle de Ritchie et Crouch (2003), qui n'a pas fait l'objet d'une évaluation directe, l'indice de compétitivité en matière de voyage et de tourisme développé par le Forum économique mondial (2017) a été appliqué pour classer les pays en fonction de leur compétitivité. Cet indice comprend un ensemble de données quantitatives, provenant tant de sources publiques que d'institutions ou d'experts du domaine du tourisme, telles que l'Organisation mondiale du tourisme (OMT), l'Association internationale du transport aérien (IATA) ou l'Organisation des nations unies pour l'éducation, la science et la culture (UNESCO). Il utilise une échelle allant de 1 à 7. En 2017, sur la base de 136 pays, l'Espagne est placée en tête du classement avec un score de 5,4, suivie par la France et l'Allemagne qui présentent un score de 5,3.

Les destinations touristiques, qui agissent de manière proactive sur leur image et la perception de leurs ressources et attractions par les touristes (film, reportages télé, etc.), doivent être également réactives, tout particulièrement dans le cas de désastres naturels et d'insécurité politique du fait de leur médiatisation à l'échelle mondiale (Cooper et Hall, 2011). Afin d'attirer les touristes, les destinations doivent donc miser sur quatre types de ressources (Cooper et Hall, 2011) : les attractions physiques et culturelles incitant les visiteurs à se rendre sur la destination ; les informations relatives aux ressources de la destination ; les infrastructures et ressources humaines influençant l'accessibilité de la destination (ressources de la région émettrice et de l'itinéraire de transit) ; les infrastructures et ressources humaines permettant le séjour des visiteurs.

Après analyse des modèles d'attractivité et de compétitivité touristiques et l'indice de compétitivité en matière du voyage et du tourisme du Forum économique mondial (WEF, 2017), il peut être déduit que l'infrastructure d'accueil, les caractéristiques sociales et culturelles, l'attitude de la population locale envers les touristes, la sûreté et la sécurité, la santé et l'hygiène, l'éducation, la formation et la disponibilité de travailleurs qualifiés sont des dimensions explicatives de l'attractivité et de la compétitivité touristique d'une destination. Ces dimensions sont présentes dans l'IDH et l'indice de la stabilité politique et l'absence de violence/terrorisme examinés ci-après.

1.3. Intérêt des indices retenus : l'IDH et l'indice de stabilité politique et d'absence de violence/terrorisme

Selon le PNUD, l'Indice de Développement Humain (IDH) a été créé pour évaluer le développement d'un pays, en mettant l'accent sur les individus et leurs capacités, et non sur la seule croissance économique. Cet indice mesure le niveau moyen atteint dans des dimensions clés du développement humain : vivre une vie longue et en bonne santé, acquérir des connaissances et jouir d'un niveau de vie décent. La moyenne géométrique des indices est normalisée pour chacune des trois dimensions suivantes : 1) la dimension de la santé, évaluée selon l'espérance de vie à la naissance ; 2) la dimension de l'éducation, mesurée au moyen du nombre d'années de scolarisation pour les adultes âgés de 25 ans et plus et des années attendues de scolarisation pour les enfants en âge d'entrer à l'école ; 3) la dimension du niveau de vie, estimée par le revenu national brut par habitant. L'IDH utilise le logarithme pour refléter son importance décroissante. Les résultats pour les trois indices de dimension de l'IDH sont ensuite agrégés pour donner un indice composite obtenu à partir de la moyenne géométrique.

Figure 1. Présentation du calcul de l'indice de développement humain

Dimensions	**Vie longue et en bonne santé**	**Connaissances**		**Niveau de vie décent**
Indicateurs	Espérance de vie à la naissance	Nombre d'années de scolarisation pour les adultes	Nombre d'années attendues de scolarisation pour les enfants	Revenu national brut par habitant
Indices des dimensions	Indice de l'espérance de vie	Indice d'éducation		Indice du revenu national brut
	Indice de développement humain (IDH)			

Source : Human Development Report (2015), work for human development.

D'après la Banque mondiale, l'indice de stabilité politique et d'absence de violence/terrorisme capte la perception de la probabilité que le gouvernement soit déstabilisé ou renversé par des moyens inconstitutionnels ou violents, y compris la violence et le terrorisme à motivation politique. Le classement des percentiles indique le rang du pays parmi tous les pays couverts par l'indicateur agrégé, avec 0 correspondant au rang le plus bas et 100 le plus élevé. Les rangs des percentiles ont été ajustés pour corriger les changements dans le temps dans la composition des pays couverts par le Worldwide Governance Indicator (Kaufmann et al., 2010).

2. MÉTHODOLOGIE DE L'ÉTUDE ÉCONOMÉTRIQUE ET ESTIMATION DU MODÈLE DE PANEL

Un modèle de panel est estimé pour expliquer le nombre d'arrivées de touristes par l'indice de développement humain et l'indice de stabilité politique et d'absence de violence/terrorisme, pour un ensemble de pays du bassin méditerranéen sur une période allant de 2003 à 2013, et dont nous vérifions sa qualité prédictive sur la période 2014-2015.

2.1. L'utilisation d'un modèle de panel

En économétrie, les données de panel comportent des avantages, par rapport aux autres méthodes économétriques destinées à l'analyse des séries temporelles adoptées pour expliquer les flux des touristes, telles que le modèle ADLM (Autoregressive Distributed Lag Model) (Song et al., 2003), le modèle VAR (Vectoriel Autoregressive) ou bien encore le modèle à correction d'erreur ECM (Error correction model) (Kulendran et Wilson, 2000 ; Kulendran et Witt, 2003 ; Lim et Mc Aleer, 2000). Les données de panel permettent en effet de combiner les données en coupe instantanée et les données temporelles (Song et Li, 2008). L'économétrie des données de panel permet de réduire les problèmes fréquents en séries temporelles de colinéarité entre les variables explicatives, grâce à la possibilité d'introduire des différences inter-individuelles.

Un panel cylindré (*balanced panel*), qui a le même nombre d'observations pour tous les individus ou un panel non-cylindré (*unbalanced panel*), lorsque certaines observations font défaut, peuvent être utilisés (Bourbonnais, 2015). Dans cette étude, notre panel est équilibré et nos données prennent en considération sept pays du bassin méditerranéen, sur une période de onze ans (2003 à 2013), soit 77 observations (7x11) pour chacune de nos trois variables d'intérêt (voir les données en annexe).

Pour N (i=1,..., N) individus et T intervalles de temps réguliers (t=1,...,T), le modèle en données de panel s'écrit comme suit : $y_{it} = a_i + b_i x_{it} + \varepsilon_{it}$, où y_{it} est la variable expliquée observée pour l'individu i à la période t ; x_{it} est le vecteur des k variables explicatives $x'_{it} = (x_{1it}, x_{2it}, \dots, x_{kit})$; a_i est la constante pour l'individu i ; b_i est le vecteur des k coefficients des k variables explicatives $b'_i = (b_{1i}, b_{2i}, \dots, b_{ki})$ et ε_{it} est le terme d'erreur.

Dans cette étude, nous essayons d'expliquer par un modèle en données de panel, pour les sept pays méditerranéens (la France, l'Espagne, l'Italie, l'Egypte, le Maroc, la Croatie et la Tunisie), la variable dépendante « le nombre d'arrivées de touristes », notée y_{it}, sur la période de 2003-2013, par les deux variables explicatives suivantes : l'indice de développement humain pour le pays i à l'année t, noté x_{1it} et l'indice de stabilité politique et d'absence du terrorisme/violence pour le pays i à l'année t, noté x_{2it} :

$$y_{it} = a_i + b_i x_{it} + \varepsilon_{it} \qquad (1)$$

On distingue généralement trois cas possibles de modèles de panel : (i) le cas de l'« homogénéité totale » où les constantes et les coefficients des variables explicatives sont identiques pour tous les individus et le modèle approprié correspond à une seule équation estimée sur les observations empilées ; (ii) le cas de l'« hétérogénéité totale » où les constantes et les coefficients des variables explicatives sont tous différents pour tous les individus et le modèle approprié correspond à une estimation d'une équation par individu (N équations) ; (iii) le cas du « modèle à effets individuels » où il y a hétérogénéité des constantes et homogénéité des coefficients des variables explicatives.

En vue de mener à bien ce test, il convient d'adopter la procédure séquentielle de tests d'homogénéité proposée par Hsiao (1986) construits à partir des statistiques de Fisher. La procédure qui a été suivie est présentée en figure 2.

Figure 2. Procédure du test d'homogénéité suivie d'après Hsiao (1986)

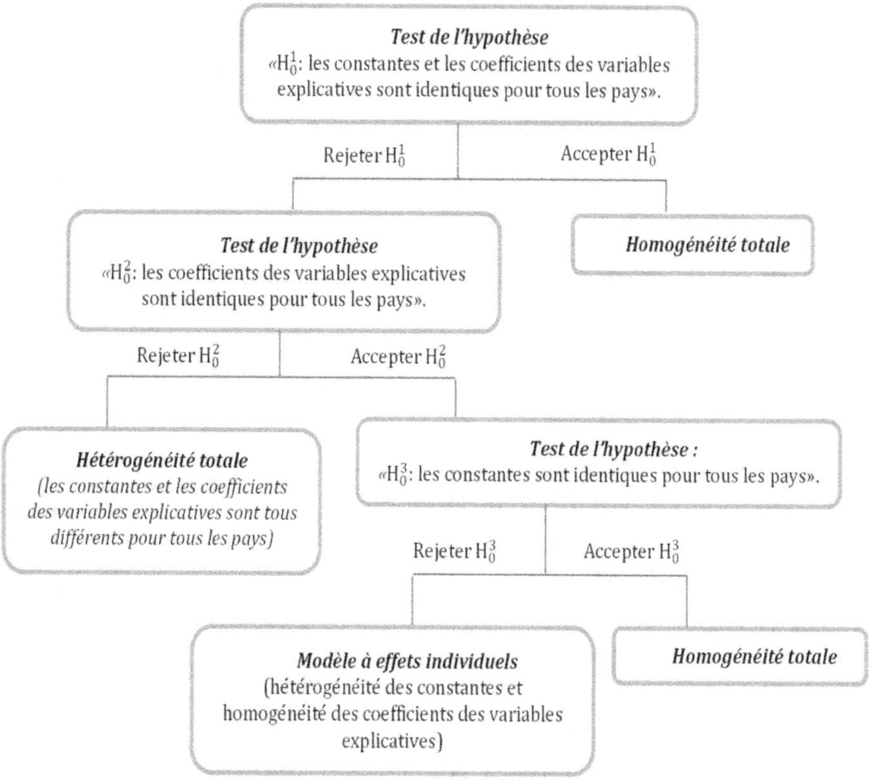

Cf. Bourbonnais (2015), pp. 347-349.

Les résultats de ces tests d'homogénéité montrent le rejet de la première hypothèse [« H_0^1: les constantes et les coefficients des variables explicatives sont identiques pour tous les pays » (H_0^1: $a_i = a_0$ *et* $b = b_i$ $\forall i$)], l'acceptation de la deuxième hypothèse [« H_0^2: les coefficients des variables explicatives sont identiques pour tous les pays » (H_0^2: $b = b_i$ $\forall i$)] et le rejet de la troisième hypothèse [« H_0^3: les constantes sont identiques pour tous les pays » (H_0^3: $a_i = a_0$ $\forall i$)].

En d'autres termes, les résultats de nos tests d'homogénéité montrent que le panel présente une structure à effets individuels. Toutefois, les modèles à effets individuels regroupent des modèles à effets fixes, où l'effet individuel est constant au cours du temps, et des modèles à effets aléatoires, où la constante est aléatoire. En vue de déterminer si les coefficients des deux estimations, fixes et aléatoires, sont statistiquement différents, nous faisons appel au test de spécification de Hausman. Le résultat de ce test montre que le modèle à effets variables *(random effect model)* constitue le modèle approprié et non le modèle à effets fixes. La prise en compte d'effets individuels aléatoires permet de combiner une spécification intermédiaire entre le modèle à effet individuel et le modèle avec effets fixes. Autrement dit, notre structure de panel n'est ni totalement homogène, ni totalement hétérogène.

Le modèle à effets aléatoires individuels estimé s'écrit comme suit :

$$y_{it} = a + a_i + b_1\, x_{1it} + b_2 x_{2it} + v_{it} \qquad (2)$$

Figure 3. Nombre d'arrivées de touristes, Indice de développement humain et indice de stabilité politique et absence de terrorisme

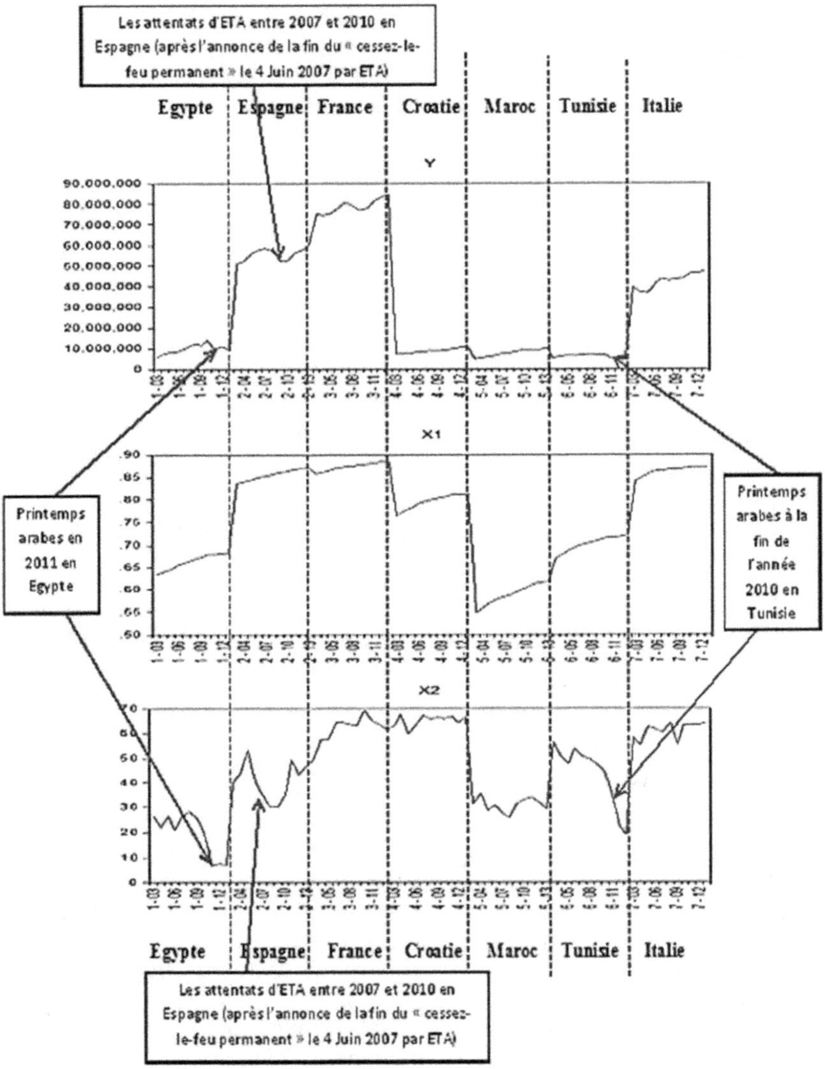

Tableau 1. Résultats de l'estimation du modèle à effets variables

Pays i	a	a_i	b_1	b_2
Egypte		-5330673		
Espagne		16016540		
France	-62030151	34245028	1.13E+08	129309.5
Croatie	[-4.451296]	-27212699	[7.638916]	[3.811791]
Maroc	(0.0000)	-575725.7	(0.0000)	(0.0003)
Tunisie		-16439555		
Italie		-702915.5		

F-statistic=31.22294 et Prob(F-statistic)=0.0000 ; [.] est la valeur de t-statistic et (.) est la valeur de la probabilité critique (Prob(T-Statistic)).

Le test de significativité individuelle des coefficients, le test de Student, et celui de la significativité globale des coefficients, le test de Fisher, indiquent respectivement que chaque coefficient des variables explicatives x_1 et x_2 de notre modèle est significativement différent de zéro et que le modèle est globalement significatif au seuil statistique usuel de 5%. L'indice de développement humain et celui de stabilité politique conditionnent donc le nombre d'arrivées de touristes dans les pays méditerranéens considérés. Les résultats sont donnés dans le tableau 1.

A titre d'illustration des relations entre les variables, la figure 3 retrace les évolutions des données empilées des deux variables explicatives définies ci-dessus, x_1 « l'indice de développement humain » et x_2 « l'indice de stabilité politique et absence du terrorisme », et de la variable dépendante, y « le nombre d'arrivées de touristes », durant la période qui s'étend de 2003 à 2013, pour les sept pays méditerranéens de notre échantillon. Il semble que le terrorisme et l'instabilité politique peuvent affecter sensiblement le nombre d'arrivées de touristes, au-delà du niveau et de l'évolution de l'IDH. A titre d'exemple, les attentats de l'ETA entre 2007 et 2010 en Espagne – années durant lesquelles l'indice de stabilité politique et absence du terrorisme a atteint son niveau le plus bas de la période d'étude – ainsi que les printemps arabes à la fin de l'année 2010 en Tunisie et en 2011 en Egypte se sont répercutés négativement sur le nombre d'arrivées de touristes dans ces pays.

2.2. Qualité prédictive du modèle

Il est intéressant de tester la qualité prédictive du modèle, défini sur la période 2003-2013, en comparant les nombres estimés d'arrivées de touristes et les nombres observés (réalisés effectivement) d'arrivées de touristes, durant les années qui suivent notre période d'étude, soit 2014 et 2015, dates des dernières statistiques disponibles auprès de la Banque mondiale et du PNUD.

Les figures 4 et 5 représentent les valeurs estimées et les valeurs observées du nombre d'arrivées de touristes pour les 7 pays de notre échantillon, en 2014 et 2015.

Figure 4. Nombres observés et estimés d'arrivées de touristes en 2014

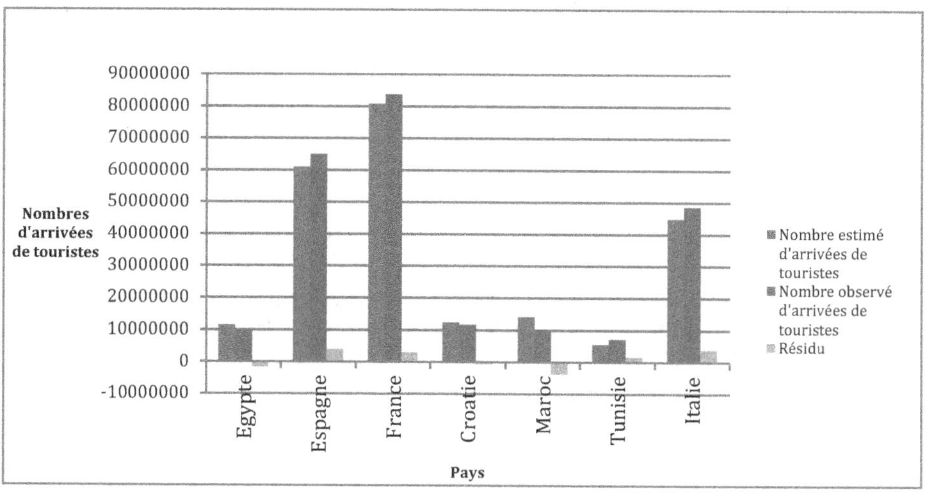

Figure 5. Nombres observés et estimés d'arrivées de touristes en 2015

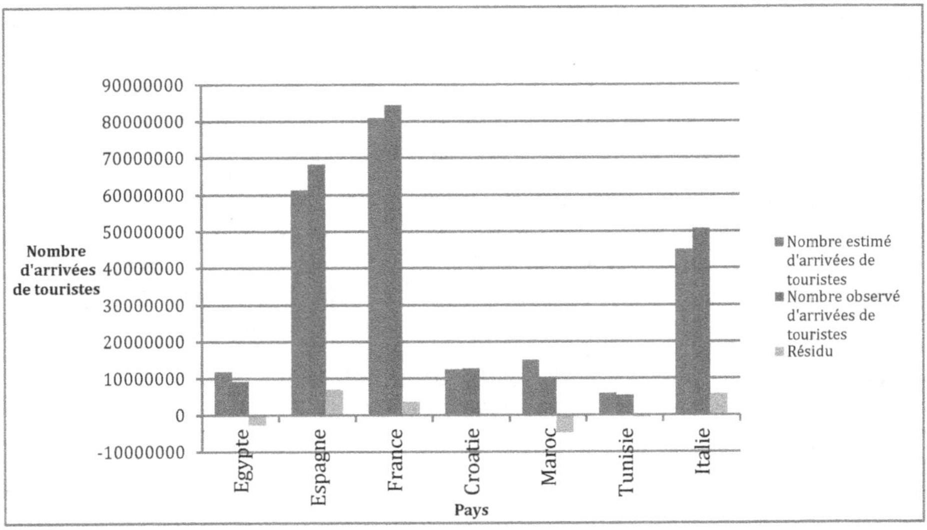

Globalement, les valeurs estimées du nombre d'arrivées de touristes sont proches de celles observées en 2014 et en 2015 pour les pays du bassin méditerranéen rassemblant des destinations touristiques supérieures à 50 millions, comme la France, l'Espagne et l'Italie, et des arrivées inférieures à 13 millions comme la Croatie, l'Egypte, le Maroc et la Tunisie.

Le pourcentage de l'erreur absolue moyenne MAE% (*Percentage of the Mean Absolute Error*) et le pourcentage d'erreur quadratique moyenne RMSE% (*Percentage of the Root Mean Square Error*) calculés sur l'ensemble des pays de notre panel, et donnés au tableau 2, sont relativement faibles en 2014 et 2015 et vont dans le sens d'une bonne qualité prédictive du modèle. Les deux variables retenues expliquent ainsi en grande partie le nombre d'arrivées de touristes.

Tableau 2. Pourcentage de l'erreur absolue moyenne et pourcentage d'erreur quadratique moyenne en 2014 et en 2015 (%)

	2014	2015
$\text{MAE\%} = \frac{\frac{1}{n}\sum \lvert e_t \rvert}{\frac{1}{n}\sum y_t} = \frac{\sum \lvert e_t \rvert}{\sum y_t}$	7,87	10,21
$\text{RMSE\%} = \frac{\sqrt{\frac{1}{n}\sum e_t^2}}{\frac{1}{n}\sum y_t}$	8,65	12,26

Les valeurs du résidu (écart entre nombre observé et nombre estimé d'arrivées de touristes) et du pourcentage d'écart absolu moyen (|(valeur estimée-valeur observée)/valeur observée|) en 2014 et en 2015 sont relativement faibles pour la plupart des pays. Pour la Croatie par exemple, les nombres estimés et observés d'arrivées approchent les 12 millions de touristes en 2014 et en 2015, le résidu s'avère inférieur à 1 million de touristes (0,69 millions en 2014 et 0,28 millions en 2015), avec un pourcentage d'écart absolu moyen égal à 5,96% en 2014 et 2,25% en 2015.

A l'opposé toutefois, le Maroc connaît un résidu égal à 3,8 et 4,8 millions de touristes en 2014 et 2015, soit un pourcentage d'écart absolu moyen relativement élevé (37,1% en 2014 et 47,4% en 2015). Ce cas suggère qu'au-delà des deux grands attributs touristiques retenus, réunissant la sûreté et la sécurité, la santé et l'hygiène, l'éducation, la formation et la disponibilité de travailleurs qualifiés et le niveau de vie, d'autres variables explicatives – notamment évoquées en section 1 – pourraient être examinées afin d'expliquer de manière plus précise l'attractivité touristique de certaines destinations.

REMARQUES CONCLUSIVES

Notre étude a tenté d'expliquer le nombre d'arrivées de touristes par l'indice de développement humain (incluant les dimensions santé, éducation et niveau de vie) et l'indice de stabilité politique et d'absence de violence/terrorisme. En vue d'expliquer l'attractivité touristique, Ritchie et Zins (1978) ont accordé une grande importance aux « caractéristiques sociales et culturelles » et à l'« attitude envers les touristes », deux attributs d'une certaine manière liés aux deux variables explicatives retenues dans notre modèle. Ces variables explicatives ont également des dimensions communes avec les trois attributs majeurs : « l'infrastructure d'accueil », « la culture de la destination et l'accueil de la population locale » et « la sécurité », considérés par Ritchie et Zins (1978), Kim (1998), Gallarza et al. (2002), Enright et Newton (2004), Cracolici et Nijkamp (2008) et Jin et al. (2012).

Notre modèle à effets individuels reprend la composition de l'indice de compétitivité touristique TTCI (Travel and Tourism Competitiveness Index) pour l'année 2017 du World Economic Forum sur la compétitivité du secteur du voyage et du tourisme (WEF, 2017). Cet indice prend essentiellement en considération les dimensions suivantes : la sûreté et la sécurité, la santé et l'hygiène, l'éducation, la formation et la disponibilité de travailleurs qualifiés. Ces dimensions sont couvertes par les deux variables explicatives de notre modèle, à savoir l'indice de stabilité politique et d'absence de violence/terrorisme et l'indice de développement humain. On peut dire ainsi que ce résultat conforte la composition de l'indice de compétitivité en matière de voyage et de tourisme TTCI du Forum économique mondial. Notre recherche présente un apport sur le plan méthodologique en regard de cet indice de compétitivité. En effet, la modélisation économétrique des données de panel, en étudiant simultanément plusieurs pays au cours d'une période, constitue un outil pratique qui permet d'élaborer un modèle explicatif valable pour plusieurs pays et qui peut être utilisé pour prévoir les flux des touristes.

Concernant les facteurs explicatifs, nous rejoignons Enright et Newton (2004) qui considèrent la sécurité comme le plus fort attribut touristique. Ce facteur, également retenu par Ritchie et Crouch (2003), illustre son importance pour le choix d'une destination touristique, ainsi que son influence sur les autres attributs. Il constitue également le centre d'intérêt de la recherche sur les perceptions dans le tourisme (Cohen et al., 2014). Nos résultats valident donc empiriquement le courant de littérature qui inclut un facteur risque par pays (Rittichainuwat et Chakraborty, 2009 ; George, 2010 ; Fuchs et Reichel, 2011), même s'il reste hétérogène. Ces résultats semblent être importants pour les acteurs politiques, qui doivent intégrer et gérer l'effet risque dans leur politique de développement touristique (Sequeira et Nunes, 2008).

Ces mesures peuvent être complétées par l'adoption de nouvelles stratégies touristiques qui s'écartent du tourisme industriel gaspillant les ressources naturelles (eau et terres) et ne respectant pas les droits humains (tourisme sexuel et pédophilie), au profit d'un tourisme équitable, solidaire et éthique basé sur des principes de développement durable. Il semble alors primordial, pour les pays méditerranéens en développement, d'adopter un tourisme durable permettant le renouvellement des ressources naturelles afin qu'elles maintiennent leur productivité future, reconnaissant la contribution des hommes, des coutumes et des modes de vie à l'expérience touristique, acceptant que les populations locales profitent équitablement des bénéfices économiques du tourisme, et répondant aux souhaits des populations et des communautés locales des destinations.

Toutefois, notre modèle tient compte d'un nombre réduit de dimensions, comme la sûreté et la sécurité, la santé et l'hygiène, l'éducation, la formation et la disponibilité de travailleurs qualifiés et le niveau de vie. Il ignore différents attributs touristiques avancés par la littérature permettant d'expliquer le nombre d'arrivées de touristes. Le cas du Maroc qui présente le plus grand pourcentage d'écart absolu moyen semble indiquer que d'autres attributs touristiques pourraient expliquer le degré d'attractivité de certains pays et son évolution. L'introduction de certains attributs comme les ressources naturelles, le patrimoine culturel, l'infrastructure touristique et l'investissement touristique (Ritchie et Crouch, 2003 ; Dwyer et Kim, 2003 ; Galarneau, 2015) serait un prolongement à notre modèle de panel expliquant le nombre d'arrivées annuelles de touristes pour les pays du bassin méditerranéen.

D'autres voies de recherche peuvent également être envisagées en élargissant notre analyse : le modèle proposé, valable globalement pour les pays du bassin méditerranéen, pourrait-il être appliqué à d'autres destinations ?

REFERENCES

Barker M., Page S., Meyer D., 2003, Urban visitor perceptions of safety during a special event, *Journal of Travel Research*, 41, 355-361.

Botti L., Boulin J-L., Castaner E., Marty N., Peypoch N., 2015, Performance des organismes de gestion de destination (OGD) : une approche par l'efficience appliquée aux offices de tourisme du Sud-Ouest de la France, *Sud-Ouest Européen Revue géographique des Pyrénées et du Sud-Ouest*. 39, 45-54.

Botti L., Peypoch N., Solonandrasana B., 2008, *Ingénierie du tourisme, concepts, méthodes, application*, Edition de boeck.

Bourbonnais R., 2015, *Econométrie*, Edition Dunod, Paris.

Cohen S. A., Prayag G., Moital M., 2014, Consumer behaviour in tourism: concepts, influences and opportunities, *Current Issues in Tourism*, 17, 872-909.

Cooper C., Hall C-M., 2011, *Le tourisme aujourd'hui*, De Boeck, Bruxelles.

Cracolici M. F., Nijkamp P., 2008, The attractiveness and competitiveness of tourist destinations: A study of Southern Italian regions, *Tourism Management*, 30, 336-344.

Dann's G., 1977, Anomie, ego-enhancement and tourism, *Annals of Tourism Research*, 4, 4, 184-194.

Dupont L., 2012, Analyse empirique de la relation entre tourisme et compétitivité : l'exemple des Antilles françaises, *Études Caribéennes*, 23.

Dwyer L., Kim C., 2003, Destination competitiveness: determinants and indicators. *Current issues in Tourism*, 6, 5, 369-414.

Eilat Y., Einav L., 2004, Determinants of international tourism: a three-dimensional panel data analysis, *Applied Economics*, 36, 12, 1315-1327.

Enright M. J., Newton J., 2004, Tourism destination competitiveness: a quantitative approach, *Tourism Management*, 25, 777-788.

Enright M. J., Newton J., 2005, Determinants of Tourism Destination Competitiveness in Asia Pacific: Comprehensiveness and Universality, *Journal of Travel Research*, 43, 4, 339-350.

Fuchs G., Reichel A., 2011, An exploratory inquiry into destination risk perceptions and risk reduction strategies of first time vs. repeat visitors to a highly volatile destination, *Tourism Management*, 32, 266–276.

Galarneau O.D., 2015, *L'attractivité du territoire touristique*. Mémoire d'une Maitrise en Sciences Géographiques (M. Sc. Géogr.), Université LAVAL, Québec, Canada.

Gallarza M. G., Gil S.I., Calderon G.H., 2002, Destination image, Towards a conceptual Framework, *Annals of Tourism Research*, 29, 1, 56-78.

George R., 2010, Visitor perceptions of crime-safety and attitudes towards risk: The case of Table Mountain National Park, Cape Town, *Tourism Management*, 31, 806–815.

Gunn C., 1988, *Vacationscape: Designing tourist regions*, Seconde edition, New York, Van Nostrand Reinhold.

Jin X., Weber K., Bauer T., 2012, Impact of clusters on exhibition destination attractiveness: Evidence from Mainland China, *Tourism Management*, 33, 6, 1429-1439.

Kaufmann D., Kraay A., Mastruzzi M., 2010, *Les indicateurs de gouvernance dans le monde : méthodologie et questions analytiques*, Document de travail de recherche sur les politiques de la Banque mondiale n° 5430.

Klenosky D. B., 2002, The 'pull' of tourism destinations: A means-end investigation, *Journal of Travel Research*, 40, 385-395.

Kulendran N., Witt S.F., 2003, Forecasting the demand for international Business tourism, *Journal of Travel Research*, 45, 265-271.

Lautier B., 2013, *L'économie informelle dans le tiers monde*, Collection repères, Edition La Découverte.

Leiper N., 1990, Tourist attraction systems, *Annals of Tourism Research*, 17, 367-384.

Lepp A., H. Gibson, 2008, Sensation seeking and tourism: Tourist role, perception of risk and destination choice, *Tourism Management*, 29, 740-750.

Lew A-A., 1987, A framework of tourist attraction research, *Annals of Tourism Research*, 14, 553-575.

Lewis, A., 1954, "Economic Development with Unlimited Supplies of Labour", Manchester School of Economic and Social Studies, 22: 139-191.

Lim C., McAleer M., 2000, A seasonal analysis of Asian tourist arrivals to Australia, *Applied Economics*, 32, 499-509.

Rittichainuwat B. N., Chakraborty G., 2009, Perceived travel risks regarding terrorism and disease: The case of Thailand, *Tourism Management*, 30, 410–418.

Ritchie J.R.B., Crouch G.I., 2003, *The competitive destination: a sustainable tourism perspective*, Oxon, UK, CABI Pub.

Ritchie, J.R., M. Zins., 1978, Culture as determinant of the attractiveness of tourism region, *Annals of Tourism Research*, April/June, 252-267.

Sequeira T.N., Nunes P., 2008, Does Country Risk Influence International Tourism? A Dynamic Panel Data Analysis, *Economic Record*, 84, 265, 223-236.

Smith V. L., 1980, Anthropology and tourism: A science-industry evaluation. *Annals of Tourism Research*, 7, 13-33.

Smith S. L.J., 1987, Regional analysis of tourism resources, *Annals of Tourism Research*, 14, 254-273.

Song H., Li G., 2008, Tourism demand modeling and forecasting-A review of recent research, *Tourism Management*, 29, 2, 203-220.

Song H., Witt S.F., Jensen T.C., 2003, Tourism forecasting: accuracy of alternative econometric models, *International Journal of Hospitality Management*, 22, 435-451.

Viceriat P., Origet Du Cluzeau C., Levy M., Doublet M., GROS D., 2007, *Attractivité touristique des grandes métropoles françaises et effets structurants sur le tourisme régional*, Rapport final - Synthèse du diagnostic, enjeux et recommandations. Paris: détente consultants, 57 pages.

Wang C-Y., Hsu M.K., 2010, The relationships of destination image, satisfaction and behavioral intentions: an integrated model. *Journal of Travel and Tourism Marketing*, 27, 829-843.

WEF (World Economic Forum), 2017, The Travel & Tourism Competitiveness Report 2017 published by the World Economic Forum within the framework of the Economic Growth and Social Inclusion System Initiative and the Future of Mobility System Initiative. World Economic Forum, Geneva, http://www3.weforum.org/docs/WEF_TTCR_2017_web_0401.pdf

Yoon Y., Uysal M., 2005, An examination of the effects of motivation and satisfaction on destination loyalty: A structural model, *Tourism Management*, 26, 45–56.

Zhang H., Gu C-L., Gu L-W., Zhang Y., 2011, The evaluation of tourism destination competitiveness by TOPSIS & information entropy – A case in the Yangtze River Delta of China, *Tourism Management*, 32, 2, 443-451.

ANNEXE : Les données de panel

Pays	Années	y	x1	x2
Egypte	2003	5746000	0,633	26,442
Egypte	2004	7795000	0,639	22,115
Egypte	2005	8244000	0,645	26,442
Egypte	2006	8646000	0,656	21,153
Egypte	2007	10610000	0,661	26,442
Egypte	2008	12296000	0,667	28,229
Egypte	2009	11914000	0,673	25,592
Egypte	2010	14051000	0,678	19,339
Egypte	2011	9497000	0,679	6,603
Egypte	2012	11196000	0,681	7,582
Egypte	2013	9174000	0,682	7,109
Espagne	2003	50854000	0,835	39,903
Espagne	2004	52430000	0,840	43,750
Espagne	2005	55914000	0,844	53,365
Espagne	2006	58004000	0,851	40,384
Espagne	2007	58666000	0,854	34,615
Espagne	2008	57192000	0,857	30,143
Espagne	2009	52178000	0,860	30,331
Espagne	2010	52677000	0,864	34,905
Espagne	2011	56177000	0,868	49,056
Espagne	2012	57701000	0,869	43,127
Espagne	2013	60661000	0,869	46,919
France	2003	75048000	0,857	49,519
France	2004	74433000	0,862	57,692
France	2005	74988000	0,867	57,692
France	2006	77916000	0,871	64,423
France	2007	80853000	0,873	64,423
France	2008	79218000	0,875	63,636
France	2009	76764000	0,877	63,033
France	2010	77648000	0,879	69,339
France	2011	81550000	0,882	65,094
France	2012	83013000	0,884	63,507
France	2013	84726000	0,884	61,611
Croatie	2003	7409000	0,764	62,980
Croatie	2004	7912000	0,773	67,788
Croatie	2005	7743000	0,781	59,615
Croatie	2006	7988000	0,791	63,461
Croatie	2007	8559000	0,796	67,307
Croatie	2008	8665000	0,801	65,550
Croatie	2009	8694000	0,804	66,350
Croatie	2010	9111000	0,806	66,037
Croatie	2011	9927000	0,812	66,981
Croatie	2012	10369000	0,812	64,454
Croatie	2013	10955000	0,812	66,350

Pays	Années	y	x1	x2
Maroc	2003	4761000	0,548	31,250
Maroc	2004	5477000	0,558	35,576
Maroc	2005	5843000	0,569	28,846
Maroc	2006	6558000	0,579	30,769
Maroc	2007	7408000	0,584	27,403
Maroc	2008	7879000	0,588	25,837
Maroc	2009	8341000	0,596	31,279
Maroc	2010	9288000	0,603	33,018
Maroc	2011	9342000	0,612	33,962
Maroc	2012	9375000	0,614	32,227
Maroc	2013	10046000	0,617	29,383
Tunisie	2003	5114000	0,670	56,250
Tunisie	2004	5998000	0,679	50,480
Tunisie	2005	6378000	0,687	47,596
Tunisie	2006	6550000	0,697	53,846
Tunisie	2007	6762000	0,701	50,480
Tunisie	2008	7050000	0,706	49,282
Tunisie	2009	6901000	0,711	47,393
Tunisie	2010	6903000	0,715	44,339
Tunisie	2011	4785000	0,716	34,433
Tunisie	2012	5950000	0,719	22,274
Tunisie	2013	6269000	0,721	18,957
Italie	2003	39604000	0,842	58,173
Italie	2004	37071000	0,850	55,288
Italie	2005	36513000	0,858	62,500
Italie	2006	41058000	0,863	61,538
Italie	2007	43654000	0,865	60,096
Italie	2008	42734000	0,868	64,114
Italie	2009	43239000	0,868	55,450
Italie	2010	43626000	0,869	63,207
Italie	2011	46119000	0,872	63,207
Italie	2012	46360000	0,872	63,033
Italie	2013	47704000	0,872	64,454

Egypte	2014	9628300	0,688	7,619
Egypte	2015	9139000	0,691	8,571
Espagne	2014	64939000	0,882	56,666
Espagne	2015	68215000	0,884	57,142
France	2014	83701000	0,894	58,095
France	2015	84452000	0,897	56,666
Croatie	2014	11623000	0,823	66,190
Croatie	2015	12683000	0,827	63,333
Maroc	2014	10283000	0,645	29,523
Maroc	2015	10177000	0,647	34,761
Tunisie	2014	7163000	0,723	18,095
Tunisie	2015	5359000	0,725	19,047
Italie	2014	48576000	0,881	61,428
Italie	2015	50732000	0,887	58,095

Source : sites de la Banque mondiale et du Programme des Nations Unies pour le Développement (PNUD). Cf. http://databank.banquemondiale.org *et* http://hdr.undp.org.

HDI, political stability and absence of violence-terrorism as explanatory factors of tourism attractiveness: The Mediterranean basin as a case study

Abstract - This article shows, through an estimated model for a panel of seven Mediterranean countries, that the number of tourist arrivals can be explained by the Human Development Index (including its three dimensions: health, education and life) and the Index of Political Stability and Absence of Violence/Terrorism. Safety and security, health and hygiene, education, training and the availability of skilled workers and the standard of living thus appear generally as strong attributes that can explain the tourist attractiveness of the destinations.

Key-words

Human development
Mediterranean basin
Panel data econometrics
Political stability
Tourism attractiveness
Violence-terrorism

Région et Développement

n° 47-2018

www.regionetdeveloppement.org

Sigma-Convergence revisited

Dimitris KALLIORAS*, Marie-Noëlle DUQUENNE, Stevi VAFEIADOU****

Abstract - *Referring to the diachronic decrease of the overall dispersion of a (regional) dataset, σ-convergence is a dominant concept in the empirical regional convergence / divergence literature. The paper revisits the σ-convergence concept, expressing the, "classical", coefficient of variation and weighted coefficient of variation formulas against the backdrop of the median. To this end, the paper specifies and proposes a pair of, "alternative", formulas for apprehending the σ-convergence concept. Such an endeavor stems from the, purely, statistical rationale that the mean is a central tendency measure highly sensitive to the eventual presence of outliers. The theory-driven propositions of the paper are supported from an illustrative empirical analysis of regional inequalities in France, at the NUTS III spatial level, for the period 2001-2015. The findings of the analysis provide valuable insight to both theory and policy-making, indicating that different expressions of the σ-convergence concept may lead to different inferences with respect to regional inequalities.*

Classification JEL

C13, C18, R11

Key Words

Regional inequalities
σ-convergence
Coefficient of variation
Weighted coefficient of variation
Mean
Median

* Department of Planning and Regional Development, University of Thessaly ; dkallior@uth.gr
** Department of Planning and Regional Development, University of Thessaly ; mdyken@uth.gr
** Department of Planning and Regional Development, University of Thessaly ; stvafeia@uth.gr

1. INTRODUCTION

Fueling the relative academic debate and providing insight to the evaluation of the relative policies, the evolution of regional inequalities is an issue of utmost importance (Islam 2003, Kostov and Le Gallo 2015, Artelaris and Petrakos 2016). Hence, the study of regional inequalities - in particular, the study of regional convergence[1] / divergence in terms of per capita Gross Domestic Product (GDP)[2] - is at the heart of regional science. From the policy viewpoint, the study of regional convergence / divergence may interpret as a sign with respect to the evaluation of the effectiveness and the efficiency of the implemented regional policy mix. Regional policy, aims, precisely, at reducing the level of regional inequalities in a growth-enhancing economic environment. From the theory viewpoint, the study of regional convergence / divergence may serve as an empirical exercise with respect to the affirmation of regional development theories. Questioning the position of the neoclassical theory that (regional) inequalities are bound to diminish with growth through the activation of market-emanating convergence mechanisms[3] in a policy-free environment, theories with sharply different policy implications, such as the endogenous (new) growth theory (Romer 1986, Lucas 1988, *inter alia*) and the new economic geography theory (Krugman 1991, Fujita 1993, *inter alia*), stress the argument[4] that growth is a spatially selective and cumulative process.

Referring to the diachronic decrease of the overall dispersion of a (regional) dataset, σ-convergence (Barro and Sala-i-Martin 1992) is a dominant concept in the empirical regional convergence / divergence literature.[5] Σ-convergence may, usually, apprehend through the coefficient of variation (CV) and the weighted coefficient of variation (wCV) formulas.[6] CV is a standardized (relative) measure of dispersion and may express as the ratio of the standard deviation of a (regional) dataset to the corresponding arithmetic mean (henceforth: mean), at a given date (Barro and Sala-i-Martin 1992). Including a weighting factor in the CV formula (Petrakos and Artelaris 2009), so as to account for the corresponding relative (regional) size[7] in the treatment of the (regional) dataset, allows for the compilation of the wCV formula, the weighted CV counterpart.

The paper revisits the σ-convergence concept, expressing the, "classical", CV and wCV formulas against the backdrop of the median (i.e. the central tendency measure

---

[1] Intuitively, the term (regional) "convergence" suggests a process whereby poor(er) (regional) economies catch-up to rich(er) ones (Abreu et al. 2005).

[2] Customarily, this is the variable under consideration in the empirical regional convergence / divergence literature.

[3] Particularly, the neoclassical convergence mechanisms are the diminishing marginal productivity of capital (Solow 1956, Swan 1956, *inter alia*), the comparative advantage in interregional trade (Heckscher 1919/1991, Ohlin 1933/1966, *inter alia*) and the interregional production factors movement (Borjas 1979, Greenwood et al. 1991, *inter alia*).

[4] Bringing earlier theories regarding the operation of economic space (Perroux 1955, Myrdal 1957, Hirschman 1958, *inter alia*) back to the forefront.

[5] Usually, σ-convergence is examined together with β-convergence. The concept of β-convergence refers to the relation between the levels of a (regional) dataset at a given date and the consequent corresponding growth rates for a given period, either in an unconditional (i.e. absolute) or in a conditional (i.e. *ceteris paribus*) fashion (Baumol 1986, Barro 1991, Barro and Sala-i-Martin 1992, Sala-i-Martin 1996). B-convergence is a necessary (though not sufficient) condition for σ-convergence (Barro and Sala-i-Martin 1995).

[6] Σ-convergence may, also, apprehend through the mean logarithmic deviation (Dalgaard and Vastrup 2001). Gini coefficient (Gini 1912), Theil index (Theil 1967) and Atkinson index (Atkinson 1970) fall, also, within the σ-convergence rationale.

[7] Customarily, in terms of relative population i.e. the ratio of the regional to the corresponding country population. In any case, the sum of regional weights is equal to 1 (i.e. 100%).

that separates the higher half of the (regional) dataset from the corresponding lower one). To this end, the paper specifies and proposes a pair of, "alternative", formulas for apprehending the σ-convergence concept. Particularly, next to the CV formula, the paper specifies and proposes the CV-median (CVmd) formula. CVmd is a standardized measure of dispersion that may express as the ratio of the standard deviation of a (regional) dataset to the corresponding median, at a given date. Correspondingly, next to the wCV formula the paper specifies and proposes the wCV-median (wCVmd) formula. Apparently, wCVmd is the weighed CVmd counterpart. Such an endeavor stems from the, purely, statistical rationale that the mean is a central tendency measure highly sensitive to the eventual presence of outliers. The theory-driven propositions of the paper are supported from an illustrative empirical analysis of regional inequalities in France, at the NUTS[8] III spatial level, for the period 2001-2013, on the basis of per capita GDP and (relative) population data obtained from EUROSTAT.

The paper proceeds as follows. The next section highlights the drawback of the "classical" CV and wCV formulas. The third section introduces the, "alternative", CVmd and wCVmd formulas for the apprehension of σ-convergence. The fourth section provides the empirical assessment of the level and the evolution of regional inequalities in France, at the NUTS III spatial level, for the period 2001-2013, on the basis of both the "classical" and the "alternative" expressions of σ-convergence. The last section offers the conclusions and discusses the inferences with respect to regional inequalities.

2. THE CLASSICAL APPROACH OF Σ-CONVERGENCE

CV and wCV are the "classical" formulas for apprehending the σ-convergence concept (Barro and Sala-i-Martin 1992, Petrakos and Artelaris 2009).

CV (equation 1.1) is a standardized (relative) measure of dispersion and may express as the ratio of the standard deviation of a (regional) dataset to the corresponding mean, at a given date. CV takes values within the interval $[0, \sqrt{n-1}]$[9], from perfect (regional) equality to perfect (regional) inequality.[10] Increasing (decreasing) values of CV diachronically, evince an increase (a decrease) of (regional) inequality.

$$CV_{c,t} = \frac{\sqrt{\sum_{r=1}^{n}\left[\frac{\left(Y_{r,t} - \overline{Y_{r,t}}\right)^2}{n}\right]}}{\overline{Y_{r,t}}} \qquad \textit{(equation 1.1)}$$

where ***CV*** is the CV(-mean), ***Y*** is the variable under consideration, $\overline{Y}$ is the mean of the variable under consideration, ***Σ*** denotes sum, ***r*** stands for regions, ***n*** is the number of regions, ***t*** stands for time (date), ***c*** stands for country.

wCV (equation 2.1) is a standardized (relative) measure of dispersion and may express as the ratio of the standard deviation of a (regional) dataset to the corresponding mean, at a given date, accounting for an included weighting factor in the

[8] NUTS (Nomenclature des Unités Territoriales Statistiques; Nomenclature of Territorial Units for Statistics) is a EUROSTAT geocode standard for referencing the subdivisions of European Union (EU) countries for statistical purposes.

[9] In essence, given than the number of regions may reach infinity, the upper value of CV may reach infinity as well. In any case, the upper value of CV is not 1, as Monfort (2008) mistakenly (or inadvertently) refers.

[10] When the mean is equal to 0, CV is not defined. In the case of using per capita GDP data, this means that CV is not defined in the theoretical case that each region under consideration has zeroed per capita GDP.

treatment of the (regional) dataset. wCV takes values within the interval [0, n-1][11], from perfect (regional) equality to perfect (regional) inequality.[12] Increasing (decreasing) values of wCV diachronically, evince an increase (a decrease) of (regional) inequality.

$$wCV_{c,t} = \frac{\sqrt{\sum_{r=1}^{n}\left[w_{r,t} \times (Y_{r,t} - \overline{Y_{r,t}})^2\right]}}{\overline{Y_{r,t}}} \qquad \textit{(equation 2.1)}$$

where ***wCV*** is the weighted CV(-mean), ***Y*** is the variable under consideration, $\overline{Y}$ is the mean of the variable under consideration, ***Σ*** denotes sum, ***r*** stands for regions, ***n*** is the number of regions, ***t*** stands for time (date), ***c*** stands for country, ***w*** is the weighting factor.

Even though both CV and wCV comply with the vast majority of the axioms (properties) of inequality indicators[13], they are subject to the criticism, stemming from a, purely, statistical rationale, that the mean is a central tendency measure highly sensitive to the eventual presence of outliers (i.e. (regional) dataset values extremely distant from the other corresponding values). This is so as the calculation of the mean is not based on any measure concerning position, and this is not without effect on standard deviation. Particularly, extremely high values connote fat- (i.e. with positive kurtosis) and right-tailed (i.e. with positive skewness) distributions[14], whereas extremely low values connote thin- (i.e. with negative kurtosis) and left-tailed (i.e. with negative skewness) distributions[15]. In other words, because the mean value gives equal weight to all observations it can be highly sensitive to outliers (Brewer et al. 2005), especially when considering regional economic data, and as a result, the distribution of the observations utilized to measure σ-convergence may exhibit skewness and/or kurtosis. Thus, given the fact that such outliers represent actual, and not erroneous regional values (that, usually, correspond to metropolitan and to outermost regions), turning to the use of the truncated mean (i.e. discarding the outliers and then taking the mean of the remaining regional dataset values) is not a risk-free, and beyond critique, methodological choice. Similarly, assuming "a priori" a normal distribution of the regional dataset values is quite often an erroneous assumption with serious consequences as regards the adequacy of the statistical treatment and their robustness: statistical parameters "appropriate with normal distributions may be misleading when applied to non-normal distributions" (Sainani, 2012:1005).

---

11 In essence, given than the number of regions may reach infinity, the upper value of wCV may reach infinity as well.

12 When the mean is equal to 0, wCV is not defined. In the case of using per capita GDP data, this means that wCV is not defined in the theoretical case that each region under consideration has zeroed per capita GDP.

13 An inequality indicator should comply with the axioms (properties) of (Litchfield 1999, Monfort 2008, Cowell 2011, *inter alia*): a) the Pigou-Dalton transfer principle: the inequality indicator increases in response to a mean-preserving spread (Pigou 1912, Dalton 1920), b) the income scale independence: the inequality indicator is invariant to uniform proportional increases or decreases (Cowell 1999), c) the principle of population: the inequality indicator is invariant to replications of the population (Dalton 1920), d) anonymity (symmetry): the inequality indicator is dependent only on the variable in terms of which inequalities are measured (Amiel and Cowell 1994), and e) decomposability: the inequality indicator may be broken down into constituent parts (Bourguignon 1979).

14 Such as the t-student, the Poisson and the Laplace distributions.

15 Such as the Bernoulli distribution.

Given that the variable under consideration is continuous and not discrete, the mean value of distributions with positive kurtosis and positive skewness is generally higher than the median value, whereas the mean value of distributions with negative kurtosis and negative skewness is generally lower than the median value. Briefly, "the mean lies towards the direction of skew (the longer tail) relative to the median" (Agresti and Finlay 1997:50)[16]. Normal distributions in contrast, represent perfectly symmetrical distributions so as the mean value is equal to the median (and the mode) value (Gunver et al. 2017). Even though normal distributions rarely exist in nature (Pearson 1920) – this is so especially with economics and social data – it is the most frequently-used distribution for explaining continuous variables. Assuming normality is effectively easier because in such a case, it is possible to only consider the mean value as measure of central tendency. But this may be "a trap" (Klatzmann 1996). It is precisely from this point of view that the classical approach of σ-convergence is subject to criticism: the measure of inequalities - as proposed through the equations 1.1 and 2.1 - is relevant to the extent that the mean value is also relevant. Consequently, when the data set is not following normal distribution, it seems useful to consider an alternative measure of σ-convergence based on the median. Following Brewer et al. (2005), it can be stipulated that because of their potential differences, it is useful to consider both mean and median in the measure of regional inequalities, thus avoiding what Klatzmann (1996) denominates "the trap of unique control". In such a context, alternative measures of regional inequalities are suggested and finally applied to the case of GDP per capita at NUTS 3 level in France, after verifying that the distribution of GDP per capita is clearly not following the normal distribution.

3. Σ-CONVERGENCE REVISITED: THE "ALTERNATIVE" FORMULAS FOR APPREHENDING S-CONVERGENCE

The paper specifies and proposes a pair of "alternative" formulas for apprehending the σ-convergence concept, expressing the, "classical", coefficient of variation (CV) and weighted coefficient of variation (wCV) formulas against the backdrop of the median. Particularly, next to the CV formula, the paper specifies and proposes the CVmd formula, and, correspondingly, next to the wCV formula, the paper specifies and proposes the wCVmd formula.

CVmd (equation 1.2) is a standardized measure of dispersion that may express as the ratio of the standard deviation of a (regional) dataset to the corresponding median, at a given date. CVmd takes values greater than (or equal to) 0, from perfect (regional) equality to perfect (regional) inequality.[17] Increasing (decreasing) values of CVmd diachronically, evince an increase (a decrease) of (regional) inequality.

$$CVmd_{c,t} = \frac{\sqrt{\sum_{r=1}^{n}\left[\frac{\left(Y_{r,t} - \widetilde{Y_{r,t}}\right)^2}{n}\right]}}{\widetilde{Y_{r,t}}} \qquad \textit{(equation 1.2)}$$

[16] Von Hippel (2005) demonstrates that this rule is quite often violated with discrete variables, while this can happen, even though continuous violations are rarer, with continuous variables, in case of multimodal continuous densities, as well.

[17] When the median is equal to 0, CVmd is not defined. In the case of using per capita GDP data, this means that CVmd is not defined in the theoretical case that the majority of regions under consideration has zeroed per capita GDP.

where CV_{md} is the CV-median, Y is the variable under consideration, $\widetilde{Y}$ is the median of the variable under consideration, Σ denotes sum, r stands for regions, n is the number of regions, t stands for time (date), c stands for country.

wCVmd (equation 2.2) is a standardized measure of dispersion that may express as the ratio of the standard deviation of a (regional) dataset to the corresponding median, at a given date, accounting for an included weighting factor in the treatment of the regional dataset. wCVmd takes values greater than (or equal to) 0, from perfect (regional) equality to perfect (regional) inequality.[18] Increasing (decreasing) values of wCVmd diachronically, evince an increase (a decrease) of (regional) inequality.

$$wCVmd_{c,t} = \frac{\sqrt{\sum_{r=1}^{n}\left[w_{r,t} \times (Y_{r,t} - \widetilde{Y_{r,t}})^2\right]}}{\widetilde{Y_{r,t}}} \qquad \text{(equation 2.2)}$$

where wCV_{md} is the weighted CV-median, Y is the variable under consideration, $\widetilde{Y}$ is the median of the variable under consideration, Σ denotes sum, r stands for regions, n is the number of regions, t stands for time (date), c stands for country, w is the weighting factor.

Both CVmd and wCVmd overcome the drawback of the "classical" CV and wCV formulas. Being in line with the fact that international organizations (EUROSTAT 1999, OECD 2007, *inter alia*) perceive the median – and not the mean – as the central tendency measure for defining thresholds, especially risk of poverty, such a methodological suggestion aims at offering an alternative perspective with respect to the empirical assessment of the level and the evolution of regional inequalities.

4. REGIONAL INEQUALITIES IN FRANCE: AN ILLUSTRATIVE EMPIRICAL ANALYSIS

4.1. General tendencies of per capita GDP during the period 2001-2015

The theory-driven propositions of the paper are supported from an illustrative empirical analysis of regional inequalities in France, at the NUTS III spatial level, for the period 2001-2015, on the basis of per capita GDP[19] and (relative) population data obtained from EUROSTAT.

France, spanning 643,801 km^2, comprises of 101 NUTS III regions (Table A1 and Figure A1 in the Annex), with Mayotte, La Réunion, Guyane, Guadeloupe, and Martinique having the status of overseas regions[20]. During the period under consideration, France exhibits a per capita GDP level ranging from 24,000 PPS/inh. (2001) to 30,600 PPS/inh. (2015) (Table 1). Systematically, Mayotte and Guyane are the poorest French regions. Paris, the capital region of France, is the richest region up to year 2006 followed by Hauts-de-Seine (i.e. the western inner suburbs of Paris) and Rhône while the Hauts-de Seine[21] is the richest French region onwards, Rhône remaining stable at the 3rd place.

[18] When the median is equal to 0, wCVmd is not defined. In the case of using per capita GDP data, this means that wCVmd is not defined in the theoretical case that the majority of regions under consideration has zeroed per capita GDP.

[19] Per capita GDP is expressed in Purchasing Power Standars per inhabitant (PPS/inh.).

[20] Overseas French regions are integral parts of France and have similar powers to the regions of metropolitan (i.e. European) France while Saint-Pierre and Miquelon hast he status of territorial collectivity.

[21] Even though it exhibits a high level of intra-regional inequalities (Feltin 2000), Hauts-de-Seine is well-known as the richest region in France including the business district of La Défense and communes such as Neuilly-sur-Seine and Saint-Cloud.

The mean value of per capita GDP ranges from 20,967 PPS/inh. (2001) to 26,300 PPS/inh. (2015), whereas the corresponding median value presents systematically lower level from 20,100 (years 2001 and 2003) to 23,800 (2016). Depending on the year, the median value in itself corresponds to different regions while some of them are throughout the whole period around the median values (between the 4th and 6th deciles), especially the departments of Cher, Loir et Cher, Morbihan Oise and Somme. Twelve other departments are also very often but not systematically near from the median: Ain, Corrèze, Haute-Marne, Hautes-Pyrénées, Haute-Vienne, Jura, Loire, Maine-et-Loire, Moselle, Sâone-et-Loire, Var and Vienne (Figure A2 in Annex).

As expected, Paris and Hauts-de-Seine are, during the entire period under consideration, high-level outliers and to a lesser extend Rhône. Val-de-Marne (2008 to 2015 except 2013), Yvelines (2008, 2015) and Essonne (2008) – all three of them are suburbs of Paris – join, sporadically, the group of high-level outliers. In contrast, Mayotte is a low-level outlier during the entire period under consideration with Guyane, also a low-level outlier thrice (2004, 2005 and 2007).

Table 1. Level and evolution of per capita GDP in France: analysis at the NUTS 3 spatial level (2001-2015)

	2001	2002	2003	2004	2005	2006	2007	2008	2009	2010	2011	2012	2013	2014	2015
p.c. GDP (PPP / inh.)	24,000	24,600	24,000	24,700	26,00	26,900	28,200	27,800	26,400	27,500	28,300	28,500	29,000	29,600	30,600
minimum	*4,200*	*4,300*	*4,500*	*4,900*	*5,500*	*6,100*	*6,400*	*7,000*	*6,700*	*7,200*	*7,300*	*7,500*	*7,900*	*8,600*	*9,400*
	FRA50	*FRA50*	*FRA50*	*FRA50*	*FRA50*	*FRA50*	*FRA50*	*FRA50*	*FRA50*	*FRA50*	*FRA50*	*FRA50*	*FRA50*	*FRA50*	*FRA50*
maximum	*68,700*	*69,200*	*66,100*	*66,600*	*70,700*	*71,300*	*76,100*	*79,200*	*74,600*	*81,100*	*81,900*	*83,600*	*86,600*	*88,300*	*90,400*
	FR101	*FR101*	*FR101*	*FR101*	*FR101*	*FR101*	*FR101*	*FR105*	*FR105*	*FR105*	*FR105*	*FR105*	*FR105*	*FR105*	*FR105*
mean	*20,967*	*21,565*	*21,035*	*21,681*	*22,805*	*23,579*	*24,569*	*23,828*	*22,710*	*23,363*	*24,129*	*24,157*	*24,604*	*25,199*	*26030*
median	*20,100*	*20,700*	*20,100*	*20,700*	*21,700*	*22,300*	*23,200*	*22,400*	*21,000*	*21,300*	*22,000*	*22,00*	*22,300*	*23,100*	*23,800*
	FR301 FR613 FR813	*FR241 FR432 FR512 FR534*	*FR432 FR711*	*FR263*	*FR825 FR626*	*FR222 FR413 FR524 FR613*	*FR222 FR263 FR512 FR711 FR715*	*FR222*	*FR245 FR263 FR631*	*FR263 FR631*	*FR245 FR263 FR633*	*FR633*	*FR263 FR414*	*FR223 F414*	*FR214 FR512*
outliers (high-level)	*3*	*3*	*3*	*3*	*3*	*3*	*3*	*6*	*4*	*4*	*4*	*4*	*3*	*5*	*2*
	FR101 FR105 FR716	*FR101 FR105 FR716*	*FR101 FR105 FR716*	*FR101 FR105 FR716*	*FR101 FR105 FR716*	*FR101 FR105 FR716*	*FR101 FR105 FR716*	*FR101 FR105 FR103 FR104 FR107 FR716*	*FR101 FR105 FR107 FR716*	*FR101 FR105 FR107 FR716*	*FR101 FR105 FR107 FR716*	*FR101 FR105 FR107 FR716*	*FR101 FR105 FR716*	*FR101 FR105 FR107 FR623 FR716*	*FR101 FR105*
outliers (low-level)	*1*	*1*	*1*	*2*	*1*	*1*	*2*	*1*	*1*	*1*	*1*	*1*	*1*		
	FRA50	*FRA50*	*FRA50*	*FRA30 FRA50*	*FRA30 FRA50*	*FRA50*	*FRA30 FRA50*	*FRA50*	*FRA50*	*FRA50*	*FRA50*	*FRA50*	*FRA50*	*FRA50*	*FRA50*

Sources: EUROSTAT / Authors' elaboration.

Observing the evolution of the mean and the median values, it comes that, between the years 2001 and 2015, the former increases by 24,1% (average annual rate of 1,6%) whereas the latter increases by 18.4% (respectively 1,2%). Apparently, the highest increase of the mean value comparatively to the median value is due to the impact of the high-level outliers. Indeed, the annual Q-Q plots[22] of the per capita GDP level of the NUTS III French regions (Figure 1) demonstrate that data do not in any case follow the normal distribution. Instead, the annual distributions of the data show positive kurtosis and positive skewness, indicating that the majority of regions considered exhibit per capita GDP level lower than the mean value.

Such an observation is considered to be perfectly awaited taking into consideration that systematically, during the entire period under consideration, the mean values are higher than the corresponding median values. This is so as the number of high-level outliers is systematically higher than the corresponding number of low-level outliers.

---

[22] Q-Q plot provides a graphical way to determine the level of normality (Wilk and Gnanadesikan 1968).

Figure 1: The annual Q-Q plots of the per capita GDP level of the NUTS III French regions, years 2001-2015

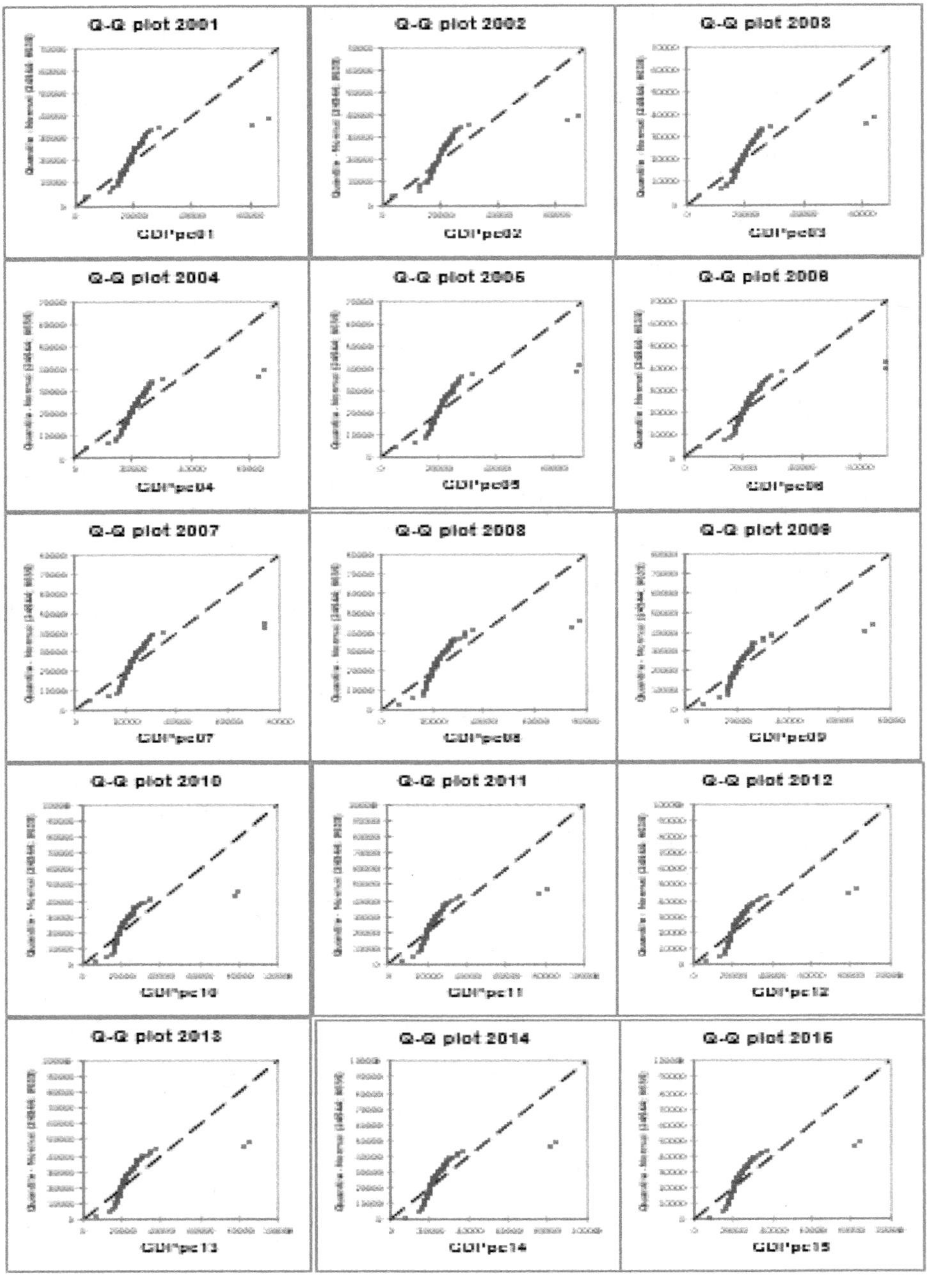

Source: EUROSTAT / Authors' elaboration.

Diachronically, the linear correlation between the per capita GDP level and the (relative) population level of the NUTS III French regions is positive, a frequent and quite logical pattern in case of countries - as France - with relatively high population's concentration in a few number of regions. Particularly, Pearson correlation coefficient[23] (Table 2) ranges from 0.544 (2002) to 0.605 (2012). Yet, it is still quite far from being characterized as perfectly positive. Such an observation indicates that the inclusion of the relative population as weighting variable in the assessment of the level and the evolution of regional inequalities may impact on the results.

Table 2. Linear correlation between the per capita GDP and the relative population of the NUTS 3 French regions (2001-2015)

	2001	2002	2003	2004	2005	2006	2007	2008	2009	2010	2011	2012	2013	2014	2015
Pearson correlation	0.545	0.544	0.551	0.552	0.555	0.568	0.567	0.597	0.598	0.601	0.600	0.605	0.597	0.579	0.582

Source: EUROSTAT / Authors' elaboration.

Towards performing the empirical analysis, both the "classical" (i.e. CV, wCV) and the "alternative" (i.e. CVmd, wCVmd) expressions of σ-convergence having be estimated (Table 3). The annual CV's variations are relatively limited with values ranging from 0.327 (2004 & 2006) to 0.394 (2013). The wCV reflects higher level of inequalities ranging from 0.514 (2006) to 0.621 (2013 & 2015), confirming that the spatial distribution of the population within the country clearly impacts the measure of inequalities. Obviously, the higher the degree of population's concentration in a limited number of metropoles, the greater is the measure of pcGDP' inequalities through the wCV coefficient, especially when the correlation between pcGDP and relative population is highly positive as it is the case for France. The two "classical" coefficient CV and wCV show the same pattern of annual fluctuations (Figure 2): during the first six years (2001-2006), they present a decreasing trend of regional inequalities about -1.0% and -1.2% per year, respectively while the next period (2006-2010) is characterized by a net increase of regional inequalities about +4,5% and +4,8% per year. Finally, from 2011, a relative stabilization can be observed.

Table 3. Regional inequalities among the NUTS 3 regions of France, estimations on the basis of both the "classical" (CV, wCV) and the alternative (CVmd, wCVmd) measures of σ-convergence (2001-2015)

		2001	2002	2003	2004	2005	2006	2007	2008	2009	2010	2011	2012	2013	2014	2015
non-weighted	CV	0.343	0.339	0.332	0.327	0.334	0.327	0.338	0.367	0.360	0.391	0.376	0.387	0.394	0.392	0.393
	CVmd	0.361	0.356	0.351	0.346	0.354	0.351	0.363	0.396	0.398	0.439	0.424	0.436	0.447	0.437	0.439
weighted	wCV	0.546	0.538	0.525	0.514	0.526	0.514	0.532	0.576	0.563	0.619	0.592	0.609	0.621	0.620	0.621
	wCVmd	0.582	0.573	0.563	0.553	0.569	0.562	0.582	0.634	0.638	0.713	0.683	0.704	0.722	0.702	0.711

Source: EUROSTAT / Authors' elaboration.

Considering the proposed "alternative" formulas, the values of the coefficient of variation based on the median (CVmd), are somewhat higher comparatively to the classical CV, ranging from 0.346 (2004) to 0.447 (2013) while the wCVmd varies from 0.553 (2004) to 0.722 (year 2013). Once again, these two alternative measures

[23] Pearson correlation coefficient is a measure of the linear correlation of two variables (Pearson 1895). It takes values in the interval [-1, 1], where -1 indicates perfectly negative linear correlation, 0 indicates no linear correlation, and 1 indicates perfectly positive linear correlation.

follow the same pattern of annual fluctuations (Figure 2) but it appears clearly that the intensity of their fluctuations differs from the classical coefficients (Table 4). Finally, with the alternative coefficients, it appears that the measure of the decline in regional inequalities is lower, while the increase in inequalities is significantly higher.

Table 4. Average annual rates of change of the "classical" (CV, wCV) and the "alternative" (CVmd, wCVmd) measures of σ-convergence (2001-2015)

Periods	"Classical"		"Alternative"	
	CV	wCV	CVmd	wCVmd
2001-2006	-0,96%	-1,22%	-0,57%	-0,72%
2006-2010	4,53%	4,76%	5,79%	6,13%
2010-2015	0,10%	0,07%	0,00%	-0,04%

Source: EUROSTAT / Authors' elaboration.

Figure 2. Regional inequalities among the NUTS III regions of France, estimation on the basis of both the "classical" (CV, wCV) and the "alternative" (CVmd, wCVmd) measures of σ-convergence period 2001-2013.

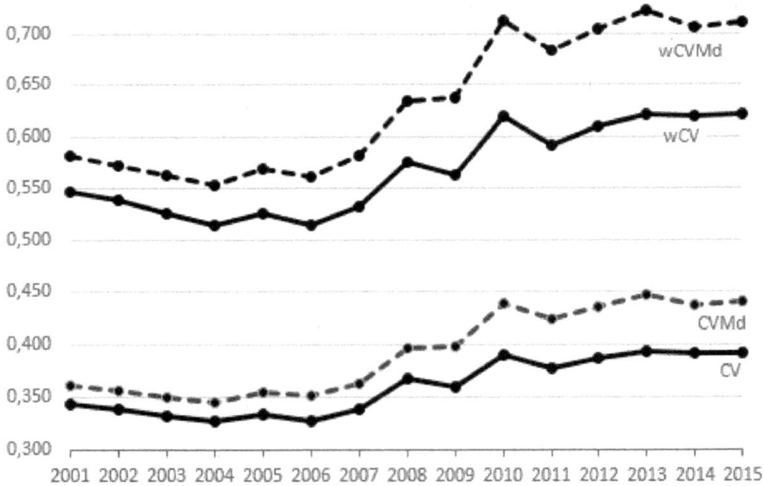

Source: EUROSTAT / Authors' elaboration.

The results of the empirical analysis evince that the level of regional inequalities in France appears to be higher in terms of the "alternative" formulas of the σ-convergence concept, comparing to the corresponding "classical" ones.[24] Particularly, the level of regional inequalities is, systematically, higher in terms of CVmd, comparing to the corresponding level in terms of CV, and in terms of wCVmd, comparing to

[24] The results of the empirical analysis, also, evince that, whilst the corresponding evolution seems to follow a similar pattern, the level of regional inequalities is higher in terms of wCV and wCVmd, comparing to the corresponding CV and CVmd formulas, respectively. In line with the considerations and the arguments of the corresponding literature (Firebaugh 2003, Sala-i-Martin 2003, Tortosa-Ausina et al. 2005, Petrakos and Artelaris 2009), it comes that the inclusion of a weighting factor (the variable of relative population, in particular) in the assessment of the level and the evolution of regional inequalities, indeed, impacts on the results.

the corresponding level in terms of wCV. Concerning the evolution of regional inequalities, it comes that the pattern is quite similar irrespective of the formula considered. Yet, a closer look indicates that the results are more sensitive, in given per capita GDP and (relative) population changes, against the backdrop of the median. Particularly, even though the median is a central tendency measure not sensitive to outliers, CVmd and wCVmd exhibit, during the whole period, higher increase than CV and wCV, respectively. The gap between CV and CVmd (as well as wCV and wCVmd) tends to widen over the years. In a nutshell, the illustrative empirical analysis of regional inequalities in France indicates that the estimation of the level and the evolution of regional inequalities with the use of the "classical" formulas of σ-convergence may mask the actual regional problem. This is so as regional inequalities appear to be lower and less sensitive against the backdrop of the mean. Even though sometimes it might be useful to policy-makers, such a discrepancy with the "alternative" formulas of σ-convergence may lead to conclusions scientifically misleading.

5. CONCLUSIONS AND INFERENCES

The paper revisits the σ-convergence concept and specifies the "alternative" CVmd and wCVmd formulas, expressing the "classical" CV and wCV formulas against the backdrop of the median. Such an endeavor stems from the, purely, statistical rationale that the mean is a central tendency measure highly sensitive to the eventual presence of outliers, and is in line with the fact that international organizations perceive the median as the central tendency measure for defining thresholds. The illustrative empirical analysis that supports the theory-driven propositions of the paper, indicates – as expected - the systematic presence of outliers and consequently the non-normal distribution of the data-sets, justifying the interest of reformulating or at least proposing a complementary measure of σ-convergence. This allows to avoid falling into "the trap of unique control" (Klatzmann, 1996). Moreover, the empirical analysis confirms that regional inequalities in France appear to be lower and less sensitive against the backdrop of the mean. Even though, sometimes, such results might be useful to policy-makers, the discrepancy between the "classical" and the "alternative" formulas of σ-convergence may mask the magnitude of the actual regional problem.

Indicating that different expressions of the σ-convergence concept may, in fact, lead to different inferences with respect to regional inequalities, the findings of the paper provide valuable insight to both theory and policy-making. Revisiting the σ-convergence concept, the paper casts strong doubts on the ability of the "classical" formulas to offer results not leading to conclusions scientifically misleading. Even though further empirical research is needed before the marginalization of the "classical" formulas of σ-convergence, the paper sets the ground for provoking the relative debate.

REFERENCES

Abreu M., de Groot H.L.F. and Florax R.J.G.M., 2005, A meta-analysis of b-convergence: The legendary 2, *Journal of Economic* Surveys, 19(3), 389-420.

Agresti A. and Finlay B., (ed), 1997, *Statistical Methods for the Social Sciences*, 3rd ed., Upper Saddle River, NJ: Prentice Hall.

Amiel Y. and Cowell F. A., 1994, Income inequality and social welfare, in Creedy J. (ed.), *Taxation, poverty and income distribution*, Cheltenham: Edward Elgar, 193-219.

Artelaris P. and Petrakos G., 2016, Intraregional spatial inequalities and regional income level in the European Union: Beyond the inverted-U hypothesis, *International Regional Science Review*, 39(3), 291-317.

Atkinson A.B., 1970, On the measurement of inequality, *Journal of Economic Theory*, 2, 244-263.

Barro R.J. (1991), Economic growth in a cross-section of countries, *Quarterly Journal of Economics*, 106, 407-443.

Barro R.J. and Sala-i-Martin X.X., 1992, Convergence, *Journal of Political Economy*, 100(2), 223-251.

Barro R.J. and Sala-i-Martin X.X., (eds.), 1995, *Economic growth*, Boston: McGraw-Hill.

Baumol W., 1986, Productivity growth, convergence and welfare: What the long-run data show? *American Economic Review*, 76(5), 1072-1085.

Borjas G., 1989, Economic theory and international migration, *International Migration Review*, 23(3), 457-485.

Bourguignon F., 1979, Decomposable income inequality measures, *Econometrica*, 47(4), 901-920.

Brewer M., Goodman A., Shaw J. and Shephard A., 2005, Poverty and inequality in Britain: 2005, *IFS*, C099.

Cowell F. A., (ed.), 2011, *Measuring inequality (3rd edition)*, New York: Oxford University Press.

Cowell F.A., 1999, Measurement of inequality, in Atkinson A. B. and Bourguignon F. (eds.), *Handbook of income distribution*, Amsterdam: North Holland, 87-166.

Dalgaard C.-J. and Vastrup J., 2001, On the measurement of σ-convergence, *Economics Letters*, 70, 283-287.

Dalton H., 1920, The measurement of inequality of incomes, *Economic Journal*, 30, 348-361.

EUROSTAT, *http://ec.europa.eu/eurostat/web/regions/overview* (*last access: January 2018*).

EUROSTAT, (ed.), 1999, *European Community Household Panel Survey: Selected Indicators from the 1995 Wave*, Luxembourg: Office for Official Publications of the EC.

Feltin M., 2002, Where do you live in the Hauts-de-Seine? 36 Cities on the test bench, *L'Express*, 03.01.2002, https://www.lexpress.fr/informations/ou-vit-on-le-mieux-dans-les-hauts-de-seine-36-villes-au-banc-d-essai_646678.html (*in French*) (*last access: January 2018*).

Firebaugh G., (ed.), 2003, *The new geography of global income inequality*, Cambridge MA: Harvard University Press.

Fujita M., 1993, Monopolistic competition and urban systems, *European Economic Review*, 37, 308-315.

Gini C. (ed.), 1912, *Variability and mutability*, C. Cuppini: Bologna (*in Italian*).

Greenwood M.J., Hunt G.L., Rickman D.S. and Treyz G.I., 1991, Migration, regional equilibrium and the estimation of compensating differentials, *American Economic Review*, 81, 1382-1390.

Gunver M.G., Senocak M.S. and Vehid S., 2017, To determine skewness, mean and deviation with a new approach on continuous data, *PONTE International Journal of Sciences and Research*, 73(2), 30-44.

Heckscher E., 1991, The effect of foreign trade on the distribution of income, in Flam H. and Flanders M. (eds.), *Heckscher - Ohlin trade theory*, Cambridge MA: MIT Press, 43-69.

Hirschman A., 1958, *The strategy of economic development*, New Haven: Yale University Press.

Islam N., 2003, What have we learned from the convergence debate? *Journal of Economic Surveys*, 17, 309-362.

Klatzmann J., 1996, *Attention Statistiques ! Comment en déjouer les pièges*, La Découverte, Paris, Poches, Essais No 17.

Kostov P. and Le Gallo J., 2015, Convergence: A story of quantiles and spillovers, *Kyklos*, 68(4), 552-576.

Krugman P.R., 1991, Increasing returns and economic geography, *Journal of Political Economy*, 99, 183-199.

Litchfield J.A., 1999, Inequality: Methods and tools, *http://siteresources.worldbank.org/INTPGI/Resources/Inequality/litchfie.pdf* (*last access: January 2018*)

Lucas R., 1988, On the mechanics of economic development, *Journal of Monetary Economics*, 22(1), 3-42.

Monfort P., 2008, Convergence of EU regions: Measures and evolution, *EU DG for Regional Policy Working Papers*, 1.

Myrdal G. (ed.), 1957, *Economic theory and underdeveloped regions*, London: Hutchinson.

OECD (ed.), 2007, *Society at a glance: OEDC Social indicators*, Paris: OECD Publishing.

Ohlin B. (ed.), 1966, *Interregional and international trade*, Cambridge MA: Harvard University Press.

Pearson K., 1895, Notes on regression and inheritance in the case of two parents, *Proceedings of the Royal Society of London*, 58, 240-242.

Pearson K., 1920, The fundamental problem of practical statistics, *Biometrika*, 13(1), 1-16.

Perroux F., 1955, Note on the notion of growth poles, *Economic Appliquée*, 1(2), 307-320 (*in French*).

Petrakos G. and Artelaris P., 2009, European regional convergence revisited: A Weighted Least Squares approach, *Growth and Change*, 40(2), 314-331.

Pigou A. F., 1912, *Wealth and welfare*, London: Macmillan.

Romer P.M., 1986, Increasing returns and long-run, *Journal of Political Economy*, 94(5), 1002-1037.

Sala-i-Martin X.X., 1996, The classical approach to convergence analysis, *Economic Journal*, 106, 1019-1036.

Sala-i-Martin X.X., 2003, Keynote speech: Convergence and divergence- theoretical underpinnings, in Tumpel-Gugerell G. and Mooslechner P. (eds.), *Economic convergence and divergence in Europe: Growth and regional development in an enlarged European Union*, Cheltenham: Edward Elgar, 117-127.

Sainani K.L., 2012, Dealing With Non-normal Data, *Physical Medicine and Rehabilitation PM&R Journal*, 4, 1001-1005.

Solow R., 1956, A contribution to the theory of economic growth, *Quarterly Journal of Economics*, 70, 65-94.

Swan T., 1956, Economic growth and capital accumulation, *Economic Record*, 32, 334-361.

Theil H., 1967, *Economics and information theory*, Amsterdam: North Holland.

Tortosa-Ausina E., Pérez F., Mas M. and Goerlich F., 2005, Growth and convergence: Profiles in the Spanish Provinces (1965–1997), *Journal of Regional Science*, 45, 147-182.

Von Hippel P.T., 2005, Mean, median and skew: Correcting a textbook rule, *Journal of Statistics Education*, 13(2).

Wilk M.B. and Gnanadesikan R., 1968, Probability plotting methods for the analysis for the analysis of data, *Biometrika*, 55(1), 1-17.

ANNEXES

Figure A1. The nomenclature of the NUTS 3 French regions (Départements)

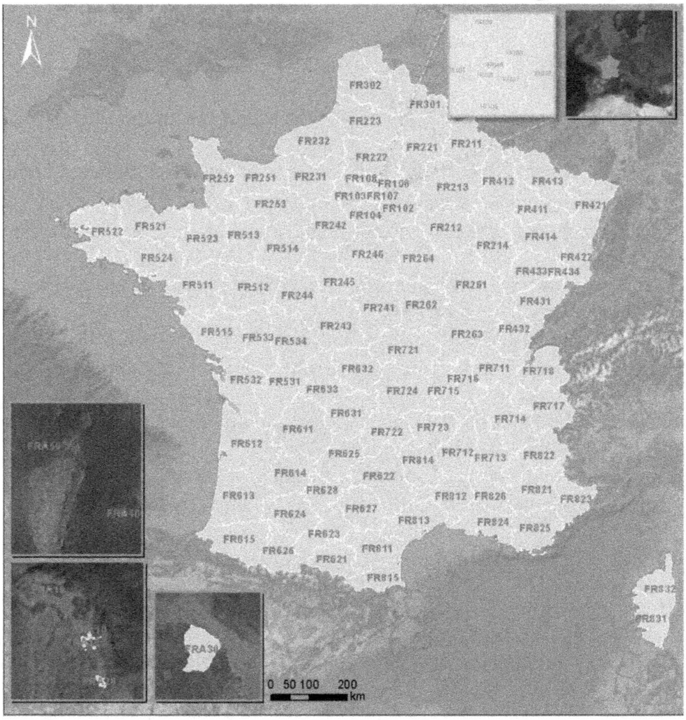

Sources: EUROSTAT / Authors' Elaboration.

Table A1. List of the 101 NUTS 3 Regions of France

FR101	Paris	FR413	Moselle	FR631	Corrèze
FR102	Seine-et-Marne	FR414	Vosges	FR632	Creuse
FR103	Yvelines	FR421	Bas-Rhin	FR633	Haute-Vienne
FR104	Essonne	FR422	Haut-Rhin	FR711	Ain
FR105	Hauts-de-Seine	FR431	Doubs	FR712	Ardèche
FR106	Seine-Saint-Denis	FR432	Jura	FR713	Drôme
FR107	Val-de-Marne	FR433	Haute-Saône	FR714	Isère
FR108	Val-d'Oise	FR434	Territoire de Belfort	FR715	Loire
FR211	Ardennes	FR511	Loire-Atlantique	FR716	Rhône
FR212	Aube	FR512	Maine-et-Loire	FR717	Savoie
FR213	Marne	FR513	Mayenne	FR718	Haute-Savoie
FR214	Haute-Marne	FR514	Sarthe	FR721	Allier
FR221	Aisne	FR515	Vendée	FR722	Cantal
FR222	Oise	FR521	Côtes-d'Armor	FR723	Haute-Loire
FR223	Somme	FR522	Finistère	FR724	Puy-de-Dôme
FR231	Eure	FR523	Ille-et-Vilaine	FR811	Aude
FR232	Seine-Maritime	FR524	Morbihan	FR812	Gard
FR241	Cher	FR531	Charente	FR813	Hérault
FR242	Eure-et-Loir	FR532	Charente-Maritime	FR814	Lozère
FR243	Indre	FR533	Deux-Sèvres	FR815	Pyrénées-Orientales
FR244	Indre-et-Loire	FR534	Vienne	FR821	Alpes-de-Haute-Provence
FR245	Loir-et-Cher	FR611	Dordogne	FR822	Hautes-Alpes
FR246	Loiret	FR612	Gironde	FR823	Alpes-Maritimes
FR251	Calvados	FR613	Landes	FR824	Bouches-du-Rhône
FR252	Manche	FR614	Lot-et-Garonne	FR825	Var
FR253	Orne	FR615	Pyrénées-Atlantiques	FR826	Vaucluse
FR261	Côte-d'Or	FR621	Ariège	FR831	Corse-du-Sud
FR262	Nièvre	FR622	Aveyron	FR832	Haute-Corse
FR263	Saône-et-Loire	FR623	Haute-Garonne	FRA10	Guadeloupe
FR264	Yonne	FR624	Gers	FRA20	Martinique
FR301	Nord	FR625	Lot	FRA30	Guyane
FR302	Pas-de-Calais	FR626	Hautes-Pyrénées	FRA40	La Réunion
FR411	Meurthe-et-Moselle	FR627	Tarn	FRA50	Mayotte
FR412	Meuse	FR628	Tarn-et-Garonne		

Source: EUROSTAT.

Figure A2. Regions with per capita GDP around the Median during the period 2001-2015

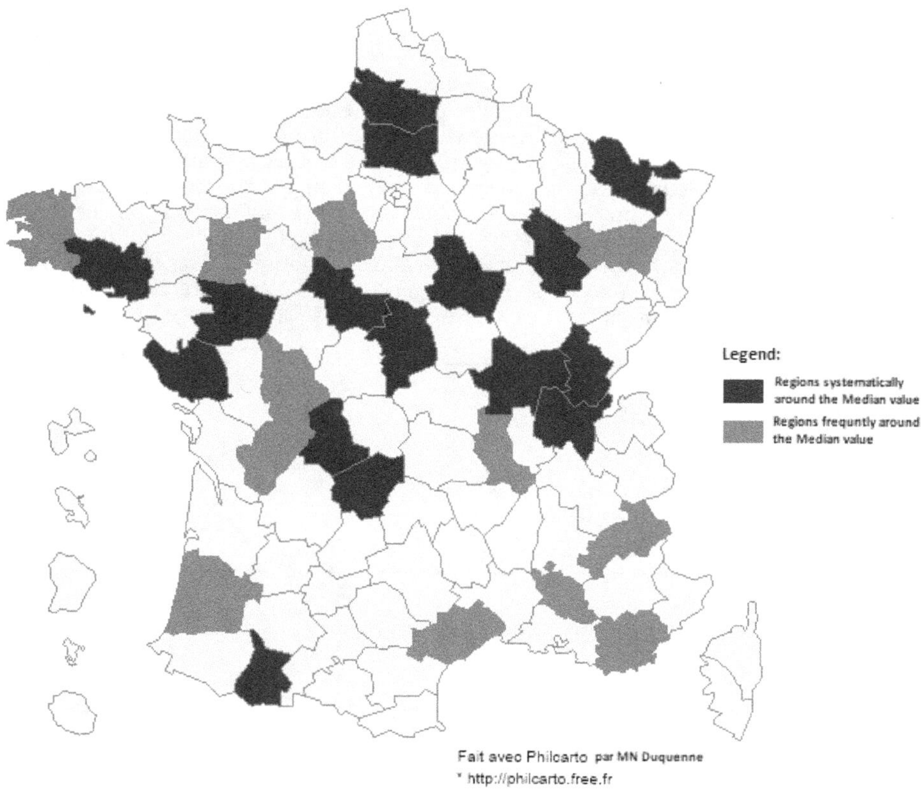

La sigma-convergence revisitée

Résumé - En se référant à l'évolution dans une période donnée de la dispersion globale d'un ensemble de données régionales, la sigma-convergence est une méthode couramment utilisée dans les analyses sur la convergence/divergence des régions. L'article revisite le concept de σ-convergence, en proposant de remplacer la moyenne arithmétique par la médiane dans les formules classiques de calcul du coefficient de variation et du coefficient de variation pondéré. À cette fin, l'article spécifie et propose une paire de formules alternatives pour appréhender le concept de σ-convergence. Une telle proposition découle de la logique purement statistique selon laquelle la moyenne est une mesure de tendance centrale très sensible à la présence éventuelle de valeurs extrêmes ou aberrantes. Cette proposition est illustrée par une analyse empirique des inégalités régionales en France à l'échelle des départements (NUTS 3) pour la période 2001-2015. Les résultats de l'analyse fournissent des indications précieuses tant sur le plan théorique que des politiques, dans la mesure où les différentes expressions du concept de σ-convergence peuvent conduire à des évaluations différentes en matière d'inégalités régionales.

Mots-clés
Inégalités régionales
Sigma-convergence
Coefficient de variation
Coefficient de variation pondéré
Moyenne arithmétique
Médiane

Région et Développement

n° 47-2018

www.regionetdeveloppement.org

Les inégalités d'éducation : une nouvelle base mondiale (1950-2015)

Wail BENAABDELAALI[*] et Maurice CATIN[**]

Résumé - Une nouvelle base mondiale sur les inégalités d'éducation est proposée ici, s'inspirant de la base élaborée par Benaabdelaali et al. (2012) et s'appuyant sur la version 2016 de la base de Barro et Lee (2013). Elle couvre la période 1950-2015 pour un ensemble de 146 pays. Elle donne une estimation des inégalités d'éducation de la population par groupe d'âge de 5 ans et par tranche d'âges agrégés, en considérant 7 niveaux d'éducation. Elle présente, outre l'indice de Gini, plusieurs indices de la famille d'entropie généralisée et de la famille d'Atkinson. Elle offre des données plus appropriées en corrigeant l'erreur de pondération utilisée par Barro et Lee dans le calcul de la moyenne d'années de scolarisation, qui peut amener un biais important pour de nombreux pays. A partir de cette base de données un panorama de la réduction des inégalités d'éducation au niveau mondial est schématiquement présenté. Dans les pays en développement, la réduction des inégalités d'éducation est essentiellement liée à la baisse de la population n'ayant aucune scolarisation. Néanmoins, l'écart entre les pays à faible niveau de développement humain dans certaines régions du monde et ceux à développement humain élevé reste important.

Classification JEL

D63, I21, J24, O15

Mots-clés

Inégalités d'éducation
Indice de Theil
Indice de Gini
Base de données mondiale

La base mondiale des inégalités d'éducation 1950-2015 présentée ici est disponible au lien : http://lead.univ-tln.fr/bdd.php

[*] Instance Nationale de l'Evaluation, Conseil Supérieur de l'Education, de la Formation et de la Recherche Scientifique, Rabat, Maroc ; wbenaabdelaali@csefrs.ma

[**] LEAD, Université de Toulon ; maurice.catin@univ-tln.fr

1. INTRODUCTION

Alors qu'elles ont été largement étudiées dans le champ de la sociologie, les inégalités éducatives ont, pendant longtemps, été peu explorées dans le champ de l'économie de l'éducation. Au départ, comme le souligne Dessus (2001), la principale raison a été le manque de données comparables au niveau international : "The measure of dispersion of qualifications is more delicate to build. Ideally the good measure would be a Gini index of education, for which the years of education of each individual would replace the traditional measure of income. To our best knowledge, this measure is unfortunately unavailable for international comparisons".

La construction d'une base mondiale sur les inégalités éducatives requiert l'existence de données homogènes sur la répartition de l'éducation pour l'ensemble des pays considérés. En ce sens, le niveau de scolarité maximum atteint semble être la seule information statistique qui paraît disponible à l'échelle mondiale. Johnes (2006) rapporte "The distribution of education is not a straightforward thing to measure. It requires information not only about the proportions of the current cohort of young people who leave education after completing various levels, but also similar information for every generation still alive. For many countries, this extent of detail in data which are quasi historic in nature has become available only very recently". De même, Meschi et Scervini (2014) notent que "the effects of the distribution of educational attainment have not been so widely studied... empirical evidence on this topic remains scarce, possibly owing to the lack of data comparing educational inequality across countries".

La première base sur les inégalités d'éducation a été développée par Lopez et al. (1998) qui ont calculé un indice de Gini de l'éducation pour un échantillon de 12 pays[1] entre 1970 et 1995. Par la suite, les auteurs l'ont étendu pour 20 pays. En utilisant aussi l'indice de Gini, Thomas et al. (2001) ont été les premiers à construire une base sur les inégalités d'éducation pour un panel de 85 pays pour la période 1960-1990. Thomas et al. (2003) ont par la suite élargi leur base jusqu'à 140 pays de 1960 à 2000 en rajoutant l'indice de Theil. De même, en utilisant l'indice de Gini de l'éducation, Castelló et Doménech (2002), Checchi (2004) et Lim et Tang (2008) ont construit une base de données comprenant respectivement 108 pays de 1960 à 2000 (935 observations), 117 pays de 1960 à 1995 (848 observations) et 99 pays de 1960 à 2000 (891 observations).

Si les inégalités éducatives sont presque toutes mesurées à partir de la répartition de la population selon le niveau d'éducation maximum atteint, les sources mobilisées pour la construction de ces bases diffèrent. Ainsi, Lopez et al. (1998, 1999), Thomas et al. (2001) et Checchi (2004) se sont appuyés sur la base de Barro et Lee (1996). Castelló et Doménech (2002), Thomas et al. (2003) et Lim et Tang (2008) ont utilisé celle de Barro et Lee (2001). Araujo et al. (2004) et Meschi et Scervini (2014) se sont appuyés sur des bases d'enquêtes ménages. D'autres auteurs comme Castelló (2010a), Benaabdelaali et al. (2012), Morrisson et Murtin (2013), Cuaresma et al. (2013), Földvári et Van Leeuwen (2014), Sauer et Zagler (2014) ont utilisé des bases plus récentes comme celles de Cohen et Soto (2007), Lutz et al. (2007) ou Barro et Lee (2013).

Plusieurs auteurs ont essayé de compiler des bases de données présentant la répartition de la population selon le niveau d'éducation maximum atteint. L'une des premières tentatives a été faite par Psacharopoulos et Arriagada (1986) qui, à partir de plusieurs recensements nationaux, ont rassemblé des données sur la composition de la population âgée de plus de 25 ans selon six niveaux d'éducation. Depuis,

[1] Brésil, Chili, Chine, Colombie, Inde, Corée, Mexique, Malaisie, Pérou, Philippines, Thaïlande et Venezuela.

de nombreux progrès ont été accomplis. Ainsi, la base de Barro et Lee (2013) présente un ensemble de données relatives à 146 pays par groupe d'âge et par genre de 1950 à 2010 sur des intervalles de cinq ans et qui donne à cet égard le pourcentage de la population – par tranche d'âge – ayant atteint, de façon achevée ou non, chacun des trois cycles d'enseignement (primaire, secondaire et supérieur). Barro et Lee ont utilisé exclusivement des données de recensements ventilées par groupe d'âge, ainsi que de nouvelles estimations des taux de mortalité et des taux d'achèvement différenciées selon l'âge et le niveau d'éducation, améliorant les données présentées dans les versions antérieures (Barro et Lee 1993, 1996, et 2001).

Il faut noter que la construction de bases internationales sur les inégalités éducatives a permis depuis l'émergence de nombreux travaux. Une littérature s'est développée pour explorer d'éventuelles relations entre les inégalités éducatives et diverses variables d'intérêt, notamment l'expansion de la scolarisation (Lim et Tang, 2008; Morrisson et Murtin, 2010, 2013; Meschi et Scervini, 2014), les inégalités de revenu (Checchi, 2004; Földvári et Van Leeuwen, 2014), la croissance économique (Castelló et Doménech, 2002; Castelló, 2010), la santé (Galea et al., 2007; Lê et al., 2010; Hori, 2011), la corruption (Patrawart, 2010), la cohésion sociale (Green et al, 2006; Vert, 2011), la migration (McKenzie et Rapoport, 2007), la démocratie (Castelló, 2008), la volatilité macroéconomique (Checchi et García-Peñalosa, 2004), voire même la rébellion populaire (Bartusevičius, 2014)...

Nous proposons dans ce qui suit une nouvelle base mondiale sur les inégalités éducatives. Elle couvre 146 pays observés tout au long de 65 années (1950-2015), et propose une estimation de l'inégalité d'éducation par tranches d'âge de 5 ans et pour les tranches d'âge agrégées. Nous partons de la base élaborée par Benaabdelaali et al. (2012) qui présentait l'indice de Gini de l'éducation pour la période 1950-2010. A la différence, la nouvelle base de données construite ici présente, sur la période 1950-2015, outre l'indice de Gini, plusieurs indices de la famille d'entropie généralisée et de la famille d'Atkinson. De plus, la moyenne d'années de scolarisation est recalculée en corrigeant l'erreur de pondération de Barro et Lee (2013) qui nous est apparue conduire à un biais pour un grand nombre de pays (section 2). De là, un panorama des inégalités au niveau mondial et de leur évolution est schématiquement présenté à partir de cette base en section 3.

2. PROPOSITION D'UNE NOUVELLE BASE MONDIALE SUR LES INÉGALITÉS ÉDUCATIVES

Pour construire notre base mondiale sur les inégalités d'éducation, nous nous sommes appuyés sur la dernière base de Barro et Lee (2013) (version 2.1 Feb, 2016) qui, comme on l'a dit précédemment, offre des estimations plus précises et actualisées sur la répartition de l'éducation selon le niveau maximum atteint pour la période 1950-2010 et présente des avantages spécifiques par rapport aux autres bases mondiales. Pour l'année 2015, nous avons reconstitué nous-même la répartition de l'éducation selon le niveau maximum atteint par groupes d'âge quinquennaux en mobilisant la ventilation de la population par tranches d'âge des différents pays de la base à partir de la révision de 2017 des estimations de population des Nations Unies (World Population Prospect) selon la démarche adoptée par Barro et Lee (2013) (voir annexe A de Barro et Lee, 2013).

Outre les années retenues jusqu'à 2015, la base mondiale sur les inégalités d'éducation que nous proposons apporte une amélioration par rapport aux bases existantes, et ce sur plusieurs plans.

• Nous avons considéré sept niveaux d'éducation. Les bases de Castelló et Doménech (2002), Checchi (2004), Castelló (2010b), Cuaresma et al. (2013) et Van Leeuwen et Földvári (2014) ont toutes été construites en s'appuyant uniquement sur quatre niveaux d'éducation. Ces auteurs ne font pas de distinction entre ceux qui ont effectivement achevé un cycle d'enseignement et ceux qui ne l'ont pas achevé puisqu'ils utilisent des données agrégées par cycle. Dans ce cas, l'inégalité estimée concerne uniquement l'inégalité inter-cycles alors que l'inégalité intra-cycles est de ce fait ignorée.

• Comme nous exploitons des données ventilées par tranches d'âge, nous prenons en compte la variation dans les durées des cycles d'enseignement. Il faut souligner qu'à l'exception de Benaabdelaali et al. (2012), l'ensemble des bases mondiales élaborées jusqu'à présent pour quantifier les inégalités éducatives ont toutes utilisé des durées des cycles d'enseignement fixes dans le temps. Tenir compte de ces changements nécessite au préalable de disposer de données désagrégées par tranches d'âge. La population âgée de 15 ans et plus est constituée d'individus, appartenant à différentes classes d'âge, n'ayant pas forcement passé au cours du temps par le même système d'éducation. En effet, durant la période 1950-2015, des restructurations du système éducatif ont été entreprises dans la plupart des pays impliquant des changements dans la durée totale de la scolarité aux cycles primaire, collégial et secondaire. Nous avons recensé 99 pays sur les 146 de la base de Barro et Lee (2013) qui ont connu des changements dans ces durées, dont 31 pays ont eu plus de trois changements. Bien entendu, ne pas tenir compte de ces changements risque de modifier significativement les estimations des indices d'inégalité. Ceci impacte aussi bien l'étendue que la répartition du nombre d'années d'études effectuées par les individus de ces différentes tranches d'âge.

• Finalement, la base de données que nous proposons est la première à offrir plusieurs indices d'inégalité de l'éducation ventilés en tranches d'âge de 5 ans, par genre, pour 146 pays, pour des groupes agrégés de pays et/ou d'intervalles d'âge, tout en tenant compte de la variation et de l'hétérogénéité au sein des groupes agrégés. Elle présente aussi pour les différents pays deux types de décomposition de quatre indices d'inégalité de l'éducation de 1950 à 2015 (Gini, indices d'entropie généralisée GE(0.5), de Theil GE(1) et d'Atkinson A(1)). Une première décomposition concerne deux groupes (les illettrés et les non illettrés) et se décompose en une inégalité intra-éduqués et une inégalité inter-éduqués-illettrés ; une seconde concerne 13 tranches d'âge, [15-19] à [75 et plus] et se décompose en une inégalité intragénérationnelle et une inégalité intergénérationnelle. Cette base est accessible en ligne sur le site du LEAD (http://lead.univ-tln.fr/bdd.php).

Nous présentons dans ce qui suit la méthodologie adoptée pour construire les différents indices d'inégalité en se basant sur la répartition de la population selon le niveau d'éducation maximum atteint.

2.1. L'erreur de pondération dans la base de Barro et Lee (2013)

Etant donné que les durées des cycles d'enseignement ne sont pas explicitement disponibles dans la base de Barro et Lee (2013), nous les avons calculées en utilisant la démarche adoptée par Benaabdelaali et al. (2012) (voir section 2.2). Elles sont appelées de manière générale :

$p^a_{c,i,t}$ la proportion de la population de la tranche d'âge "a" du pays "c" ayant atteint le niveau d'éducation "i" à la date "t" ;

$y^a_{c,i,t}$ est le nombre d'années de scolarisation cumulées de la tranche d'âge "a" du pays "c" pour atteindre le niveau d'éducation "j" à la date "t".

Afin de calculer un indice d'inégalité de l'éducation pour des grands groupes d'âge (15 ans et plus, 25 ans et plus, 15 à 65 ans, ...), la plupart des auteurs, même ceux qui ont utilisé la base de Barro et Lee (2013) comme Sauer et Zagler (2014), ne prennent pas en considération la variation par tranches d'âge des durées des cycles d'enseignement. Par exemple pour calculer l'indice de Theil de l'éducation pour la population âgée de 15 ans et plus, ils supposent des « $y^a_{c,j,t}$ » invariants à la fois par tranche d'âge et dans le temps ($y^{15+}_{c,j,t} = y^a_{c,j} = y_{c,j}\ \forall a \in [1-13], \forall t \in [1950 - 2010]$).

Toutefois, même s'il s'agit du même pays "c" à la même date "t", les durées des cycles d'enseignement peuvent être différentes d'une tranche d'âge à l'autre. De manière générale, sur les 146 pays considérés, 99 pays ont procédé à des changements dans les durées des cycles d'enseignement.

Une première approche serait alors de calculer une moyenne des « $y^a_{c,j,t}$ » de manière à tenir compte de ces éventuelles variations par rapport aux différents groupes d'âge. Ainsi, comme $p^{15+}_{c,j,t} = \sum_{a=1}^{A} l^a_{c,t} p^a_{c,j,t}$, on pourrait a priori penser que $y^{15+}_{c,j,t}$ serait de même égale à $\sum_{a=1}^{A} l^a_{c,t} y^a_{c,j,t}$.

Or on peut montrer que Barro et Lee (2013) n'ont pas utilisé la pondération adéquate dans le calcul des durées $y^{15+}_{c,j,t}$. Après avoir déduit les durées $y^a_{c,j,t}$ à partir de leur base de données[2], il apparaît bien que nos moyennes d'années de scolarisation par tranches d'âge quinquennales ($MAS^a_{c,t}$) correspondent à celles calculées par Barro et Lee (2013). Toutefois, lorsqu'il s'agit de calculer la moyenne d'années de scolarisation de la tranche d'âge agrégée de 15 ans et plus, en appliquant la formule utilisée dans leur article $MAS^{15+}_{c,t} = \sum_{a=1}^{A} l^a_{c,t} MAS^a_{c,t}$ (la moyenne des moyennes d'années de scolarisation par tranches d'âge quinquennales) ainsi que leurs propres données (répartition de la population selon les niveaux d'éducation) nous ne retrouvons pas les mêmes résultats.

Il s'avère que, pour la population âgée de 15 ans et plus, les auteurs ont utilisé une autre formule tout aussi valable qui est égale à la somme des produits entre les durées et les proportions $MAS^{15+}_{c,t} = \sum_{j=1}^{n} p^{15+}_{c,j,t} y^{15+}_{c,j,t}$. Auquel cas, le problème proviendrait des durées agrégées $y^{15+}_{c,j,t}$. Il semble que les auteurs se soient appuyés sur une pondération qui correspondrait à celle utilisée pour les $p^{15+}_{c,j,t}$ ($p^{15+}_{c,j,t} = \sum_{a=1}^{A} l^a_{c,t} p^a_{c,j,t}$). Afin de le vérifier, nous avons recalculé les durées agrégées en utilisant cette dernière pondération tel que $\tilde{y}^{15+}_{c,j,t} = \sum_{a=1}^{A} l^a_{c,t} y^a_{c,j,t}$. Nous retrouvons alors bien les mêmes valeurs des moyennes d'années de scolarisation des 15 ans et plus que celles des auteurs[3].

En partant des formules de la moyenne d'années de scolarisation de la tranche d'âge "a" ($MAS^a_{c,t} = \sum_{j=1}^{n} p^a_{c,j,t} y^a_{c,j,t}$) et de celle de la population âgée de 15 ans et plus ($MAS^{15+}_{c,t} = \sum_{a=1}^{A} l^a_{c,t} MAS^a_{c,t} = \sum_{j=1}^{n} p^{15+}_{c,j,t} y^{15+}_{c,j,t}$), on peut démontrer que l'agrégation des « $y^a_{c,j,t}$ » pour l'ensemble de la population âgée de 15 ans et plus doit s'écrire comme suit :

$$y^{15+}_{c,j,t} = \sum_{a=1}^{A} \left[\frac{l^a_{c,t}\, p^a_{c,j,t}}{\sum_{b=1}^{A} l^b_{c,t}\, p^b_{c,j,t}} \right] y^a_{c,j,t}$$

Certes, l'erreur de pondération faite par Barro et Lee (2013) peut, pour certains pays, ne pas avoir d'impact si les $y^a_{c,j,t}$ restent les mêmes pour l'ensemble des tranches d'âge. Toutefois comme les systèmes éducatifs de la majorité des pays ont subi des aménagements quant aux durées des cycles d'enseignement depuis 65 ans,

---

[2] La démarche de calcul des $y^a_{c,j,t}$ est présentée dans la section 2.2.

[3] On a refait les calculs avec les versions précédentes de la base de Barro et Lee {1.0, 1.1, 1.2, 1.3, 2.0 et 2.1} et on obtient les mêmes résultats.

cette erreur peut changer significativement les résultats et ceci peut être illustré à travers l'exemple qui suit.

Tableau 1. Répartition de la population par tranche d'âge selon le niveau d'éducation maximum atteint pour le cas de la Bulgarie en 1990

Groupe d'âge	Pop.	Poids du groupe d'âge (l^a)	Proportion de la population selon le niveau d'éducation maximum atteint (en %) ($p^a_{c,j,t}$) {c=120,t=1990}						
			Non Scol. (p^a_1)	Prim. inachevé (p^a_2)	Prim. achevé (p^a_3)	Sec. inachevé (p^a_4)	Sec. achevé (p^a_5)	Sup. inachevé (p^a_6)	Sup. achevé (p^a_7)
15-19	641	9.24	1.90	6.40	63.50	22.76	5.24	0.09	0.01
20-24	585	8.43	1.40	2.80	17.30	14.97	57.13	4.26	2.04
25-29	580	8.36	1.40	2.70	17.40	12.35	46.35	6.33	13.37
30-34	606	8.74	1.40	2.70	17.40	13.59	45.11	6.33	13.37
35-39	625	9.01	1.40	3.40	25.70	14.34	34.06	6.72	14.18
40-44	638	9.20	1.40	3.40	25.70	16.46	31.94	6.72	14.18
45-49	527	7.60	2.70	6.80	37.90	16.70	19.00	5.37	11.33
50-54	513	7.40	2.70	6.80	37.90	18.73	16.97	5.37	11.33
55-59	560	8.07	5.60	16.30	42.80	14.26	9.64	3.63	7.67
60-64	529	7.63	5.60	16.30	42.80	14.86	9.04	2.75	8.55
65-69	474	6.83	12.00	32.30	36.70	8.55	3.75	1.61	4.99
70-74	240	3.46	12.00	32.30	36.70	8.95	3.35	1.09	5.51
75 et +	418	6.03	12.00	32.30	36.70	9.45	2.85	1.25	5.35
15 et +	**6936**	-	**4.03**	**9.13**	**35.00**	**18.44**	**20.19**	**4.96**	**8.11**

Source : Base de données de Barro et Lee (2013) (v. 2.1, Feb. 2016).

Tableau 2. Répartition de la population par tranche d'âge selon le niveau d'éducation maximum atteint pour le cas de la Bulgarie en 1990

Groupe d'âge	Moyenne d'années de scolarisation (l^a)	Nombre d'années cumulées de scolarisation ($y^a_{c,j,t}$) {c=120, t=1990}						
		Non Scol. (y^a_1)	Prim. inachevé (y^a_2)	Prim. achevé (y^a_3)	Sec. inachevé (y^a_4)	Sec. achevé (y^a_5)	Sup. inachevé (y^a_6)	Sup. achevé (y^a_7)
15-19	5.08	0.0	2.0	4.0	8.0	11.0	13.0	15.0
20-24	10.06	0.0	4.0	8.0	9.5	11.0	13.0	15.0
25-29	10.60	0.0	4.0	8.0	9.5	11.0	13.0	15.0
30-34	10.58	0.0	4.0	8.0	9.5	11.0	13.0	15.0
35-39	10.30	0.0	4.0	8.0	9.5	11.0	13.0	15.0
40-44	8.84	0.0	2.0	4.0	7.5	11.0	13.0	15.0
45-49	8.88	0.0	2.0	4.0	10.0	14.0	16.0	18.0
50-54	8.80	0.0	2.0	4.0	10.0	14.0	16.0	18.0
55-59	6.78	0.0	2.0	4.0	10.0	14.0	16.0	18.0
60-64	6.77	0.0	2.0	4.0	10.0	14.0	16.0	18.0
65-69	4.65	0.0	2.0	4.0	10.0	14.0	16.0	18.0
70-74	4.64	0.0	2.0	4.0	10.0	14.0	16.0	18.0
75 et +	4.62	0.0	2.0	4.0	10.0	14.0	16.0	18.0
15 et + **Auteurs**	**7.96**	**0.0**	**2.2**	**4.8**	**9.3**	**11.6**	**14.1**	**16.3**
Barro et Lee	**8.42**	**0.0**	**2.7**	**5.4**	**9.4**	**12.4**	**14.4**	**16.4**
Surestimation	**0.46**	**0.0**	**0.5**	**0.6**	**0.1**	**0.8**	**0.3**	**0.1**

Source: Calcul des auteurs à partir de la base de données de Barro et Lee (2013) (v. 2.1, Feb. 2016).

Les tableaux n°1 et n°2 présentent le cas de la Bulgarie en 1990 {c=120, t=1990}. Le tableau n°1 fournit la répartition de la population de la Bulgarie en 1990 par tranche d'âge selon le niveau d'éducation maximum atteint « $p^a_{c,j,t}$ » ainsi que les poids de chaque tranche d'âge dans la population âgée de 15 ans et plus « $l^a_{c,t}$ ». Le tableau n°2 présente les nombres d'années cumulées de scolarisation par tranche d'âge et selon chaque niveau d'éducation « $y^a_{c,j,t}$ » ainsi que la moyenne d'années de scolarisation par tranche d'âge. La différence entre les deux pondérations est ainsi présentée dans le tableau n°2.

Prenons par exemple le cas du primaire achevé *j=3*, $y^{15+}_{c,3,t}$. Selon Barro et Lee (2013), sa valeur est égale à $\sum_{a=1}^{A} l^a_{c,t} y^a_{c,3,t} = 5.4$ alors qu'elle doit plutôt être égale à $\sum_{a=1}^{A} \left[\frac{l^a_{c,t} p^a_{c,3,t}}{\sum_{b=1}^{A} l^b_{c,t} p^b_{c,3,t}}\right] y^a_{c,3,t} = 4.8$. Il en va de même du calcul pour les autres $y^{15+}_{c,j,t}$. La moyenne d'années de scolarisation de la population âgée de 15 ans et plus peut passer ainsi de 7.96 à 8.42 (différence de 0.46). Cette différence est relativement importante, puisqu'une moyenne d'années de scolarisation n'augmente en moyenne que d'une année de scolarisation tous les dix ans. D'où l'ampleur du biais dû à l'utilisation d'une pondération non adéquate.

2.2. Calcul des durées des cycles d'enseignement

Nous présentons dans cette section la démarche adoptée pour reconstituer les durées des cycles d'enseignement « $y^a_{c,j,t}$ » pour l'ensemble des 146 pays de 1950 à 2015. Celles-ci n'étant pas explicitement présentées dans la base de données de Barro et Lee (2013), nous les avons calculées – et mises à disposition dans notre base de données en ligne.

Nous avons adopté la même approche que Benaabdelaali et al. (2012). Nous fusionnons les deux bases de la population totale {MF} et féminine {F} considérées par Barro et Lee (2013) et utilisons les moyennes d'années de scolarisation par tranches d'âge de chaque cycle. Nous avons ainsi construit un ensemble de 24674 systèmes d'équations à sept inconnues chacun, ce qui nous a permis de retrouver « $y^a_{c,j,t}$ » qui correspond au nombre nécessaire d'années cumulées de scolarisation pour atteindre le niveau d'éducation "j" par la tranche d'âge "a" du pays "c" à la date "t" tel que j =1…7, a=1…13, c=1…146 et t=1950, 1955…2010.

Nous nous sommes basés sur les formules des moyennes d'années de scolarisation par cycle. Toutefois, il faut d'abord disposer des proportions d'individus qui n'ont pas achevé les trois cycles d'enseignement. En effet, la base de Barro et Lee (2013) ne les présente pas explicitement. Nous les avons calculées en faisant la différence entre la proportion de ceux qui ont atteint le cycle d'enseignement {notée "lp" "ls" "lh" pour les cycles primaire, secondaire et supérieur respectivement} en question et ceux qui l'ont terminé {notée "lpc" "lsc" "lhc" pour les cycles primaire, secondaire et supérieur respectivement}.

Ainsi, la moyenne d'années de scolarisation du cycle primaire peut être définie comme étant la somme du nombre d'années de scolarisation correspondant aux individus qui n'ont pas achevé le cycle primaire « $y^a_{c,2,t} - y^a_{c,1,t}$ » pondéré par la proportion de ces derniers « $p^a_{c,2,t}$ » plus le nombre d'années de scolarisation correspondant aux individus qui ont achevé le cycle primaire « $y^a_{c,3,t} - y^a_{c,1,t}$ » pondéré par la proportion des individus ayant au moins complété ce même niveau « $\sum_{j=3}^{7} p^a_{c,j,t}$ », d'où la formule ci-après :

$$aysp^a_{c,t} = \underbrace{p^a_{c,2,t}\left[y^a_{c,2,t} - y^a_{c,1,t}\right]}_{\text{Cycle primaire inachevé}} + \underbrace{\left(\sum_{j=3}^{7} p^a_{c,j,t}\right)\left[y^a_{c,3,t} - y^a_{c,1,t}\right]}_{\text{Cycle primaire achevé}} \qquad (1)$$

Les moyennes d'années de scolarisation des cycles secondaire et supérieur peuvent être obtenues en suivant le même raisonnement :

$$ayss^{a}_{c,t} = \underbrace{p^{a}_{c,4,t}\left[y^{a}_{c,4,t} - y^{a}_{c,3,t}\right]}_{\text{Cycle secondaire inachevé}} + \underbrace{\left(\sum_{j=5}^{7} p^{a}_{c,j,t}\right)\left[y^{a}_{c,5,t} - y^{a}_{c,3,t}\right]}_{\text{Cycle secondaire achevé}} \quad (2)$$

$$ayst^{a}_{c,t} = \underbrace{p^{a}_{c,6,t}\left[y^{a}_{c,6,t} - y^{a}_{c,5,t}\right]}_{\text{Cycle supérieur inachevé}} + \underbrace{p^{a}_{c,7,t}\left[y^{a}_{c,7,t} - y^{a}_{c,5,t}\right]}_{\text{Cycle supérieur achevé}} \quad (3)$$

L'objectif est de calculer les « $y^{a}_{c,j,t}$ » pour chaque quadruplet (a,c,t,j) où "a" est la tranche d'âge, "c" le pays, "t" la date et "j" le niveau d'éducation. Ceci revient à retrouver pour chaque triplet (a,c,t) les sept inconnues :
$y^{a}_{c,1,t}; y^{a}_{c,2,t}; y^{a}_{c,3,t}; y^{a}_{c,4t}; y^{a}_{c,5,t}; y^{a}_{c,6,t}; y^{a}_{c,7,t}$.

On note ainsi :
$aysp_{(mf)}{}^{a}_{t}$ la moyenne d'années de scolarisation du cycle primaire de la tranche d'âge « a » de la population totale à la date « t ».
$ayss_{(mf)}{}^{a}_{t}$ la moyenne d'années de scolarisation du cycle secondaire de la tranche d'âge « a » de la population totale à la date « t ».
$ayst_{(mf)}{}^{a}_{t}$ la moyenne d'années de scolarisation du cycle supérieur de la tranche d'âge « a » de la population totale à la date « t ».
$aysp_{(f)}{}^{a}_{t}$ la moyenne d'années de scolarisation du cycle primaire de la tranche d'âge « a » de la population féminine à la date « t ».
$ayss_{(f)}{}^{a}_{t}$ la moyenne d'années de scolarisation du cycle secondaire de la tranche d'âge « a » de la population féminine à la date « t ».
$ayst_{(f)}{}^{a}_{t}$ la moyenne d'années de scolarisation du cycle supérieur de la tranche d'âge « a » de la population féminine à la date « t ».
$p_{(mf)}{}^{a}_{j,t}$ la proportion de la population totale appartenant à la tranche d'âge « a » ayant atteint le niveau d'éducation « j » à la date « t ».
$p_{(f)}{}^{a}_{j,t}$ la proportion de la population féminine appartenant à la tranche d'âge « a » ayant atteint le niveau d'éducation « j » à la date « t ».

Etant donné que le nombre d'années de scolarisation cumulées $y^{a}_{c,j,t}$ est le même pour les hommes que pour les femmes $y_{(mf)}{}^{a}_{c,j,t} = y_{(m)}{}^{a}_{c,j,t} = y_{(f)}{}^{a}_{c,j,t}$, nous avons reproduit les trois équations relatives à la moyenne d'années de scolarisation des trois cycles pour la population totale et féminine ($3 \times 2 = 6$ équations). En outre, la dotation éducative de la population non scolarisée est nulle ($y^{a}_{c,1,t} = 0$). Au total, nous pouvons obtenir pour chaque triplet (a,c,t) un système de sept équations et de sept inconnues :

$$aysp_{(mf)}{}^{a}_{c,t} = p_{(mf)}{}^{a}_{c,2,t}\left[y^{a}_{c,2,t} - y^{a}_{c,1,t}\right] + \left(\sum_{j=3}^{7} p_{(mf)}{}^{a}_{c,j,t}\right)\left[y^{a}_{c,3,t} - y^{a}_{c,1,t}\right]$$

$$aysp_{(f)}{}^{a}_{c,t} = p_{(f)}{}^{a}_{c,2,t}\left[y^{a}_{c,2,t} - y^{a}_{c,1,t}\right] + \left(\sum_{j=3}^{7} p_{(f)}{}^{a}_{c,j,t}\right)\left[y^{a}_{c,3,t} - y^{a}_{c,1,t}\right]$$

$$ayss_{(mf)}{}^{a}_{c,t} = p_{(mf)}{}^{a}_{c,4,t}\left[y^{a}_{c,4,t} - y^{a}_{c,3,t}\right] + \left(\sum_{j=5}^{7} p_{(mf)}{}^{a}_{c,j,t}\right)\left[y^{a}_{c,5,t} - y^{a}_{c,3,t}\right]$$

$$ayss_{(f)}{}^{a}_{c,t} = p_{(f)}{}^{a}_{c,4,t}\left[y^{a}_{c,4,t} - y^{a}_{c,3,t}\right] + \left(\sum_{j=5}^{7} p_{(f)}{}^{a}_{c,j,t}\right)\left[y^{a}_{c,5,t} - y^{a}_{c,3,t}\right]$$

$$ayst_{(mf)}{}^{a}_{c,t} = p_{(mf)}{}^{a}_{c,6,t}\left[y^{a}_{c,6,t} - y^{a}_{c,5,t}\right] + p_{(mf)}{}^{a}_{c,7,t}\left[y^{a}_{c,7,t} - y^{a}_{c,5,t}\right]$$

$$ayst_{(f)}{}_{c,t}^{a} = p_{(f)}{}_{c,6,t}^{a}\left[y_{c,6,t}^{a} - y_{c,5,t}^{a}\right] + p_{(f)}{}_{c,7,t}^{a}\left[y_{c,7,t}^{a} - y_{c,5,t}^{a}\right]$$

$$y_{c,1,t}^{a} = 0$$

On peut ainsi résoudre ce système d'équations pour chaque triplet (a,c,t) et les sept inconnues $\{y_{c,1,t}^{a}; y_{c,2,t}^{a}; y_{c,3,t}^{a}; y_{c,4t}^{a}; y_{c,5,t}^{a}; y_{c,6,t}^{a}; y_{c,7,t}^{a}\}$ sont retrouvées comme suit :

$$y_{c,1,t}^{a} = 0$$

$$y_{c,2,t}^{a} = \frac{\left(\sum_{j=3}^{7} p_{(f)}{}_{c,j,t}^{a}\right)\left(aysp_{(mf)}{}_{c,t}^{a}\right) - \left(\sum_{j=3}^{7} p_{(mf)}{}_{c,j,t}^{a}\right)\left(aysp_{(f)}{}_{c,t}^{a}\right)}{p_{(mf)}{}_{c,2,t}^{a}\left(\sum_{j=3}^{7} p_{(f)}{}_{c,j,t}^{a}\right) - p_{(f)}{}_{c,2,t}^{a}\left(\sum_{j=3}^{7} p_{(mf)}{}_{c,j,t}^{a}\right)}$$

$$y_{c,3,t}^{a} = \frac{p_{(mf)}{}_{c,2,t}^{a}\left(aysp_{(f)}{}_{c,t}^{a}\right) - p_{(f)}{}_{c,2,t}^{a}\left(aysp_{(mf)}{}_{c,t}^{a}\right)}{p_{(mf)}{}_{c,2,t}^{a}\left(\sum_{j=3}^{7} p_{(f)}{}_{c,j,t}^{a}\right) - p_{(f)}{}_{c,2,t}^{a}\left(\sum_{j=3}^{7} p_{(mf)}{}_{c,j,t}^{a}\right)}$$

$$y_{c,4,t}^{a} = y_{c,3,t}^{a} + \frac{\left(\sum_{j=5}^{7} p_{(f)}{}_{c,j,t}^{a}\right)\left(ayss_{(mf)}{}_{c,t}^{a}\right) - \left(\sum_{j=5}^{7} p_{(mf)}{}_{c,j,t}^{a}\right)\left(ayss_{(f)}{}_{c,t}^{a}\right)}{p_{(mf)}{}_{c,4,t}^{a}\left(\sum_{j=5}^{7} p_{(f)}{}_{c,j,t}^{a}\right) - p_{(f)}{}_{c,4,t}^{a}\left(\sum_{j=5}^{7} p_{(mf)}{}_{c,j,t}^{a}\right)}$$

$$y_{c,5,t}^{a} = y_{c,3,t}^{a} + \frac{p_{(mf)}{}_{c,4,t}^{a}\left(ayss_{(f)}{}_{c,t}^{a}\right) - p_{(f)}{}_{c,4,t}^{a}\left(ayss_{(mf)}{}_{c,t}^{a}\right)}{p_{(mf)}{}_{c,4,t}^{a}\left(\sum_{j=5}^{7} p_{(f)}{}_{c,j,t}^{a}\right) - p_{(f)}{}_{c,4,t}^{a}\left(\sum_{j=5}^{7} p_{(mf)}{}_{c,j,t}^{a}\right)}$$

$$y_{c,6,t}^{a} = y_{c,5,t}^{a} + \frac{p_{(f)}{}_{c,7,t}^{a}\left(ayst_{(mf)}{}_{c,t}^{a}\right) - p_{(mf)}{}_{c,7,t}^{a}\left(ayst_{(f)}{}_{c,t}^{a}\right)}{p_{(mf)}{}_{c,6,t}^{a}\, p_{(f)}{}_{c,7,t}^{a} - p_{(f)}{}_{c,6,t}^{a}\, p_{(mf)}{}_{c,7,t}^{a}}$$

$$y_{c,7,t}^{a} = y_{c,5,t}^{a} + \frac{p_{(mf)}{}_{c,6,t}^{a}\left(ayst_{(f)}{}_{c,t}^{a}\right) - p_{(f)}{}_{c,6,t}^{a}\left(ayst_{(mf)}{}_{c,t}^{a}\right)}{p_{(mf)}{}_{c,6,t}^{a}\, p_{(f)}{}_{c,7,t}^{a} - p_{(f)}{}_{c,6,t}^{a}\, p_{(mf)}{}_{c,7,t}^{a}}$$

Il faut préciser que lorsque le dénominateur est nul, on peut retrouver la valeur de $y_{c,j,t}^{a}$ par l'équation suivante $y_{c,j,t-5}^{a-1} = y_{c,j,t}^{a} = y_{c,j,t+5}^{a+1}$, puisqu'il s'agit de la même cohorte.

2.3. Indices d'inégalité d'éducation pour des groupes agrégés

Répétons que l'erreur de pondération qu'on a pu déceler dans la base de Barro et Lee ne remet pas en question la qualité des données sur la répartition de l'éducation mais concerne plus particulièrement les moyennes d'années de scolarisation de la population âgée de 15 ans et plus et de 25 ans et plus. Pour calculer les indices d'inégalité nous avons donc utilisé les données de Barro et Lee sur la répartition de l'éducation et nous avons mené les corrections nécessaires pour les moyennes d'années de scolarisation.

Ceci étant, afin de calculer les indices d'inégalité d'éducation de la population âgée de 15 ans et plus, on pourrait opter pour une solution qui consiste à calculer la moyenne des « $y_{c,j,t}^{a}$ » avec les bonnes pondérations pour obtenir « $y_{c,j,t}^{15+}$ » puis l'utiliser par la suite pour l'évaluation de l'indice d'inégalité. Toutefois, cette solution consiste à agréger les données avant de calculer l'indice d'inégalité du groupe d'âge agrégé et ne permet pas de prendre en considération les inégalités inter-tranches d'âge ni d'exploiter la richesse des données désagrégées. Aussi, afin d'en tenir compte, nous utilisons une autre approche, en utilisant une formulation plus adaptée. Les indices d'inégalité considérés se déclinent alors comme suit.

2.3.1. Indice de Gini de l'éducation pour des groupes agrégés

$$Gini_{c,t}^{G}=\frac{\sum_{a\in G}\sum_{a'\in G}\sum_{i=1}^{n}\sum_{j=1}^{n}n_{c,i,t}^{a}\left|y_{c,i,t}^{a}-y_{c,j,t}^{a'}\right|n_{c,j,t}^{a'}}{2\,N_{c,t}^{G}\left[\sum_{a\in G}\sum_{i=1}^{n}n_{c,i,t}^{a}y_{c,i,t}^{a}\right]}$$

avec :
- $Gini_{c,t}^{G}$ l'indice de Gini de l'éducation du grand groupe d'âge "G"[4] appartenant au pays "c" à la date "t".
- a=1 (a'=1) pour le groupe d'âge 15-19 ans, a=2 (a'=2) pour le groupe d'âge 20-24 ans, ..., et a=13 (a'=13) pour le groupe d'âge 75 et plus.
- *i* et *j* sont les niveaux d'éducation : i=1 pour les illettrés, i=2 pour le primaire inachevé, i=3 pour le primaire achevé, i=4 pour le secondaire inachevé, i=5 pour le secondaire achevé, i=6 pour le supérieur inachevé, and i=7 pour le supérieur achevé.
- $n_{c,i,t}^{a}$ représente la taille de la population de la tranche d'âge "a" du pays "c" ayant atteint le niveau d'éducation "i" à la date "t".
- $y_{c,i,t}^{a}$ traduit le nombre d'années de scolarisation cumulées de la tranche d'âge "a" du pays "c" pour atteindre le niveau d'éducation "j" à la date "t".

De même pour des groupes de pays, qu'ils soient considérés selon la zone géographique, le niveau de revenu ou de développement, des auteurs comme Földvári et Van Leeuwen (2014) calculent une moyenne des indices de Gini par pays au lieu de calculer un indice de Gini sur la distribution de l'ensemble des pays appartenant au groupe en question et ignorent de ce fait, les inégalités inter-pays. Pour rendre compte du niveau d'inégalités pour un groupe de pays, il nous paraît plus approprié de calculer un indice de Gini sur la distribution de l'ensemble des pays du groupe :

$$Gini_{R,t}^{a}=\frac{\sum_{c\in R}\sum_{c'\in R}\sum_{i=1}^{n}\sum_{j=1}^{n}n_{c,i,t}^{a}\left|y_{c,i,t}^{a}-y_{c',j,t}^{a}\right|n_{c',j,t}^{a}}{2\,N_{R,t}^{a}\left[\sum_{c\in R}\sum_{i=1}^{n}n_{c,i,t}^{a}y_{c,i,t}^{a}\right]}$$

avec, outre les symboles déjà définis :
- $Gini_{R,t}^{a}$ l'indice de Gini de l'éducation du groupe d'âge "a" appartenant à la région "R" à la date "t".
- c (c') représente les pays appartenant à la région "R".
- *n* est le nombre des niveaux d'éducation retenus qui correspond ici à 7.
- $N_{R,t}^{a}$ représente la taille de la population du groupe d'âge "a" appartenant à la région "R" à la date "t". ($N_{R,t}^{a}=\sum_{c\in R}\sum_{i=1}^{n}n_{c,i,t}^{a}=\sum_{c\in R}N_{c,t}^{a}$).

On peut généraliser la formule du calcul de l'indice de Gini pour des groupes agrégés à la fois par pays et par grands groupes d'âge (par exemple, pour la population âgée de 15 ans et plus) tout en utilisant une formule qui, en plus de prendre en considération les inégalités inter-niveaux d'éducation des individus, tienne compte à la fois des inégalités inter-pays et inter-tranches d'âge :

[4] Par exemple G peut être la population âgée entre 15 et 65 ans, de 25 à 65 ans, 15 à 24 ans, ou encore la population âgée de 15 ans et plus ou 25 ans et plus...

$$Gini_{R,t}^{G} = \frac{\sum_{c\in R}\sum_{c'\in R}\sum_{a\in G}\sum_{a'\in G}\sum_{i=1}^{n}\sum_{j=1}^{n} n_{c,i,t}^{a}\left|y_{c,i,t}^{a} - y_{c',j,t}^{a'}\right| n_{c',j,t}^{a'}}{2\, N_{R,t}^{G}\left[\sum_{c\in R}\sum_{a\in G}\sum_{i=1}^{n} n_{c,i,t}^{a}\, y_{c,i,t}^{a}\right]}$$

où :

- $Gini_{R,t}^{G}$ est l'indice de Gini de l'éducation du grand groupe d'âge "G" appartenant à la région "R" à la date "t".
- $N_{R,t}^{G}$ représente la taille de la population du grand groupe d'âge "G" appartenant à la région "R" à la date "t". ($N_{R,t}^{G} = \sum_{c\in R}\sum_{a\in G}\sum_{i=1}^{n} n_{c,i,t}^{a} = \sum_{c\in R} N_{c,t}^{G} = \sum_{c\in R} N_{R,t}^{a}$).

2.3.2. Les indices d'entropie généralisée et d'Atkinson de l'éducation

En suivant la même approche adoptée pour le calcul de l'indice de Gini de l'éducation d'un groupe d'âge quinquennal d'un pays donné ou d'un groupe agrégé de pays et/ou de groupes d'âge, nous pouvons calculer d'autres indices d'inégalité comme ceux appartenant à la famille d'entropie généralisée ou d'Atkinson.

Les indices d'entropie généralisée et d'Atkinson de l'éducation sont :

$$GE(r)_{c,t}^{a} = \frac{{N_{c,t}^{a}}^{(r-1)}}{r(r-1)}\left[\frac{\sum_{j=1}^{n} n_{c,j,t}^{a}\left(y_{c,j,t}^{a}\right)^{r}}{\left(\sum_{j=1}^{n} n_{c,j,t}^{a}\, y_{c,j,t}^{a}\right)^{r}} - 1\right]$$

$$\text{et } A(\varepsilon)_{c,t}^{a} = 1 - \frac{1}{\left[N_{c,t}^{a}\right]^{\left(\frac{\varepsilon}{1-\varepsilon}\right)}}\left[\frac{\left[\sum_{j=1}^{n} n_{c,j,t}^{a}\left(y_{c,j,t}^{a}\right)^{(1-\varepsilon)}\right]^{\left(\frac{1}{1-\varepsilon}\right)}}{\sum_{j=1}^{n} n_{c,j,t}^{a}\, y_{c,j,t}^{a}}\right]$$

avec :

- $GE(r)_{c,t}^{a}$ l'indice d'entropie généralisée de l'éducation d'ordre *r* du groupe d'âge "a" appartenant au pays "c" à la date "t".
- $A(\varepsilon)_{c,t}^{a}$ l'indice Atkinson de l'éducation d'ordre ε du groupe d'âge "a" appartenant au pays "c" à la date "t".
- a=1 pour le groupe d'âge 15–19 ans, a=2 pour le groupe d'âge 20–24 ans, ..., et a=13 pour le groupe d'âge 75 et plus.
- *n* est le nombre des niveaux d'éducation retenus qui correspond ici à 7.
- *i* et *j* sont les niveaux d'éducation tel que: i=1 pour les illettrés, i=2 pour le primaire inachevé, i=3 pour le primaire achevé, i=4 pour le secondaire inachevé, i=5 pour le secondaire achevé, i=6 pour le supérieur inachevé, and i=7 pour le supérieur achevé.
- $n_{c,i,t}^{a}$ représente la taille de la population de la tranche d'âge "a" du pays "c" ayant atteint le niveau d'éducation "i" à la date "t".
- $N_{c,t}^{a}$ représente la taille de la population de la tranche d'âge "a" du pays "c" à la date "t" ($N_{c,t}^{a} = \sum_{i=1}^{n} n_{c,i,t}^{a}$).
- $y_{c,i,t}^{a}$ indique le nombre d'années de scolarisation cumulées de la tranche d'âge "a" du pays "c" pour atteindre le niveau d'éducation "j" à la date "t".

Les indices d'entropie généralisée et d'Atkinson de l'éducation peuvent être établis pour des groupes agrégés.

Grand groupe d'âge d'un pays

$$GE(r)_{c,t}^{G}=\frac{N_{c,t}^{G\,(r-1)}}{r(r-1)}\left[\frac{\sum_{a\in G}\sum_{j=1}^{n}n_{c,j,t}^{a}\left(y_{c,j,t}^{a}\right)^{r}}{\left(\sum_{a\in G}\sum_{j=1}^{n}n_{c,j,t}^{a}y_{c,j,t}^{a}\right)^{r}}-1\right]$$

$$A(\varepsilon)_{c,t}^{G}=1-\frac{1}{\left[N_{c,t}^{G}\right]^{\left(\frac{\varepsilon}{1-\varepsilon}\right)}}\left[\frac{\left[\sum_{a\in G}\sum_{j=1}^{n}n_{c,j,t}^{a}\left(y_{c,j,t}^{a}\right)^{(1-\varepsilon)}\right]^{\left(\frac{1}{1-\varepsilon}\right)}}{\sum_{a\in G}\sum_{j=1}^{n}n_{c,j,t}^{a}y_{c,j,t}^{a}}\right]$$

où :
- $GE(r)_{c,t}^{G}$ l'indice d'entropie généralisée de l'éducation d'ordre *r* du grand groupe d'âge "G" appartenant au pays "c" à la date "t".
- $A(\varepsilon)_{c,t}^{G}$ l'indice Atkinson de l'éducation d'ordre ε du grand groupe d'âge "G" appartenant au pays "c" à la date "t".
- a=1 (a'=1) pour le groupe d'âge 15–19 ans, a=2 (a'=2) pour le groupe d'âge 20–24 ans, ..., et a=13 (a'=13) pour le groupe d'âge 75 et plus.
- $N_{c,t}^{G}$ représente la taille de la population du grand groupe d'âge "G" du pays "c" à la date "t" ($N_{c,t}^{G}=\sum_{a\in G}\sum_{i=1}^{n}n_{c,i,t}^{a}=\sum_{a\in G}N_{c,t}^{a}$).

Groupe d'âge quinquennal d'une zone géographique

$$GE(r)_{R,t}^{a}=\frac{N_{R,t}^{a\,(r-1)}}{r(r-1)}\left[\frac{\sum_{c\in R}\sum_{j=1}^{n}n_{c,j,t}^{a}\left(y_{c,j,t}^{a}\right)^{r}}{\left(\sum_{c\in R}\sum_{j=1}^{n}n_{c,j,t}^{a}y_{c,j,t}^{a}\right)^{r}}-1\right]$$

$$A(\varepsilon)_{R,t}^{a}=1-\frac{1}{\left[N_{R,t}^{a}\right]^{\left(\frac{\varepsilon}{1-\varepsilon}\right)}}\left[\frac{\left[\sum_{c\in R}\sum_{j=1}^{n}n_{c,j,t}^{a}\left(y_{c,j,t}^{a}\right)^{(1-\varepsilon)}\right]^{\left(\frac{1}{1-\varepsilon}\right)}}{\sum_{c\in R}\sum_{j=1}^{n}n_{c,j,t}^{a}y_{c,j,t}^{a}}\right]$$

où :
- $GE(r)_{R,t}^{a}$ l'indice d'entropie généralisée de l'éducation d'ordre *r* du groupe d'âge "a" appartenant à la région "R" à la date "t".
- $A(\varepsilon)_{R,t}^{a}$ l'indice Atkinson de l'éducation d'ordre ε du groupe d'âge "a" appartenant à la région "R" à la date "t".
- c (c') les pays appartenant à la région "R".
- *n* est le nombre des niveaux d'éducation retenus qui correspond ici à 7.
- $N_{R,t}^{a}$ représente la taille de la population du groupe d'âge "a" appartenant à la région "R" à la date "t". ($N_{R,t}^{a}=\sum_{c\in R}\sum_{i=1}^{n}n_{c,i,t}^{a}=\sum_{c\in R}N_{c,t}^{a}$).

Grand groupe d'âge d'une zone géographique

$$GE(r)_{c,t}^{G}=\frac{N_{R,t}^{G\ (r-1)}}{r(r-1)}\left[\frac{\sum_{c\in R}\sum_{a\in G}\sum_{j=1}^{n}n_{c,j,t}^{a}\left(y_{c,j,t}^{a}\right)^{r}}{\left(\sum_{c\in R}\sum_{a\in G}\sum_{j=1}^{n}n_{c,j,t}^{a}y_{c,j,t}^{a}\right)^{r}}-1\right]$$

$$A(\varepsilon)_{R,t}^{G}=1-\frac{1}{\left[N_{R,t}^{G}\right]^{\left(\frac{\varepsilon}{1-\varepsilon}\right)}}\left[\frac{\left[\sum_{c\in R}\sum_{a\in G}\sum_{j=1}^{n}n_{c,j,t}^{a}\left(y_{c,j,t}^{a}\right)^{(1-\varepsilon)}\right]^{\left(\frac{1}{1-\varepsilon}\right)}}{\sum_{c\in R}\sum_{a\in G}\sum_{j=1}^{n}n_{c,j,t}^{a}y_{c,j,t}^{a}}\right]$$

où :

- $GE(r)_{R,t}^{G}$ l'indice d'entropie généralisée de l'éducation d'ordre r du grand groupe d'âge "G" appartenant à la région "R" à la date "t".
- $A(\varepsilon)_{R,t}^{G}$ l'indice Atkinson de l'éducation d'ordre ε du grand groupe d'âge "G" appartenant à la région "R" à la date "t".
- a=1 pour le groupe d'âge 15-19 ans, a=2 pour le groupe d'âge 20-24 ans, ..., et a=13 pour le groupe d'âge 75 et plus.
- n est le nombre des niveaux d'éducation retenus qui correspond ici à 7.
- $N_{R,t}^{G}$ représente la taille de la population du grand groupe d'âge "G" appartenant à la région "R" à la date "t". ($N_{R,t}^{G}=\sum_{c\in R}\sum_{a\in G}\sum_{i=1}^{n}n_{c,i,t}^{a}=\sum_{c\in R}N_{c,t}^{G}=\sum_{c\in R}N_{R,t}^{a}$).

L'annexe n°1 présente une synthèse de l'ensemble des formules proposées pour le calcul des indices d'inégalité éducative.

3. TENDANCES DES INÉGALITES ÉDUCATIVES AU NIVEAU MONDIAL

A partir de la base que nous avons construite, le tableau n° 3 présente l'évolution de l'inégalité mondiale de l'éducation mesurée à travers quatre indices d'entropie généralisée, l'indice de Gini et deux indices d'Atkinson.

Tableau 3. Evolution des inégalités mondiales d'éducation, 1950-2015

Année	Indices d'entropie généralisée				Indice	Indices d'Atkinson	
	GE(0)	GE(0.5)	GE(1)	GE(2)	de Gini	A(0.5)	A(1)*
1950	13.61	1.23	0.81	0.78	0.64	0.52	0.37
1960	12.02	1.08	0.70	0.64	0.60	0.47	0.36
1975	9.34	0.83	0.53	0.44	0.52	0.37	0.35
1990	7.44	0.65	0.41	0.31	0.45	0.30	0.32
2005	4.85	0.43	0.27	0.19	0.35	0.20	0.25
2015	3.60	0.33	0.20	0.15	0.31	0.16	0.21

* *L'indice d'Atkinson d'ordre 1 est calculé en ajoutant une année de scolarisation à l'ensemble de la distribution.*
Source : Calcul des auteurs à partir de la base mondiale des inégalités d'éducation, 1950-2015.

Il apparaît que, durant ces soixante-cinq années, d'importants efforts ont été entrepris par les pays sur le plan de l'accès à l'éducation. Une baisse de l'inégalité mondiale de l'éducation s'observe en général quels que soient les indices présentés. Elle s'est accompagnée d'une augmentation significative de la moyenne d'années de scolarisation : cette dernière a augmenté de 3.14 en 1950 à 8.49 années en 2015 pour la population âgée de 15 ans et plus. En parallèle, le taux d'analphabétisme à largement baissé : entre 1950 et 2015 ce taux est passé de 48% à 12% pour la population âgée de 15 ans et plus.

La figure n° 1 présente ainsi une carte de l'indice de Theil de l'éducation (GE(1)) à travers le monde en 1950 et en 2015. De manière générale, l'indice de Theil de l'éducation de la population mondiale âgée de 15 et plus a été divisé par quatre, il est passé de 0.81 en 1950 à 0.20 en 2015.

Figure 1 : Indice de Theil de l'éducation de la population âgée de 15 ans et plus à l'échelle mondiale entre 1950 et 2015

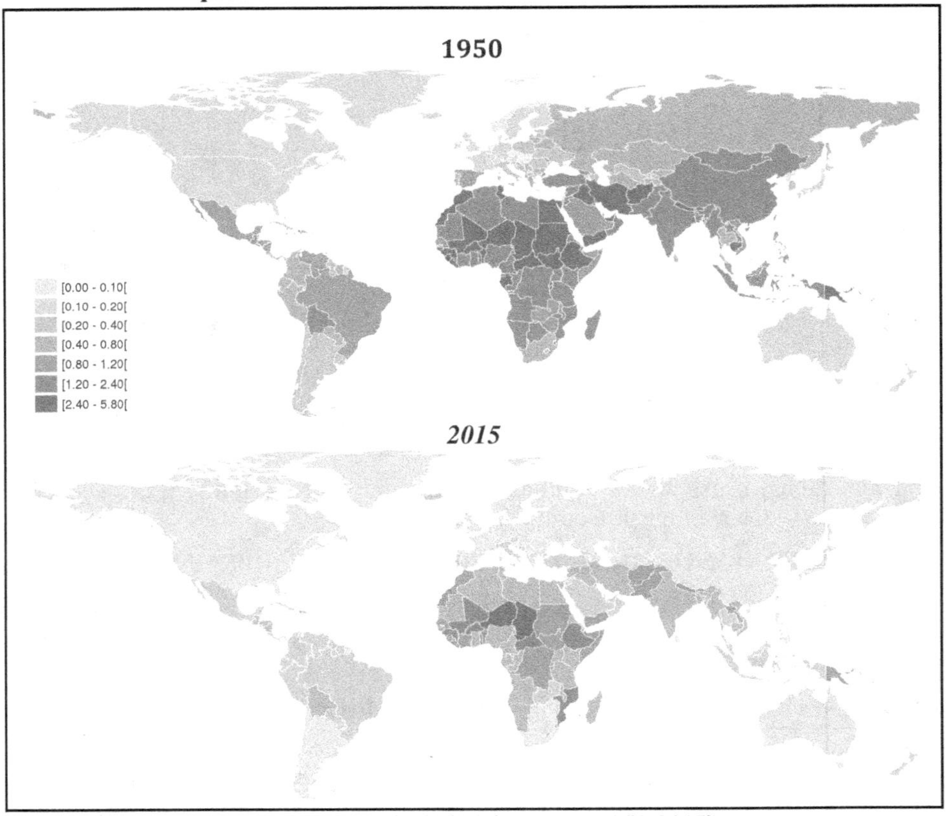

Source : Auteurs (Base mondiale des inégalités d'éducation, 1950-2015).

3.1. Les inégalités mondiales d'éducation par sous-régions

L'annexe n°2 présente les valeurs des différents indices d'inégalité entre 1950 et 2015 pour l'ensemble des 20 sous-régions du monde, en se référant au nouveau découpage de l'ONU du programme de développement durable 2015-2030. A l'exception de l'indice d'Atkinson d'ordre 1, A(1), qui paraît revêtir une certaine spécificité, tous les autres indices montrent une tendance à la baisse des inégalités d'éducation. L'indice d'Atkinson d'ordre 1 dévoile plutôt une courbe en cloche au fil du temps dans le cas des sous-régions de l'Afrique « non australe », de l'Asie du sud et de l'Océanie. Ainsi, lorsque le taux d'analphabétisme est très élevé (supérieur à 90%), l'inégalité d'éducation mesurée par l'indice d'Atkinson A(1) est atypiquement faible alors que les autres indices considérés présentent des niveaux d'inégalité très élevés. Lorsque le niveau d'analphabétisme diminue au fil du temps, l'indice d'Atkinson A(1) augmente jusqu'à atteindre un certain pic[5]. Au-delà de ce pic, sa tendance globale rejoint celle des autres indices d'inégalité de l'éducation. Il convient de noter que cette tendance particulière est principalement expliquée par le mode de calcul de cet indice. En effet, l'indice d'Atkinson d'ordre 1 correspond au rapport entre la moyenne géométrique et la moyenne arithmétique de l'éducation. Étant donné que la moyenne géométrique n'accepte pas des valeurs nulles[6] ($y_1 = 0$), la distribution de l'éducation subit au préalable une transformation avant le calcul de l'indice[7], ce qui est de nature à affecter la sensibilité à l'extrémité inférieure de cette distribution.

Graphique n°1 : Changement de l'indice de Theil de l'éducation selon les sous-régions du monde, 1950-2015

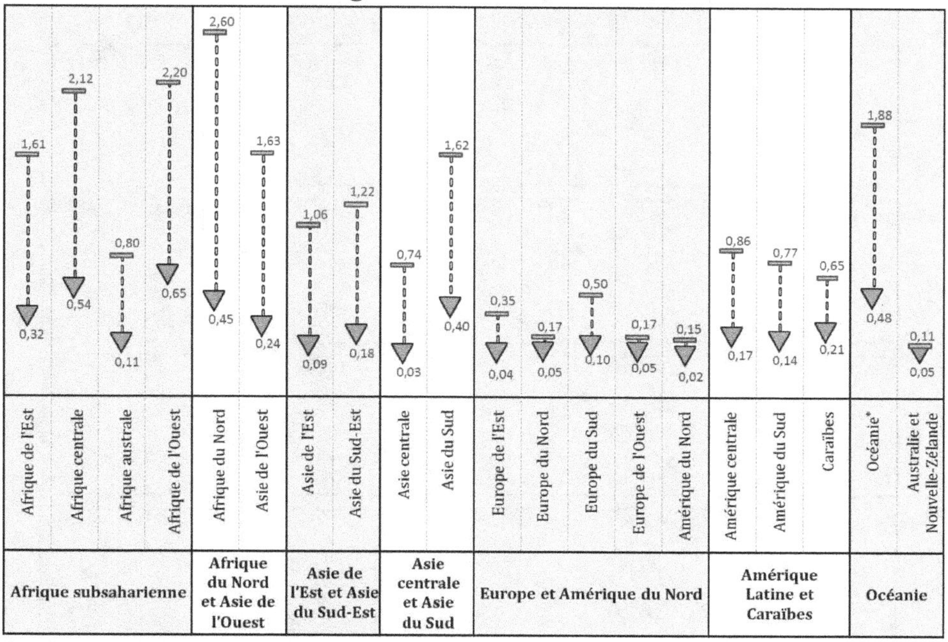

** Océanie sauf Australie et Nouvelle-Zélande.*
Source : Calcul des auteurs à partir de la base mondiale des inégalités d'éducation 1950-2015.

La réduction importante des inégalités dans l'éducation globalement observée montre notamment un certain mouvement de rattrapage des pays en retard d'éducation mais ne doit pas cacher l'existence encore de profondes disparités.

Comme le montrent la figure n° 1 et le graphique n°1, c'est le continent africain qui a enregistré la réduction la plus importante en matière d'inégalité d'éducation.

[5] Ce point de retournement est de l'ordre de 0.36 pour l'Afrique de l'Est, de 0.39 pour l'Afrique centrale, de 0.46 pour l'Afrique de l'Ouest de 0.44 pour l'Afrique du Nord, de 0.43 pour l'Asie du Sud et de 0.42 pour l'Océanie (sauf Australie et Nouvelle-Zélande).

[6] Contrairement à l'indice d'Atkinson d'ordre 1, l'indice de Theil même s'il n'est pas compatible avec les valeurs nulles, accepte néanmoins une limite finie lorsque les valeurs nulles sont considérées comme étant infiniment petites (y_1 tend vers 0).

[7] Cette transformation consiste à ajouter une année de scolarisation à l'ensemble de la distribution de l'éducation pour éviter le problème des valeurs nulles ($y_i \rightarrow y_i + 1$). Cette même transformation a été adoptée par le PNUD pour évaluer la perte due à l'inégalité dans la « composante éducation » de l'indice de développement humain ajusté aux inégalités.

L'indice de Theil de l'éducation de l'Afrique du Nord en particulier est passé de 2.60 en 1950 à 0.45 en 2015, soit une réduction de 2.15 points. Les indices de Theil de l'éducation de l'Afrique de l'Ouest, de l'Afrique centrale et de l'Afrique de l'Est ont baissé significativement de 1.55, 1.58 et 1.29 points sur la même période. Le niveau d'inégalité d'éducation reste toutefois élevé en Afrique, sauf en Afrique australe qui présente en 2015 une distribution de l'éducation relativement équitable (indice de Theil de 0.11). Soulignons que cette région est la seule du continent africain à présenter une moyenne d'années de scolarisation supérieure à la moyenne mondiale (9.88 années). L'Asie et l'Océanie ont connu aussi une baisse sensible des inégalités éducatives depuis les années 1950-1960.

Graphique n°2 : La courbe de Lorenz de l'éducation de la population âgée de 15 ans et plus selon les sous-régions du monde, 1950-2015

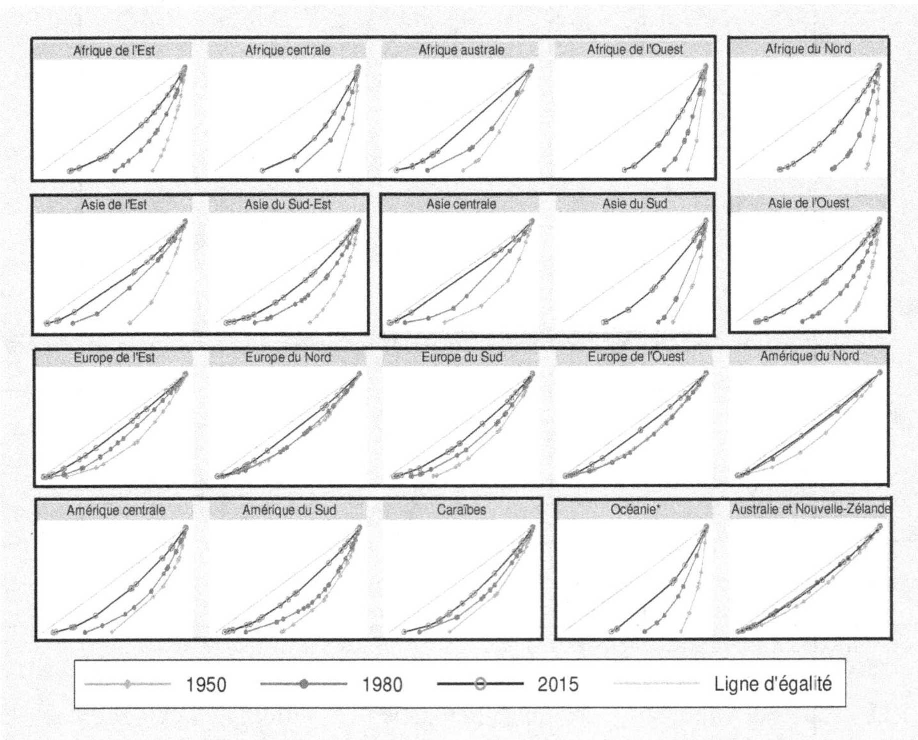

** Océanie sauf Australie et Nouvelle-Zélande.*
Source : Calcul des auteurs à partir de la base mondiale des inégalités d'éducation 1950-2015.

Par ailleurs, le graphique n°2 présente la courbe de Lorenz de l'éducation pour la population âgée de 15 ans et plus de chacune des vingt sous-régions du monde. Il apparaît nettement un déplacement de ces courbes entre 1950 et 2015 vers la bissectrice qui représente la ligne égalitaire.

Toutefois, pour l'Amérique du Nord, l'Europe du Nord, l'Europe de l'Est, l'Europe de l'Ouest et l'Australie/Nouvelle-Zélande, les courbes de Lorenz se déplacent au cours du temps à travers la partie supérieure de la distribution. Ces courbes sont pratiquement reliées à l'origine du graphique, ce qui traduit pour ces pays un niveau d'alphabétisation relativement élevé dès le début des années 1950. Il semblerait que l'amélioration de l'accès à l'éducation dans les pays de ce groupe soit passée par une proportion plus grande de la population ayant atteint le niveau d'enseignement supérieur. Pour tous les autres pays, les courbes se déplacent plutôt à travers la partie inférieure de la distribution de l'éducation. Ces pays ont beaucoup plus élargi l'éducation de base, c'est-à-dire la partie inférieure de la distribution de l'éducation. En conséquence, l'inégalité de l'éducation dans ces pays s'est réduite en raison notamment d'une baisse sensible de la proportion de la population n'ayant aucune scolarisation.

3.2. L'inégalité d'éducation selon le niveau de développement et les groupes d'âge

Le graphique n°3 présente une déclinaison de l'indice de Theil de l'éducation selon le niveau de revenu et le niveau de développement humain des pays entre 1950 et 2015. De manière générale, le groupe de pays qui dispose du revenu national brut (d'après la classification de la Banque mondiale), et du niveau de développement humain (selon la classification du PNUD) les plus élevés présente un niveau d'inégalité de l'éducation faible. Dès lors la réduction de cette même inégalité apparaît relativement limitée entre 1950 et 2015.

Graphique n°3 : Changement de l'indice de Theil de l'éducation selon le niveau de revenu, le niveau de développement humain et les groupes d'âge, 1950-2015

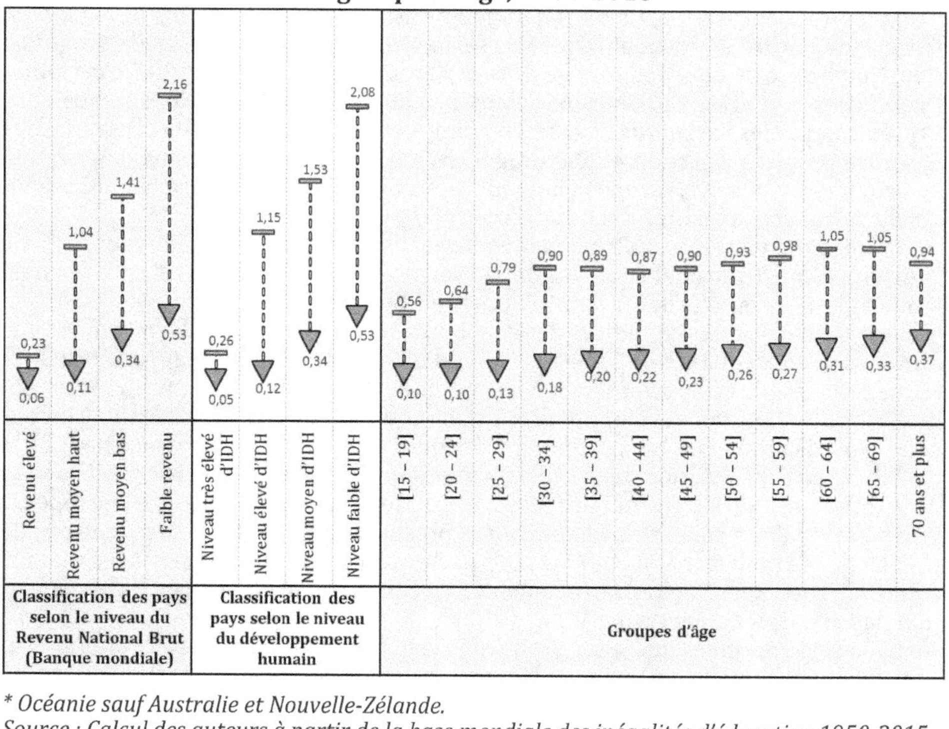

** Océanie sauf Australie et Nouvelle-Zélande.*
Source : Calcul des auteurs à partir de la base mondiale des inégalités d'éducation 1950-2015.

En revanche l'indice de Theil de l'éducation des pays à faible niveau de développement humain est passé de 2.08 à 0.53, soit une baisse sensible de 1.55 points. Néanmoins, malgré cette réduction significative des inégalités éducatives, l'écart entre pays à niveau de développement humain très élevé et ceux à niveau faible demeure assez important puisque la différence entre les deux indices de Theil est de l'ordre de 0.48.

Le graphique n°3 présente également l'indice de Theil de l'éducation au niveau mondial selon les différents groupes d'âge. Si la réduction des inégalités d'éducation est perceptible pour l'ensemble des groupes d'âge, le niveau d'inégalité le plus faible s'observe pour les tranches 15-19 ans et 20-24 ans. Ainsi c'est la population des jeunes qui a le plus bénéficié de la progression liée au développement de l'éducation de base tandis que la population âgée de 60 ans et plus constitue le groupe d'âge pour lequel le niveau d'inégalité est le plus élevé : l'indice de Theil mondial de l'éducation est passé de 0.56 en 1950 à 0.10 en 2015 pour le groupe d'âge 15-19 ans, et de 0.64 à 0.10 pour les 20-24 ans. Il est passé de 1.05 en 1950 à 0.31 en 2015 pour les 60-64 ans, à 0.33 pour les 65-69 ans, et de 0.94 à 0.37 pour les 70 ans et plus.

CONCLUSION

Cet article propose une nouvelle base de données, disponible en ligne, comportant plusieurs indicateurs caractéristiques des inégalités éducatives couvrant 146 pays sur la période 1950-2015. Par rapport aux autres bases existantes, nous avons cherché à améliorer sensiblement les estimations des indices d'inégalité d'éducation et de la moyenne d'années de la scolarisation. Nous avons montré que la pondération utilisée par Barro et Lee (2013), pour obtenir les durées cumulées de scolarisation d'une tranche d'âge agrégée, conduit à un biais dans l'estimation de la moyenne d'années de scolarisation. Ce biais peut même atteindre pour certains pays une différence de l'ordre d'une demi-année en termes de moyenne d'années de scolarisation. Notre base de données corrige cette erreur de pondération et relâche certaines hypothèses peu vraisemblables adoptées par plusieurs auteurs. Nous avons ainsi pris en compte les variations au cours du temps et entre les différentes classes d'âge des durées de scolarisation et l'hétérogénéité par rapport aux niveaux d'éducation au sein d'un même cycle d'enseignement. Nous avons ainsi amélioré la méthodologie du calcul des inégalités d'éducation.

En résultat, cette base offre de nouvelles estimations de l'inégalité mondiale de l'éducation par tranche d'âge et selon les sous-régions du monde. A l'exception de l'indice d'Atkinson d'ordre 1, dont l'interprétation liée à sa méthode de calcul est plus particulière, tous les indices d'inégalité présentés dans la base confirment une diminution conséquente de l'inégalité mondiale de l'éducation. Il apparaît que les réductions les plus importantes, repérées entre 1950 et 2015, sont principalement dues pour les pays en développement à une réduction de la population n'ayant aucune scolarisation et du taux d'analphabétisme, ce que montre le déplacement de la distribution de l'éducation dans la partie inférieure de la courbe de Lorenz. Les pays de l'Amérique du Nord, de l'Europe du Nord, de l'Europe de l'Est, de l'Europe de l'Ouest et de l'Australie/Nouvelle-Zélande présentent en revanche des courbes de Lorenz qui se déplacent au cours du temps à travers la partie supérieure de la distribution, correspondant essentiellement à une progression de la part de la population dans l'enseignement supérieur.

La base de données que nous proposons renseigne, de la manière la plus appropriée possible, sur le degré de scolarisation à travers différents indicateurs d'inégalité et peut aider à différentes études, mais certes ne renseigne pas sur la qualité de l'éducation et a fortiori sur les résultats, les performances scolaires et les « profits » de l'éducation.

REFERENCES

Araujo C., Ferreira F., Schady N., 2004, Is the World Becoming More Unequal? Changes in the World Distribution of Schooling", *World Bank*. Washington, DC.

Barro R.J., Lee J.W., 1993, International Comparisons of Educational Attainment, *Journal of Monetary Economics*, 32, 3, 363–394.

Barro R.J., Lee J.W., 1996, International Measures of Schooling Years and Schooling Quality", *American Economic Review*, 86, 2, 218–223.

Barro R.J., Lee J.W., 2001, International Data on Educational Attainment: Updates and Implications", *Oxford Economic Papers*, 53, 3, 541–563.

Barro R.J., Lee J.W., 2013, A New Data Set of Educational Attainment in the World, 1950-2010", *Journal of Development Economics*, 104, 3, 184–198.

Bartusevičius H., 2014, The Inequality-Conflict Nexus Re-Examined: Income, Education and Popular Rebellions, *Journal of Peace Research*, 51, 1, 35–50.

Benaabdelaali W., Hanchane S., Kamal A., 2012, Educational Inequality in the World, 1950–2010: Estimates from a New Dataset, in John A. Bishop, Rafael Salas , ed., Inequality, Mobility and Segregation: Essays in Honor of Jacques Silber , *Research on Economic Inequality*, 20, Emerald Group Publishing Limited, Chapter 13, 337-366.

Castelló A., Doménech R., 2002, Human Capital Inequality and Economic Growth: Some New Evidence, *The Economic Journal*, 112, 478, 187–200.

Castelló A., 2008, On the distribution of education and democracy, *Journal of Development Economics*, 87, 179–190.

Castelló A., 2010a, Channels Through Which Human Capital Inequality Influences Economic Growth, *Journal of Human Capital*, 4, 4, 394–450.

Castelló A., 2010b, Inequality and Growth in Advanced Economies: An Empirical Investigation, *Journal of Economic Inequality*, 8, 3, 293–321.

Checchi D., 2004, Does educational achievement help to explain income inequality?, In A. Cornia , eds., Inequality, Growth and Poverty in an Era of Liberalization and Globalization., Oxford University Press, Chapter 4.

Checchi D., García-Peñalosa C., 2004, Risk and the distribution of human capital, *Economics Letters* 82, 53–61.

Cohen D., Soto M., 2007, Growth and Human Capital: Good Data, Good Results, *Journal of Economic Growth*, 12, 1, 51–76.

Cuaresma J.C., Samir K.C., Sauer P., 2013, Age-Specific Education Inequality, Education Mobility and Income Growth, *Welfare, Wealth and Work for Europe*, Working Paper no 6.

Dessus S., 2000, Capital humain et croissance : le rôle retrouvé du système éducatif, *Economie publique* 6, 2, 95-114.

Földvári P., Van Leeuwen B., 2014, Educational and income inequality in Europe, ca. 1870–2000, Cliometrica, 8, 3, 271–300.

Galea S., Ahern J., Tracy M., Rudenstine S., Vlahov D., 2007, Education Inequality and Use of Cigarettes, Alcohol, and Marijuana, *Drug and Alcohol Dependence*, 90, 1, 4–15.

Green A., 2011, Lifelong Learning, Equality and Social Cohesion, *European Journal of Education*, 46, 2, 228–243.

Hori T., 2011, Educational Gender Inequality and Inverted U-Shaped Fertility Dynamics, *The Japanese Economic Review* 62, 1, 126–150.

Johnes G., 2006, Education and Economic Growth, Working Paper 2006/019 Lancaster University Management School

Lê F., Ahern J., Galea S., 2010, Neighborhood education inequality and drinking behavior, *Drug and Alcohol Dependence* 112, 1, 18–26.

Lim A.S.K., Tang K.K., 2008, Human Capital Inequality And The Kuznets Curve, *The Developing Economies*, 46, 1, 26–51.

López R., Thomas V., Wang Y., 1998, Addressing the Education Puzzle: the Distribution of Education and Economic Reforms, *World Bank Working Paper Series* No. 2031, World Bank, Washington, DC.

Lutz W., Goujon A., Samir K. C., Sanderson W., 2007, Reconstruction of populations by age, sex and level of educational attainment for 120 countries for 1970–2000, *Vienna Yearbook of Population Research* 2007 : 193–235.

McKenzie D., Rapoport H., 2007, Network Effects and the Dynamics of Migration and Inequality: Theory and Evidence from Mexico, *Journal of Development Economics*, 84, 1, 1–24.

Meschi E. Scervini F., 2014, A New Dataset on Educational Inequality, *Empirical Economics*, 47, 2, 695–716.

Morrisson C., Murtin F., 2010, he Kuznets Curve of Education: A Global Perspective on Education Inequalities, Centre for the Economics of Education, *London School of Economics*, CEE DP 116.

Morrisson C., Murtin F., 2013, The Kuznets curve of human capital inequality: 1870–2010, *Journal of Economic Inequality*, 11, 3, 283–301.

Patrawart K., 2010, Can Equality in Education Be a New Anti-Corruption Tool? Cross-Country Evidence, 1990-2005, *NACC Journal*, 3, 2, 127–157.

Psacharopoulos G., Arriagada A. M., 1986, The Educational Composition of the Labour Force: An international Comparison, *International Labour Review*, 125, 5, 561–574.

Sauer P., 2016, The Role of Age and Gender in Education Expansion". *INEQ Working Paper Series*, 4. WU Vienna University of Economics and Business, Vienna.

Thomas V., Wang Y., Fan X., 2001, Measuring Education Inequality: Gini Coefficients of Education., *Policy Research Working Paper*, N°. 2525, World Bank Institute

Thomas V., Wang Y., Fan X., 2003, Measuring Education Inequality: Gini Coefficients of Education for 140 Countries (1960–2000), *Journal of Education Planning and Administration*, 17, 1, 5–33.

ANNEXE 1.

Synthèse des formules de l'entropie généralisée de l'éducation selon les différents cas de figure

Type	Entropie généralisée de l'éducation
Groupe d'âge quinquennal « a » d'un pays « c »	$GE(r)^a_{c,t} = \frac{N^{a\ (r-1)}_{c,t}}{r(r-1)} \left[\frac{\sum_{j=1}^{n} n^a_{c,j,t} \left(y^a_{c,j,t}\right)^r}{\left(\sum_{j=1}^{n} n^a_{c,j,t} y^a_{c,j,t}\right)^r} - 1 \right]$
Grand groupe d'âge « G » d'un pays « c »	$GE(r)^G_{c,t} = \frac{N^{G\ (r-1)}_{c,t}}{r(r-1)} \left[\frac{\sum_{a\in G}\sum_{j=1}^{n} n^a_{c,j,t} \left(y^a_{c,j,t}\right)^r}{\left(\sum_{a\in G}\sum_{j=1}^{n} n^a_{c,j,t} y^a_{c,j,t}\right)^r} - 1 \right]$
Groupe d'âge quinquennal « a » d'une zone géographique « R »	$GE(r)^a_{R,t} = \frac{N^{a\ (r-1)}_{R,t}}{r(r-1)} \left[\frac{\sum_{c\in R}\sum_{j=1}^{n} n^a_{c,j,t} \left(y^a_{c,j,t}\right)^r}{\left(\sum_{c\in R}\sum_{j=1}^{n} n^a_{c,j,t} y^a_{c,j,t}\right)^r} - 1 \right]$
Grand groupe d'âge « G » d'une zone géographique « R »	$GE(r)^G_{c,t} = \frac{N^{G\ (r-1)}_{R,t}}{r(r-1)} \left[\frac{\sum_{c\in R}\sum_{a\in G}\sum_{j=1}^{n} n^a_{c,j,t} \left(y^a_{c,j,t}\right)^r}{\left(\sum_{c\in R}\sum_{a\in G}\sum_{j=1}^{n} n^a_{c,j,t} y^a_{c,j,t}\right)^r} - 1 \right]$

Synthèse des formules de l'indice de Gini de l'éducation selon les différents cas de figure

Type	Indice de Gini de l'éducation
Groupe d'âge quinquennal « a » d'un pays « c »	$Gini^a_{c,t} = \frac{\sum_{i=1}^{n}\sum_{j=1}^{n} n^a_{c,i,t} \left\lvert y^a_{c,i,t} - y^a_{c,j,t} \right\rvert n^a_{c,j,t}}{2\ N^a_{c,t} \sum_{i=1}^{n} n^a_{c,i,t} y^a_{c,i,t}}$
Grand groupe d'âge « G » d'un pays « c »	$Gini^G_{c,t} = \frac{\sum_{a\in G}\sum_{a'\in G}\sum_{i=1}^{n}\sum_{j=1}^{n} n^a_{c,i,t} \left\lvert y^a_{c,i,t} - y^{a'}_{c,j,t} \right\rvert n^{a'}_{c,j,t}}{2\ N^G_{c,t} \left[\sum_{a\in G}\sum_{i=1}^{n} n^a_{c,i,t} y^a_{c,i,t}\right]}$
Groupe d'âge quinquennal « a » d'une zone géographique « R »	$Gini^a_{R,t} = \frac{\sum_{c\in R}\sum_{c'\in R}\sum_{i=1}^{n}\sum_{j=1}^{n} n^a_{c,i,t} \left\lvert y^a_{c,i,t} - y^a_{c',j,t} \right\rvert n^a_{c',j,t}}{2\ N^a_{R,t} \left[\sum_{c\in R}\sum_{i=1}^{n} n^a_{c,i,t} y^a_{c,i,t}\right]}$
Grand groupe d'âge « G » d'une zone géographique « R »	$Gini^G_{R,t} = \frac{\sum_{c\in R}\sum_{c'\in R}\sum_{a\in G}\sum_{a'\in G}\sum_{i=1}^{n}\sum_{j=1}^{n} n^a_{c,i,t} \left\lvert y^a_{c,i,t} - y^{a'}_{c',j,t} \right\rvert n^{a'}_{c',j,t}}{2\ N^G_{R,t} \left[\sum_{c\in R}\sum_{a\in G}\sum_{i=1}^{n} n^a_{c,i,t} y^a_{c,i,t}\right]}$

Synthèse des formules de la famille des indices d'Atkinson de l'éducation selon les différents cas de figure

Type	Indice d'Atkinson de l'éducation (ε≠1)
Groupe d'âge quinquennal « a » d'un pays « c »	$A(\varepsilon)^{a}_{c,t}=1-\frac{1}{\left[N^{a}_{c,t}\right]^{\left(\frac{\varepsilon}{1-\varepsilon}\right)}}\left[\frac{\left[\sum_{j=1}^{n} n^{a}_{c,j,t}\left(y^{a}_{c,j,t}\right)^{(1-\varepsilon)}\right]^{\left(\frac{1}{1-\varepsilon}\right)}}{\sum_{j=1}^{n} n^{a}_{c,j,t}\,y^{a}_{c,j,t}}\right]$
Grand groupe d'âge « G » d'un pays « c »	$A(\varepsilon)^{G}_{c,t}=1-\frac{1}{\left[N^{G}_{c,t}\right]^{\left(\frac{\varepsilon}{1-\varepsilon}\right)}}\left[\frac{\left[\sum_{a\in G}\sum_{j=1}^{n} n^{a}_{c,j,t}\left(y^{a}_{c,j,t}\right)^{(1-\varepsilon)}\right]^{\left(\frac{1}{1-\varepsilon}\right)}}{\sum_{a\in G}\sum_{j=1}^{n} n^{a}_{c,j,t}\,y^{a}_{c,j,t}}\right]$
Groupe d'âge quinquennal « a » d'une zone géographique « R »	$A(\varepsilon)^{a}_{R,t}=1-\frac{1}{\left[N^{a}_{R,t}\right]^{\left(\frac{\varepsilon}{1-\varepsilon}\right)}}\left[\frac{\left[\sum_{c\in R}\sum_{j=1}^{n} n^{a}_{c,j,t}\left(y^{a}_{c,j,t}\right)^{(1-\varepsilon)}\right]^{\left(\frac{1}{1-\varepsilon}\right)}}{\sum_{c\in R}\sum_{j=1}^{n} n^{a}_{c,j,t}\,y^{a}_{c,j,t}}\right]$
Grand groupe d'âge « G » d'une zone géographique « R »	$A(\varepsilon)^{G}_{R,t}=1-\frac{1}{\left[N^{G}_{R,t}\right]^{\left(\frac{\varepsilon}{1-\varepsilon}\right)}}\left[\frac{\left[\sum_{c\in R}\sum_{a\in G}\sum_{j=1}^{n} n^{a}_{c,j,t}\left(y^{a}_{c,j,t}\right)^{(1-\varepsilon)}\right]^{\left(\frac{1}{1-\varepsilon}\right)}}{\sum_{c\in R}\sum_{a\in G}\sum_{j=1}^{n} n^{a}_{c,j,t}\,y^{a}_{c,j,t}}\right]$

Synthèse des formules de l'indice d'Atkinson de l'éducation d'ordre 1 selon les différents cas de figure

Type	Indice d'Atkinson de l'éducation (ε=1)
Groupe d'âge quinquennal « a » d'un pays « c »	$A(\varepsilon)^{a}_{c,t}=1-\left[\prod_{j=1}^{n}\left(y^{a}_{c,j,t}+1\right)^{\left(\frac{n^{a}_{c,j,t}}{N^{a}_{c,t}}\right)}\right]\Big/\left[\sum_{j=1}^{n}\left(\frac{n^{a}_{c,j,t}}{N^{a}_{c,t}}\right)\left(y^{a}_{c,j,t}+1\right)\right]$
Grand groupe d'âge « G » d'un pays « c »	$A(\varepsilon)^{G}_{c,t}=1-\left[\prod_{a\in G}\prod_{j=1}^{n}\left(y^{a}_{c,j,t}+1\right)^{\left(\frac{n^{a}_{c,j,t}}{N^{G}_{c,t}}\right)}\right]\Big/\left[\sum_{a\in G}\sum_{j=1}^{n}\left(\frac{n^{a}_{c,j,t}}{N^{G}_{c,t}}\right)\left(y^{a}_{c,j,t}+1\right)\right]$
Groupe d'âge quinquennal « a » d'une zone géographique « R »	$A(\varepsilon)^{a}_{R,t}=1-\left[\prod_{c\in R}\prod_{j=1}^{n}\left(y^{a}_{c,j,t}+1\right)^{\left(\frac{n^{a}_{c,j,t}}{N^{a}_{R,t}}\right)}\right]\Big/\left[\sum_{c\in R}\sum_{j=1}^{n}\left(\frac{n^{a}_{c,j,t}}{N^{a}_{R,t}}\right)\left(y^{a}_{c,j,t}+1\right)\right]$
Grand groupe d'âge « G » d'une zone géographique « R »	$A(\varepsilon)^{G}_{R,t}=1-\left[\prod_{c\in R}\prod_{a\in G}\prod_{j=1}^{n}\left(y^{a}_{c,j,t}+1\right)^{\left(\frac{n^{a}_{c,j,t}}{N^{G}_{R,t}}\right)}\right]\Big/\left[\sum_{c\in R}\sum_{a\in G}\sum_{j=1}^{n}\left(\frac{n^{a}_{c,j,t}}{N^{G}_{R,t}}\right)\left(y^{a}_{c,j,t}+1\right)\right]$

Source : Auteurs.

ANNEXE 2.

Inégalité de l'éducation par sous-région, 1950-2015

Région	Année	Indices d'entropie généralisée				Indice de Gini	Indices d'Atkinson	
		GE(0)	GE(0.5)	GE(1)	GE(2)		A(0.5)	A(1)
Afrique de l'Est	**1950**	21.11	2.16	1.61	2.37	0.83	0.79	0.28
	1955	20.36	2.04	1.49	2.03	0.81	0.76	0.30
	1960	19.12	1.85	1.31	1.60	0.77	0.71	0.31
	1965	18.05	1.71	1.18	1.35	0.74	0.67	0.32
	1970	16.77	1.56	1.05	1.12	0.71	0.63	0.33
	1975	15.66	1.43	0.95	0.97	0.68	0.59	0.35
	1980	14.37	1.29	0.84	0.80	0.65	0.54	0.36
	1985	13.03	1.15	0.74	0.67	0.61	0.49	0.36
	1990	11.65	1.02	0.65	0.56	0.57	0.45	0.35
	1995	10.41	0.90	0.57	0.47	0.53	0.40	0.34
	2000	9.40	0.81	0.51	0.41	0.50	0.37	0.32
	2005	8.29	0.72	0.45	0.36	0.47	0.33	0.31
	2010	6.93	0.61	0.39	0.31	0.44	0.28	0.28
	2015	5.61	0.51	0.32	0.26	0.40	0.24	0.26
Afrique centrale	**1950**	23.20	2.57	2.12	4.30	0.90	0.87	0.22
	1955	22.47	2.41	1.92	3.46	0.87	0.84	0.24
	1960	21.65	2.26	1.73	2.79	0.85	0.81	0.27
	1965	20.63	2.08	1.55	2.25	0.82	0.77	0.30
	1970	19.39	1.90	1.37	1.80	0.78	0.72	0.32
	1975	17.76	1.69	1.18	1.41	0.74	0.67	0.35
	1980	16.03	1.49	1.01	1.10	0.70	0.61	0.37
	1985	14.46	1.32	0.87	0.86	0.66	0.55	0.39
	1990	12.95	1.17	0.77	0.72	0.62	0.50	0.38
	1995	11.83	1.06	0.69	0.63	0.60	0.46	0.37
	2000	11.54	1.03	0.67	0.60	0.59	0.45	0.37
	2005	11.18	1.00	0.65	0.57	0.58	0.44	0.37
	2010	10.99	0.98	0.63	0.55	0.57	0.43	0.37
	2015	9.42	0.84	0.54	0.46	0.53	0.38	0.35
Afrique australe	**1950**	14.69	1.28	0.80	0.68	0.62	0.54	0.42
	1955	13.83	1.19	0.74	0.61	0.59	0.51	0.41
	1960	13.34	1.14	0.71	0.58	0.58	0.49	0.41
	1965	12.19	1.06	0.66	0.55	0.57	0.46	0.39
	1970	10.94	0.95	0.60	0.50	0.54	0.42	0.37
	1975	9.39	0.82	0.51	0.41	0.50	0.37	0.33
	1980	7.79	0.69	0.43	0.34	0.46	0.31	0.30
	1985	5.84	0.54	0.35	0.29	0.42	0.25	0.25
	1990	3.77	0.36	0.24	0.18	0.34	0.17	0.21
	1995	2.00	0.22	0.15	0.12	0.27	0.11	0.15
	2000	4.42	0.39	0.24	0.17	0.32	0.18	0.23
	2005	3.34	0.30	0.18	0.13	0.27	0.14	0.19
	2010	2.11	0.21	0.13	0.09	0.22	0.10	0.14
	2015	1.62	0.16	0.11	0.07	0.18	0.08	0.12
Afrique de l'Ouest	**1950**	23.53	2.62	2.20	4.68	0.91	0.88	0.25
	1955	23.26	2.56	2.11	4.26	0.90	0.87	0.26
	1960	22.69	2.43	1.94	3.50	0.88	0.85	0.28
	1965	22.18	2.31	1.79	2.91	0.86	0.82	0.34
	1970	21.53	2.18	1.64	2.37	0.84	0.79	0.39
	1975	20.58	2.03	1.48	1.92	0.81	0.76	0.42
	1980	19.78	1.91	1.35	1.62	0.79	0.73	0.44
	1985	18.82	1.78	1.23	1.37	0.76	0.69	0.45
	1990	17.99	1.67	1.13	1.19	0.73	0.66	0.46
	1995	17.04	1.56	1.04	1.05	0.71	0.63	0.45
	2000	16.16	1.46	0.96	0.93	0.69	0.60	0.45
	2005	15.36	1.37	0.88	0.81	0.66	0.57	0.45
	2010	13.96	1.22	0.77	0.66	0.61	0.52	0.44
	2015	12.35	1.05	0.65	0.53	0.56	0.46	0.42

Région	Année	Indices d'entropie généralisée				Indice	Indices d'Atkinson	
		GE(0)	GE(0.5)	GE(1)	GE(2)	de Gini	A(0.5)	A(1)
Afrique du Nord	**1950**	24.27	2.85	2.60	7.60	0.94	0.92	0.22
	1955	24.02	2.76	2.45	6.45	0.93	0.90	0.25
	1960	23.83	2.69	2.34	5.65	0.92	0.89	0.28
	1965	23.28	2.54	2.12	4.34	0.90	0.87	0.32
	1970	22.24	2.33	1.84	3.14	0.87	0.83	0.36
	1975	20.88	2.10	1.57	2.27	0.84	0.77	0.40
	1980	18.84	1.80	1.27	1.51	0.78	0.70	0.43
	1985	16.53	1.51	1.01	1.01	0.70	0.61	0.44
	1990	14.96	1.33	0.86	0.79	0.65	0.56	0.44
	1995	13.50	1.18	0.74	0.64	0.61	0.50	0.43
	2000	12.08	1.04	0.65	0.53	0.56	0.45	0.41
	2005	10.95	0.93	0.57	0.45	0.53	0.41	0.40
	2010	9.94	0.84	0.51	0.40	0.50	0.38	0.38
	2015	8.72	0.73	0.45	0.33	0.46	0.33	0.36
Asie de l'Ouest	**1950**	21.16	2.15	1.63	2.44	0.84	0.79	0.37
	1955	20.08	1.99	1.46	1.97	0.81	0.75	0.38
	1960	18.81	1.81	1.28	1.56	0.78	0.70	0.39
	1965	17.45	1.64	1.13	1.27	0.74	0.65	0.40
	1970	16.20	1.49	1.01	1.06	0.71	0.61	0.40
	1975	14.63	1.32	0.87	0.85	0.66	0.55	0.40
	1980	13.08	1.17	0.76	0.69	0.62	0.50	0.40
	1985	10.81	0.96	0.62	0.54	0.57	0.42	0.38
	1990	9.37	0.83	0.53	0.44	0.52	0.37	0.36
	1995	8.04	0.71	0.45	0.37	0.48	0.32	0.33
	2000	6.47	0.59	0.37	0.30	0.44	0.27	0.29
	2005	5.60	0.50	0.32	0.25	0.40	0.24	0.27
	2010	4.75	0.43	0.27	0.21	0.37	0.20	0.25
	2015	4.04	0.37	0.24	0.18	0.34	0.18	0.22
Asie de l'Est	**1950**	17.07	1.58	1.06	1.09	0.71	0.63	0.38
	1955	15.37	1.39	0.91	0.87	0.67	0.57	0.37
	1960	13.77	1.22	0.78	0.70	0.62	0.52	0.37
	1965	11.66	1.01	0.63	0.53	0.56	0.44	0.35
	1970	9.61	0.82	0.51	0.40	0.50	0.37	0.32
	1975	8.06	0.69	0.42	0.33	0.45	0.32	0.29
	1980	6.16	0.53	0.33	0.25	0.39	0.25	0.26
	1985	5.68	0.49	0.30	0.22	0.38	0.23	0.25
	1990	5.58	0.48	0.30	0.22	0.37	0.23	0.25
	1995	4.07	0.37	0.23	0.17	0.32	0.18	0.21
	2000	2.85	0.27	0.18	0.13	0.28	0.13	0.17
	2005	2.04	0.21	0.14	0.11	0.25	0.10	0.14
	2010	1.42	0.16	0.11	0.09	0.22	0.08	0.11
	2015	0.92	0.12	0.09	0.07	0.21	0.06	0.09
Asie du Sud-Est	**1950**	18.15	1.74	1.22	1.45	0.76	0.68	0.32
	1955	16.82	1.59	1.09	1.22	0.73	0.64	0.33
	1960	15.57	1.44	0.97	1.02	0.69	0.59	0.33
	1965	13.42	1.23	0.82	0.81	0.65	0.52	0.33
	1970	11.23	1.02	0.67	0.63	0.59	0.45	0.32
	1975	9.66	0.88	0.58	0.52	0.55	0.39	0.31
	1980	7.90	0.74	0.49	0.43	0.51	0.33	0.29
	1985	8.13	0.75	0.50	0.43	0.51	0.34	0.31
	1990	7.93	0.74	0.48	0.41	0.51	0.33	0.31
	1995	6.35	0.60	0.39	0.33	0.46	0.28	0.28
	2000	5.01	0.49	0.33	0.27	0.42	0.23	0.25
	2005	3.68	0.38	0.26	0.21	0.37	0.18	0.22
	2010	2.70	0.30	0.21	0.17	0.33	0.14	0.19
	2015	2.17	0.26	0.18	0.14	0.30	0.12	0.17

Région	Année	Indices d'entropie généralisée				Indice de Gini	Indices d'Atkinson	
		GE(0)	GE(0.5)	GE(1)	GE(2)		A(0.5)	A(1)
Asie centrale	**1950**	10.97	1.06	0.74	0.78	0.62	0.46	0.34
	1955	9.59	0.94	0.66	0.67	0.59	0.42	0.33
	1960	8.13	0.82	0.58	0.56	0.56	0.37	0.32
	1965	7.01	0.73	0.52	0.49	0.53	0.33	0.31
	1970	5.79	0.63	0.44	0.40	0.49	0.29	0.30
	1975	4.44	0.50	0.35	0.30	0.43	0.24	0.27
	1980	3.40	0.40	0.28	0.22	0.37	0.19	0.24
	1985	2.50	0.31	0.22	0.17	0.32	0.15	0.20
	1990	1.74	0.24	0.17	0.13	0.27	0.12	0.17
	1995	1.00	0.15	0.11	0.08	0.20	0.07	0.12
	2000	0.40	0.08	0.06	0.04	0.14	0.04	0.07
	2005	0.15	0.05	0.04	0.03	0.11	0.02	0.04
	2010	0.11	0.04	0.03	0.02	0.10	0.02	0.03
	2015	0.08	0.03	0.03	0.02	0.10	0.02	0.03
Asie du Sud	**1950**	20.88	2.14	1.62	2.53	0.84	0.78	0.28
	1955	20.58	2.10	1.57	2.38	0.83	0.77	0.28
	1960	20.21	2.03	1.50	2.16	0.82	0.76	0.29
	1965	19.92	1.98	1.45	1.99	0.81	0.75	0.32
	1970	18.96	1.84	1.30	1.61	0.78	0.71	0.35
	1975	18.82	1.79	1.25	1.43	0.76	0.70	0.39
	1980	18.57	1.73	1.18	1.25	0.74	0.68	0.42
	1985	16.58	1.49	0.98	0.94	0.68	0.61	0.42
	1990	14.84	1.31	0.83	0.74	0.63	0.55	0.41
	1995	13.81	1.20	0.76	0.65	0.61	0.51	0.42
	2000	12.72	1.08	0.67	0.54	0.57	0.47	0.43
	2005	10.83	0.91	0.55	0.42	0.51	0.40	0.39
	2010	9.63	0.80	0.48	0.36	0.47	0.36	0.37
	2015	8.20	0.68	0.40	0.29	0.43	0.31	0.34
Europe de l'Est	**1950**	4.96	0.51	0.35	0.31	0.43	0.24	0.23
	1955	3.43	0.39	0.28	0.25	0.40	0.19	0.20
	1960	2.91	0.36	0.26	0.23	0.38	0.17	0.19
	1965	2.43	0.31	0.23	0.20	0.36	0.15	0.18
	1970	1.93	0.27	0.20	0.17	0.33	0.13	0.16
	1975	1.86	0.25	0.18	0.15	0.31	0.12	0.16
	1980	1.78	0.22	0.16	0.12	0.28	0.11	0.15
	1985	1.70	0.20	0.14	0.11	0.26	0.10	0.14
	1990	1.56	0.18	0.12	0.09	0.23	0.09	0.13
	1995	1.14	0.14	0.10	0.07	0.20	0.07	0.11
	2000	0.55	0.09	0.06	0.05	0.17	0.04	0.07
	2005	0.39	0.07	0.05	0.04	0.15	0.03	0.06
	2010	0.30	0.06	0.05	0.04	0.14	0.03	0.05
	2015	0.26	0.05	0.04	0.03	0.13	0.02	0.04
Europe du Nord	**1950**	1.23	0.21	0.17	0.16	0.31	0.10	0.13
	1955	1.11	0.20	0.17	0.16	0.31	0.10	0.13
	1960	1.02	0.19	0.16	0.15	0.30	0.09	0.13
	1965	0.98	0.19	0.16	0.15	0.30	0.09	0.13
	1970	0.93	0.18	0.15	0.14	0.30	0.09	0.13
	1975	0.91	0.18	0.15	0.14	0.29	0.09	0.13
	1980	1.03	0.18	0.14	0.13	0.28	0.09	0.13
	1985	0.96	0.17	0.13	0.12	0.27	0.08	0.12
	1990	0.87	0.16	0.13	0.11	0.27	0.08	0.12
	1995	0.89	0.15	0.12	0.10	0.26	0.07	0.11
	2000	0.89	0.14	0.11	0.10	0.25	0.07	0.11
	2005	0.46	0.10	0.08	0.07	0.20	0.05	0.08
	2010	0.29	0.08	0.06	0.05	0.17	0.04	0.06
	2015	0.31	0.07	0.05	0.04	0.15	0.03	0.06
Europe du Sud	**1950**	8.69	0.78	0.50	0.43	0.50	0.35	0.29
	1955	8.12	0.73	0.47	0.40	0.49	0.33	0.29
	1960	7.37	0.67	0.43	0.36	0.47	0.30	0.28
	1965	6.58	0.60	0.38	0.32	0.44	0.28	0.27
	1970	5.78	0.53	0.34	0.29	0.42	0.25	0.25
	1975	5.10	0.48	0.31	0.26	0.40	0.22	0.24

	1980	4.38	0.42	0.28	0.22	0.38	0.20	0.23
	1985	4.32	0.40	0.26	0.21	0.36	0.19	0.23
	1990	4.00	0.38	0.24	0.19	0.35	0.18	0.22
	1995	3.41	0.33	0.21	0.17	0.33	0.16	0.20
	2000	2.79	0.28	0.18	0.14	0.30	0.13	0.18
	2005	1.49	0.18	0.13	0.10	0.26	0.09	0.13
	2010	1.34	0.17	0.12	0.10	0.25	0.08	0.12
	2015	0.95	0.14	0.10	0.08	0.23	0.07	0.10
Europe de l'Ouest	**1950**	1.73	0.23	0.17	0.16	0.31	0.11	0.14
	1955	0.66	0.15	0.13	0.13	0.28	0.07	0.10
	1960	0.64	0.16	0.14	0.14	0.29	0.08	0.11
	1965	0.73	0.17	0.14	0.14	0.29	0.08	0.11
	1970	1.04	0.19	0.16	0.15	0.30	0.09	0.13
	1975	1.09	0.20	0.17	0.16	0.31	0.10	0.14
	1980	1.09	0.21	0.18	0.16	0.32	0.10	0.14
	1985	1.49	0.23	0.18	0.16	0.32	0.11	0.16
	1990	1.79	0.24	0.17	0.14	0.30	0.11	0.16
	1995	1.57	0.20	0.14	0.11	0.27	0.10	0.15
	2000	1.29	0.17	0.12	0.09	0.24	0.08	0.13
	2005	1.10	0.12	0.08	0.06	0.19	0.06	0.10
	2010	0.55	0.08	0.06	0.05	0.16	0.04	0.07
	2015	0.43	0.07	0.05	0.04	0.15	0.03	0.05
Amérique du Nord	**1950**	0.78	0.18	0.15	0.13	0.29	0.09	0.13
	1955	0.75	0.17	0.14	0.12	0.28	0.08	0.12
	1960	0.68	0.15	0.13	0.11	0.26	0.08	0.12
	1965	0.56	0.12	0.10	0.08	0.22	0.06	0.10
	1970	0.48	0.09	0.07	0.06	0.19	0.05	0.08
	1975	0.42	0.07	0.06	0.05	0.16	0.04	0.06
	1980	0.31	0.06	0.04	0.03	0.14	0.03	0.05
	1985	0.35	0.06	0.05	0.04	0.15	0.03	0.05
	1990	0.38	0.07	0.05	0.04	0.15	0.03	0.06
	1995	0.21	0.04	0.03	0.03	0.12	0.02	0.04
	2000	0.17	0.03	0.03	0.02	0.11	0.02	0.03
	2005	0.16	0.03	0.03	0.02	0.11	0.02	0.03
	2010	0.13	0.03	0.02	0.02	0.10	0.01	0.03
	2015	0.12	0.03	0.02	0.02	0.09	0.01	0.02

Région	Année	Indices d'entropie généralisée				Indice de Gini	Indices d'Atkinson	
		GE(0)	GE(0.5)	GE(1)	GE(2)		A(0.5)	A(1)
Amérique centrale	**1950**	13.49	1.26	0.86	1.02	0.64	0.53	0.30
	1955	12.85	1.19	0.82	0.94	0.63	0.51	0.30
	1960	12.18	1.13	0.78	0.87	0.62	0.49	0.30
	1965	11.22	1.06	0.73	0.82	0.61	0.46	0.32
	1970	10.14	0.96	0.66	0.69	0.58	0.42	0.31
	1975	9.57	0.90	0.62	0.61	0.57	0.40	0.33
	1980	8.44	0.80	0.53	0.49	0.53	0.36	0.33
	1985	6.87	0.66	0.44	0.38	0.48	0.30	0.31
	1990	5.54	0.54	0.36	0.30	0.44	0.25	0.28
	1995	4.59	0.46	0.31	0.25	0.40	0.22	0.25
	2000	3.78	0.39	0.27	0.22	0.37	0.19	0.23
	2005	2.94	0.32	0.22	0.17	0.33	0.15	0.20
	2010	2.58	0.29	0.20	0.16	0.32	0.14	0.19
	2015	2.24	0.25	0.17	0.14	0.30	0.12	0.17
Amérique du Sud	**1950**	12.86	1.16	0.77	0.75	0.62	0.50	0.34
	1955	11.89	1.08	0.71	0.69	0.60	0.47	0.33
	1960	10.75	0.98	0.65	0.62	0.58	0.43	0.32
	1965	9.56	0.88	0.59	0.55	0.56	0.39	0.31
	1970	8.13	0.77	0.51	0.47	0.52	0.35	0.30
	1975	6.27	0.66	0.48	0.48	0.51	0.30	0.28
	1980	5.93	0.64	0.46	0.45	0.51	0.29	0.28
	1985	5.42	0.56	0.39	0.35	0.47	0.26	0.27
	1990	4.91	0.50	0.35	0.30	0.44	0.24	0.26
	1995	4.36	0.44	0.30	0.24	0.40	0.21	0.24
	2000	3.65	0.37	0.25	0.19	0.36	0.18	0.22
	2005	2.76	0.29	0.19	0.15	0.31	0.14	0.18
	2010	2.11	0.23	0.16	0.12	0.28	0.11	0.16
	2015	1.74	0.20	0.14	0.11	0.26	0.10	0.14

Caraïbes	**1950**	11.73	1.03	0.65	0.58	0.56	0.45	0.29
	1955	11.24	0.98	0.62	0.55	0.55	0.43	0.29
	1960	10.49	0.92	0.58	0.51	0.53	0.41	0.29
	1965	9.65	0.85	0.55	0.48	0.52	0.38	0.30
	1970	8.63	0.77	0.50	0.43	0.50	0.35	0.30
	1975	7.35	0.67	0.44	0.37	0.48	0.31	0.29
	1980	6.00	0.56	0.37	0.30	0.44	0.26	0.28
	1985	4.85	0.48	0.32	0.26	0.41	0.22	0.26
	1990	4.49	0.45	0.30	0.24	0.39	0.21	0.25
	1995	4.12	0.42	0.28	0.22	0.38	0.20	0.24
	2000	3.81	0.39	0.26	0.20	0.36	0.19	0.23
	2005	3.64	0.37	0.24	0.19	0.35	0.18	0.23
	2010	3.41	0.35	0.23	0.17	0.33	0.17	0.22
	2015	2.96	0.31	0.21	0.16	0.32	0.15	0.21
Océanie (sauf Australie et Nouvelle-Zélande)	**1950**	22.47	2.38	1.88	3.26	0.87	0.84	0.31
	1955	21.73	2.24	1.72	2.70	0.85	0.81	0.33
	1960	20.59	2.06	1.52	2.13	0.82	0.76	0.35
	1965	19.24	1.87	1.33	1.66	0.78	0.72	0.37
	1970	17.91	1.70	1.18	1.34	0.75	0.67	0.39
	1975	17.05	1.58	1.06	1.11	0.72	0.63	0.41
	1980	15.99	1.44	0.95	0.91	0.68	0.59	0.42
	1985	14.55	1.27	0.81	0.71	0.63	0.54	0.41
	1990	13.40	1.15	0.71	0.59	0.58	0.49	0.41
	1995	12.17	1.03	0.63	0.51	0.55	0.45	0.39
	2000	10.89	0.93	0.58	0.47	0.53	0.41	0.36
	2005	9.75	0.81	0.49	0.38	0.47	0.36	0.34
	2010	9.38	0.78	0.47	0.36	0.46	0.35	0.33
	2015	9.59	0.80	0.48	0.37	0.47	0.36	0.34
Australie et Nouvelle-Zélande	**1950**	0.50	0.13	0.11	0.10	0.25	0.06	0.09
	1955	0.45	0.12	0.10	0.09	0.25	0.06	0.09
	1960	0.42	0.12	0.10	0.09	0.24	0.06	0.09
	1965	0.39	0.11	0.09	0.08	0.22	0.05	0.08
	1970	0.35	0.09	0.08	0.07	0.20	0.05	0.08
	1975	0.35	0.07	0.06	0.05	0.16	0.04	0.06
	1980	0.30	0.06	0.05	0.04	0.14	0.03	0.05
	1985	0.34	0.06	0.05	0.04	0.15	0.03	0.05
	1990	0.32	0.07	0.05	0.04	0.16	0.03	0.06
	1995	0.39	0.07	0.06	0.05	0.16	0.04	0.06
	2000	0.32	0.07	0.05	0.04	0.16	0.03	0.06
	2005	0.29	0.06	0.05	0.04	0.15	0.03	0.05
	2010	0.29	0.06	0.05	0.04	0.16	0.03	0.05
	2015	0.31	0.06	0.05	0.04	0.16	0.03	0.05

Source : Auteurs, base mondiale des inégalités d'éducation 1950-2015.

Educational inequalities: A new world database (1950-2015)

Abstract - A new world database on educational inequalities is proposed, inspired by the dataset of Benaabdelaali et al. (2012) and based on the 2016 version of the database of Barro and Lee (2013). Our database covers the period 1950-2015 for 146 countries and provides an estimation of educational inequality of the population by 5-year age intervals and by aggregated age groups, considering seven levels of education. In addition to the Gini index, our database presents several indices of the generalized entropy family and the Atkinson family. It provides more accurate data by correcting the weighting error made by Barro and Lee in calculating the average years of schooling which can lead to a significant bias for many countries. From this database a panorama of the reduction of educational inequalities at the global level is schematically presented. It is mainly linked in developing countries to the decline of the population with no schooling. Nevertheless, the gap remains high between countries with low levels of human development in some parts of the world and those with high human development.

Mots-clés

Educational inequalities
Theil index
Gini index
World database

En souvenir de Philippe Hugon

Philippe Hugon nous a quittés en avril 2018. Il a été une des figures majeures, dans une certaine tradition à la française, de l'économie du développement. Son magistère intellectuel, sa connaissance profonde de l'Afrique, son approche plurielle du développement élargissant les travaux instrumentalisés et formalisés des économistes aujourd'hui, son activité inlassable dans les conférences et les médias, l'élégance et la clarté de ses propos, vont nous manquer cruellement.

Philippe Hugon a été un membre important du comité scientifique de la revue Région et Développement dès sa création en 1995 et jusqu'à récemment.

Il a coordonné un numéro spécial de la revue, le n° 22-2005 *Intégrations régionales dans les pays en développement*. Région et Développement a donné un compte rendu de quelques-uns de ses nombreux ouvrages : *Les économies en développement à l'heure de la régionalisation* (n° 18-2003), *Géopolitique de l'Afrique* (n° 25-2007), *Les Suds dans la crise* (n° 31-2010) et son dernier livre *Afriques : entre puissance et vulnérabilité* (n° 44-2016). J'avais aussi présenté ses *Mémoires solidaires et solitaires. Trajectoires d'un économiste du développement* en 2014 dans le n° 39, livre qui est un témoignage intime de l'homme, du parcours de l'universitaire imprégné d'une vraie culture humaniste et de son engagement social.

Le bel hommage que je peux lui rendre comme traduction de notre estime mutuelle est de reprendre, en parallèle de notre vocation scientifique, ce qu'il a écrit en conclusion de ses *Mémoires* : « Vivre, c'est recevoir, créer et transmettre, être un passeur de sens, de valeurs et de vie avant le grand passage » (p. 287).

Maurice Catin
Professeur émérite, Université de Toulon
Directeur de la revue *Région et Développement*

REVUE RÉGION ET DÉVELOPPEMENT

Site Web : www.regionetdeveloppement.org

Recommandations aux auteurs

La Revue Région et Développement publie en français ou en anglais des articles originaux, des notes et documents et des comptes rendus de lecture. Pour soumission à publication, l'auteur doit adresser à la rédaction de la revue le texte par courrier électronique (ou le manuscrit dactylographié en deux exemplaires). La présentation des chapitres, des références bibliographiques et des notes de bas de page doit être conforme à celle de la revue. Les articles doivent être accompagnés d'un résumé en français et en anglais d'une dizaine de lignes, des mots-clés correspondants et de la classification du JEL. Le nom de l'auteur, l'institution à laquelle il appartient et l'adresse complète doivent figurer en page de garde.
Les articles proposés à la revue Région et Développement sont évalués par le Comité de rédaction puis soumis de manière anonyme à un ou deux referees. L'auteur reçoit un rapport d'évaluation, lui aussi anonyme, concluant à publication, révision ou refus.
Après avis favorable à la publication dans la revue, il sera demandé à l'auteur un envoi par mail du texte en Word (y compris figures, tableaux et formules mathématiques compatibles avec Word 2010).

Les propositions d'articles doivent être adressées à la rédaction de la revue :

Professeur Maurice Catin
Revue Région et Développement
Université de Toulon
Laboratoire d'Economie Appliquée au Développement (LEAD)
Faculté de Sciences Économiques et de Gestion
70 Avenue Roger Decouvoux - 83000 Toulon

Mail : maurice.catin@univ-tln.fr

BULLETIN D'ABONNEMENT

Revue Région et Développement

• **Je désire souscrire un abonnement pour l'année 2018 (deux numéros) :**

☐ France, DOM-TOM : 44 €   ☐ Étranger : 47 €

• **Règlement :**

Pour la France

- Chèque bancaire
- Virement sur le compte *CCP 23 625 44 N Paris*
- Paypal sur le lien *paiement.harmattan.fr*
- Carte Bancaire sur le lien *paiement.harmattan.fr*

Pour l'étranger

- Virement (en euros uniquement) sur le compte *CCP 23 625 44 N Paris*
- Paypal sur le lien *paiement.harmattan.fr*
- Carte Internationale Visa/Mastercard sur le lien *paiement.harmattan.fr*

Nom et Prénom : ....
Adresse : ....
....
Code Postal : .... Ville : ....
Pays : ....

Date :   Signature :

Ce bulletin d'abonnement à la revue Région et Développement et votre règlement sont à retourner à :

Éditions L'HARMATTAN - 7, rue de l'École-Polytechnique, 75005 PARIS
Tél. : 01 40 46 79 14 - fax : 01 43 29 86 20 - site web : www.editions-harmattan.fr

Abonnement annuel : 2 numéros
France, DOM-TOM : 44 € ; Étranger : 47 €

Structures éditoriales du groupe L'Harmattan

L'Harmattan Italie
Via degli Artisti, 15
10124 Torino
harmattan.italia@gmail.com

L'Harmattan Hongrie
Kossuth l. u. 14-16.
1053 Budapest
harmattan@harmattan.hu

L'Harmattan Sénégal
10 VDN en face Mermoz
BP 45034 Dakar-Fann
senharmattan@gmail.com

L'Harmattan Cameroun
TSINGA/FECAFOOT
BP 11486 Yaoundé
inkoukam@gmail.com

L'Harmattan Burkina Faso
Achille Somé – tengnule@hotmail.fr

L'Harmattan Guinée
Almamya, rue KA 028 OKB Agency
BP 3470 Conakry
harmattanguinee@yahoo.fr

L'Harmattan RDC
185, avenue Nyangwe
Commune de Lingwala – Kinshasa
matangilamusadila@yahoo.fr

L'Harmattan Congo
67, boulevard Denis-Sassou-N'Guesso
BP 2874 Brazzaville
harmattan.congo@yahoo.fr

L'Harmattan Mali
Sirakoro-Meguetana V31
Bamako
syllaka@yahoo.fr

L'Harmattan Togo
Djidjole – Lomé
Maison Amela
face EPP BATOME
ddamela@aol.com

L'Harmattan Côte d'Ivoire
Résidence Karl – Cité des Arts
Abidjan-Cocody
03 BP 1588 Abidjan
espace_harmattan.ci@hotmail.fr

L'Harmattan Algérie
22, rue Moulay-Mohamed
31000 Oran
info2@harmattan-algerie.com

L'Harmattan Maroc
5, rue Ferrane-Kouicha, Talaâ-Elkbira
Chrableyine, Fès-Médine
30000 Fès
harmattan.maroc@gmail.com

Nos librairies en France

Librairie internationale
16, rue des Écoles – 75005 Paris
librairie.internationale@harmattan.fr
01 40 46 79 11
www.librairieharmattan.com

Librairie l'Espace Harmattan
21 bis, rue des Écoles – 75005 Paris
librairie.espace@harmattan.fr
01 43 29 49 42

Lib. sciences humaines & histoire
21, rue des Écoles – 75005 Paris
librairie.sh@harmattan.fr
01 46 34 13 71
www.librairieharmattansh.com

Lib. Méditerranée & Moyen-Orient
7, rue des Carmes – 75005 Paris
librairie.mediterranee@harmattan.fr
01 43 29 71 15

Librairie Le Lucernaire
53, rue Notre-Dame-des-Champs – 75006 Paris
librairie@lucernaire.fr
01 42 22 67 13

www.ingramcontent.com/pod-product-compliance
Lightning Source LLC
LaVergne TN
LVHW051358061026
849535LV00009B/3242